This Is the Life!

This Is the Life!

by Lila Goodspeed
Curriculum Branch, Home Economics
Department of Education, Manitoba

and Eleanor Smith
Secondary School Home Economics Teacher
Winnipeg, Manitoba

Revised and adapted by Jeanne Brinkley
Home economics writer
Former teacher educator, Florida State University
and Assistant State Director for Home Economics, Florida

Bennett Publishing Company

Peoria, IL 61615

Original edition copyright © Copp Clark Pitman, Toronto, 1977
This edition copyright © Bennett Publishing Company, 1981
All rights reserved

81 82 83 84 85 KP 5 4 3 2 1
ISBN 87002-342-X
Library of Congress Catalog No. 80-69719

This edition:
Editor/Ramona Gibbs
Production Manager/Gordon Guderjan
Production Assistants/Carol Owen, Pat Schultz

Printed in the United States of America

To our mothers, Madeline MacDonald and Reta Robertson
—L. G. and E. S.

Acknowledgments

Photo Credits

Sincere appreciation is extended to all the people who assisted us directly or indirectly in the development of this book. We especially appreciate the contribution of Grant Park High School students who provided us with their ideas, feelings, and reactions.

Linda Scott provided invaluable assistance with her cheerful supportive attitudes and her thoughtful editorial work. Thanks to Irmgard Kasdorff who was our creative typist. Finally, this book could not have been written without the vital interest, patience, and support of our immediate families—Wesley and Melanie Goodspeed and Jim, Roxanne, Greg, and Andrea Smith.

L. G. and E. S.

The authors wish to acknowledge their indebtedness for some of the ideas expressed in this book to J. C. Penney, E. Erikson, V. Satir, J. Tanner, R. Havighurst, and Kingsley Davis.

"X: A Fabulous Child's Story" by Lois Gould is reprinted by permission of Lois Gould c/o International Creative Management. Copyright © 1978 by Lois Gould.

CBC, 2 (right), 3, 7, 13 (right), 30–1, 48–9 (upper), 62–3, 201 (upper), 219
Board of Jewish Education, Toronto, 10 (lower)
Peter Paterson, 24–5, 154
Jim Macdonald, 39
Canadian Press, 48–9 (lower)
New Brunswick Provincial Archives, 65, 85 (lower), 121 (upper and lower)
Canadian Conklin Shows, 69
Public Archives of Canada, 90
John Murtagh, 2 (left), 109, 131 (upper left and right), 141, 198–9
John Dashwood, 126
Y.M.C.A., 130 (left)
CHCH–TV, 200–1 (lower)
Miller Services, 205
Mattel Toys, 2 (left)
Girl Scouts of the U.S.A./Nanci Hertzog, 12; Kristyne J. Stevenson, 54; Pete Beren, 55; Susan Kurys, 67; Nancy Corbin, 80; Sharon Stirek, 86; Nydia Ann Gonzalez, 131 (lower left)
Boy Scouts of America, 13 (left)
United Way, 32, 66
Northwoods Management Co., 81
U.S. Dept. of Labor, 68, 85 (upper), 123, 131 (lower right), 138–9
Sears, Roebuck and Co., 91, 101 (lower), 120 (left and right), 130 (right), 142, 155, 181
March of Dimes, 101 (upper)
Cape Cod Health Care Coalition/Reginald Carter, Photographer, 114, 115 (right)
Voice of the People in Uptown, Inc./Thom Clark, Photographer, 115 (left)

Every effort has been made to acknowledge all sources of illustrations, photographs, and textual materials used in this book. The publisher would be grateful if any errors or omissions were pointed out so that they may be corrected in future printings.

Contents

1 Who Are You? — 1
1. Who Are You? — 2
2. Adolescence — 12
3. The Socialization of You — 30

2 You and Yourself — 36
4. Developmental Tasks of Adolescence — 38
5. Heredity and Environment — 46
6. The Parts You Play — 54
7. Self-Concept — 66
8. Values — 76
9. Emotions — 94
10. Coping with Change — 106

3 You and Your Family — 116
11. Family Facts — 118
12. Influences on You — 128
13. Siblings — 144
14. Baby-Sitting — 154

4 You and Your Friends — 172
15. A Place in the Crowd — 174
16. Dating — 182

5 You and Communication — 192
17. Communication: It's a Two-Way Street — 194
18. Developing Your Communication Skills — 206
19. A Series of Decisions — 218

Appendix
"X: A Fabulous Child's Story" by Lois Gould — 235
Bibliography — 241
Index — 243

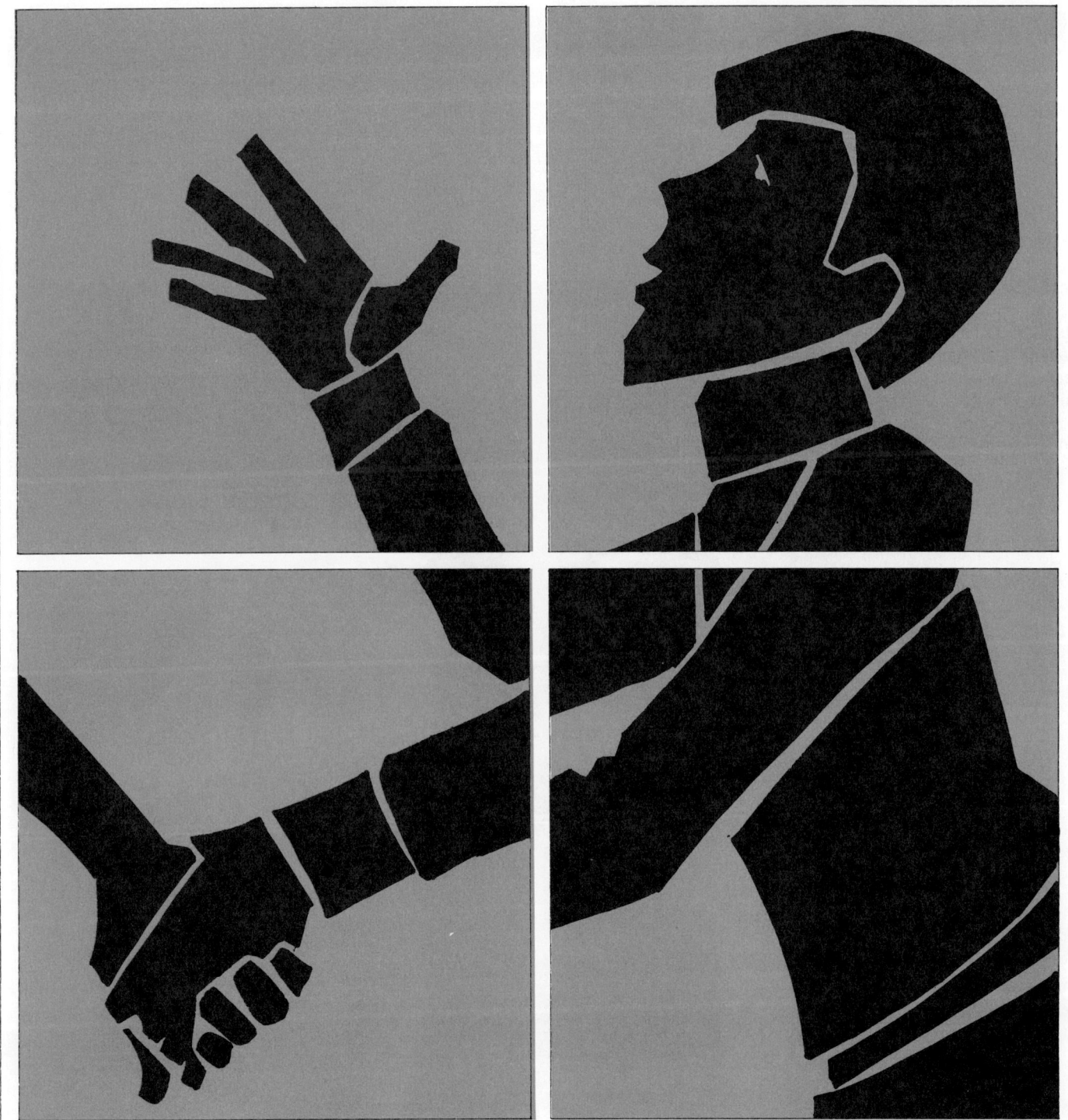

1 Who Are You?

I am a daydreamer . . . funny . . . kind . . . athletic . . . slow to anger . . . stubborn . . . moody . . . quiet . . . patient . . . I enjoy children . . . have big feet . . . believe in superstitions . . . am self-conscious . . . talkative . . . enjoy life . . . have a long nose . . . am concerned and perplexed.

- Do any of these points describe you?
- Are you changeable?
- Do you act differently with different people and in different places at different times?

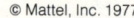
© Mattel, Inc. 1977

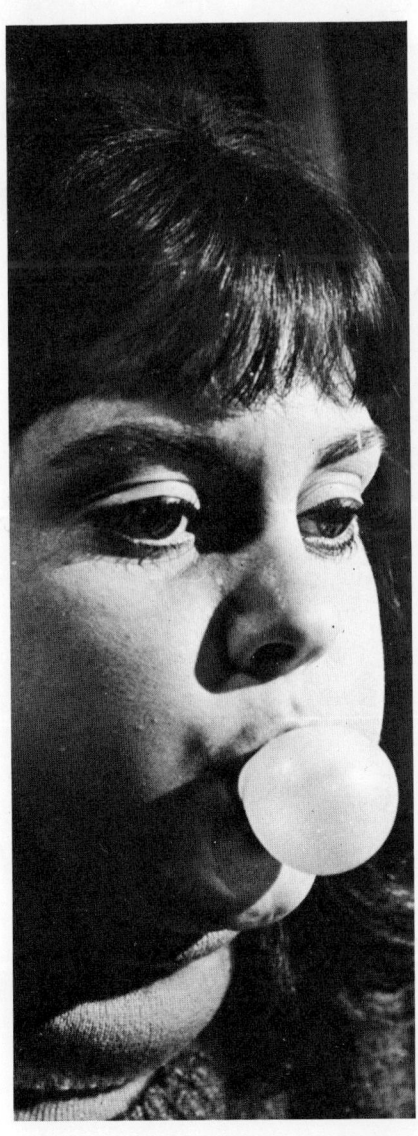

These are the kinds of questions that only you can answer as you find out more about who *you* are. Adolescence involves learning more about yourself. The period of adolescence has been described as one of storm and stress – a time of conflict and frustration. Is this your experience? Would you agree that the things you don't fully understand are the most worrisome?

Adolescence is full of changes: if you learn the facts about the changes that occur to young people at this stage, and realize that these changes are natural – they are happening to all your friends, too – then the worry is reduced. This period can then be a fairly undisturbed path between childhood and adulthood with a minimum of conflict and frustration. This book is for you, now, as you move through adolescence.

Many issues, needs, difficulties, and joys related to youth will be discussed in this book. You may not find *all* the answers here, but you will find many suggestions that will help you choose the right answers for you.

This Is the Life! in many ways is about your life – your growth, development, difficulties, and joys. In this book you will read about situations that are familiar to you or to people you know. You will also find reasons why you are experiencing, or may expect to experience, certain joys or difficulties. More than anything, it is hoped you will discover more about yourself, the life of adolescents, their interrelationship in families, with others, and in the changing world. Much of the discussion in the book and many of the examples are about young children. Learning how you developed as a child will help you understand why you are the kind of person you are today. This whole book is designed to help you think about the way you are developing and the way you interact with others, and to prepare you for the kind of adult person you can become. Read on and discover yourself!

Tracy
- small, fragile, blue-eyed, dark-blonde hair, very smart
- kind of tomboyish – she likes to compete and play with the boys
- in the upper group in the class
- in the choir
- very lively, not at all shy
- polite and does not argue with the teacher or me

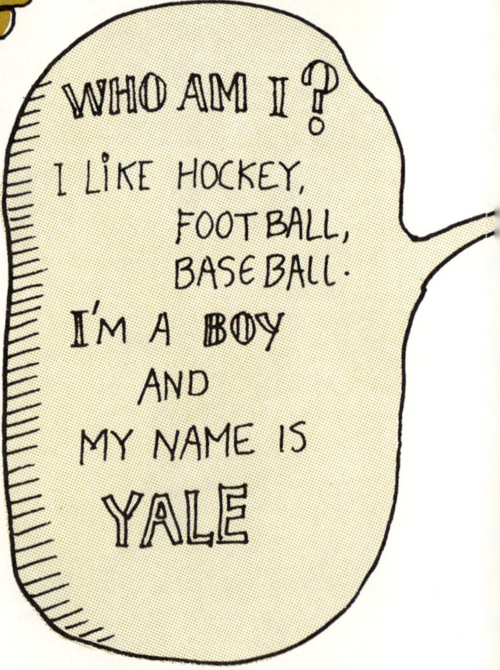

Take a piece of paper and write down the numbers from one to twenty. Now fill in twenty words or phrases that describe you. Are any of your descriptive phrases similar to those at the beginning of the chapter?

What seems important to second grade students? Are these things important to you? Would you tell anyone if your nickname were "Skunky"? Would you state your sex? Can you remember how pleased you were at school when someone told you he or she loved you? The way you describe yourself at each age will change, because the things you emphasize and are interested in change.

A senior high school student asked Tracy and Yale to do this "Who am I?" exercise. This is the way the senior student, a teacher volunteer, described these children. See if you can tell what is important to this student.

WHO AM I?
I'VE GOT TWO EYES AND TWO ARMS.
MY NICKNAME IS SKUNKY
MY MIDDLE NAME IS LEA.
I HAVE BLUE SNEAKERS.

OWEN LOVES ME!

WHO AM I?
I LIKE HOCKEY, FOOTBALL, BASEBALL.
I'M A BOY AND MY NAME IS YALE

Yale
- small, fragile, blue-eyed, longish brown hair
- also in the upper group in the class
- does not ask questions or talk out loud
- does all his work without asking anything of anyone
- is shy with adults, but not with friends

Barb Bone, a fourteen-year-old junior high school student, expressed her feelings about "Who am I?" in a poem.

Who Am I?

Who am I? I wouldn't know,
I am one of many with a long way to go.
I live my life in many ways,
Doing a mixture of things on different days.
With mixed emotions, and constant fears,
I live my life with its joys and tears,
Who am I? I am me,
That's the way it will always be.

- What does this poem say to you?
- Do you live your life in many ways?
- Do you have mixed emotions?

Barb also described the image she has of her friend, Shirley.

Shirley

Shirley is a giggly one,
She can be lots of fun.
Always has a joke to say,
Like sunshine on a cloudy day.

When she takes a laughing fit,
She never quite gets over it.
She's still chuckling when she goes to bed.
Shirley, is there something wrong in your head?

So any time you're feeling down,
And need someone to wipe away that frown,
Just look over Shirley's way,
That smile will cure your day.

- Does this poem tell you any more about Barb?
- Do you think that Shirley would describe herself in this way?

Elementary-school-age children are very natural in expressing their feelings, and often say and do things that an adolescent would find embarrassing to say and do. Children are full of a sense of discovery and are keen to reach out around them. They are learning about the world and are more interested in their external world than in themselves. Their lives revolve around the family, whereas adolescents are widening their social contacts and gaining independence. Often children have fewer concerns and inhibiting feelings than adolescents. The main reason why you are so self-conscious about what you say, what you do, how you dress, and what others think of you is because you are entering the unsettling growth period called *puberty*. Let's find out what physical developments you can expect to occur in this adolescent period. It is often the unknown that is worrisome. Knowing the facts can make you realize that these changes are common to all adolescents.

Pubescence and Puberty

Physical Development

Some general terms can be used to describe this stage of your life and the stages you will be going through before becoming an adult. Some people refer to the "preteen" or "preadolescent" years, or they use the term "pubescence." Pubescence is derived from the Latin word *pubescere,* which means to grow hairy. It refers to the approximately two-year period prior to puberty. During this period, your reproductive functions mature. Puberty is derived from the Latin word *pubertas,* which means the age of manhood.

The pubescent period is a time during which a great many changes take place. Some of the physical changes that occur are shown in the following table.

Physical Changes during Pubescence

Girls	*Boys*
Growth in skeleton	Growth in skeleton
Breast development	Enlargement of testes
Straight pubic hair	Straight pubic hair
Height and mass gain	Voice change
Kinky pubic hair	Ejaculation
Thyroid enlargement	Kinky pubic hair
Menstruation	Maximum annual growth
Axillary hair (under the arms)	Downy facial hair
	Axillary and chest hair

The normal range for puberty is from age ten to sixteen in girls and from age twelve to eighteen in boys. This wide range in age means that children vary widely in beginning the growth spurt, reaching the peak, and finishing their growth. The average boy grows 20 cm [8 in.] between ages thirteen and fifteen and a half, and the average girl grows 9 cm [3.5 in.] between eleven and thirteen and a half.

Jim and Ed had been best friends since birth, as their mothers were also best friends. They were always in the same room at school and played the same sports. Jim and Ed were the same height at age thirteen. Jim increased rapidly in height for a year and shot ahead of Ed, whose growth was not as noticeable. Eventually Ed overtook Jim and became the taller of the two.

1. What does this story tell you about growth rates?
2. Can you see examples of such growth patterns in yourself and your friends?

Your growth spurts may amaze you, your family, and your friends. Your slacks quickly become too short, and you rapidly outgrow your new shoes! A spurt in head length and breadth may make your eyes look smaller. Your nose and jaw may grow more than other parts of your face, changing your facial proportion from childish to more mature. Another interesting physical change takes place in the voice. Boys usually add nine low notes to their voices before they reach adulthood, while girls add only three. The boy loses four high notes, and the girl adds one.

The school social worker arrived at Carmella's house to discuss Carmella's three-week absence from school. Carmella's mother had died during the summer, and the family seemed to have adjusted well. Carmella had attended school regularly in September and October.

When Carmella entered the room, she had her arms crossed in front of her, and she maintained this posture throughout the conversation. The social worker noticed that Carmella's breasts were developing and that she was very self-conscious about her appearance. The counselor realized that Carmella's dad was not aware of her figure changes. It seemed that some new clothing styles were needed to help Carmella feel more comfortable with her appearance. The counselor helped Carmella to recognize that her friends were also going through the same physical changes, and that they too were learning to adjust to changes in their appearance.

1. What was Carmella's problem?
2. Where could Carmella get information about her physical development?

Did you consider the following?
- family doctor
- school nurse
- adult of the same sex
- booklets sent from the U.S. Dept. of Health, Education, and Welfare
- books in sections 301.431 in the public or school library which deal specifically with adolescence
- family clergyman

Studies show that adolescents are overconcerned and dissatisfied with their appearance. A group of students discussing this dissatisfaction said, "Who wouldn't be, when you look around and see some really beautiful people?" The students analyzed the reasons for their discontent and were able to pin it down to the unreal world of Hollywood and advertising. Advertisements, TV, movies, fashions, beauty contests, and magazines concern themselves with the ideal human body. The students decided not to be trapped by advertising slogans, and took comfort in knowing that theater makeup and special photography can make people look fantastic.

Students also decided that they weren't very realistic about their own appearance. They were often overcritical. A survey on body mass showed that although 50 percent of the class thought they were too heavy, in reality, only 16 percent were.

Why are people in advertisements and on TV usually more "beautiful" than real people? How do they affect you?

Tom not only accepts his nickname, "Boy," but jokes with friends about his lack of beard and his cracking voice. He participates in all activities with his classmates, who have already matured, and is well-accepted because he is sensitive to others and is independent. Tom did not make any school teams because of his small build, but he helps with the management of a team.

1. What disadvantages does Tom experience because of his late development?
2. How does Tom make up for these disadvantages?
3. Based on Tom's case, do you think it is a serious problem to physically mature later than others your own age?

Times, and People, Are Changing

An American teenager today reaches puberty at a much earlier chronological age than those who lived a century ago. One study shows that the average age at first menstruation of Norwegian girls in 1840 was seventeen years. In 1968, the average American age was less than thirteen years. Why is this an important fact?

Another interesting example of the changes in our physical development is evident in the famous La Scala Opera House in Milan, which has seats that are only 33 cm [13 in.] wide. Today the standard width of seats is 61 cm [24 in.]. Perhaps you have noticed, when you have visited an American pioneer museum, that shoe sizes were much smaller in the past. Remember to check this the next time you visit one of these places.

Today's teenager reaches adult height earlier than ever before. Can you suggest reasons for this?

1. At what age did your grandparents and parents reach puberty?
2. List some ways in which adults can help you at this stage of development.
3. What suggestions and advice would you give to a younger brother or sister to help them understand the changes that occur in puberty?

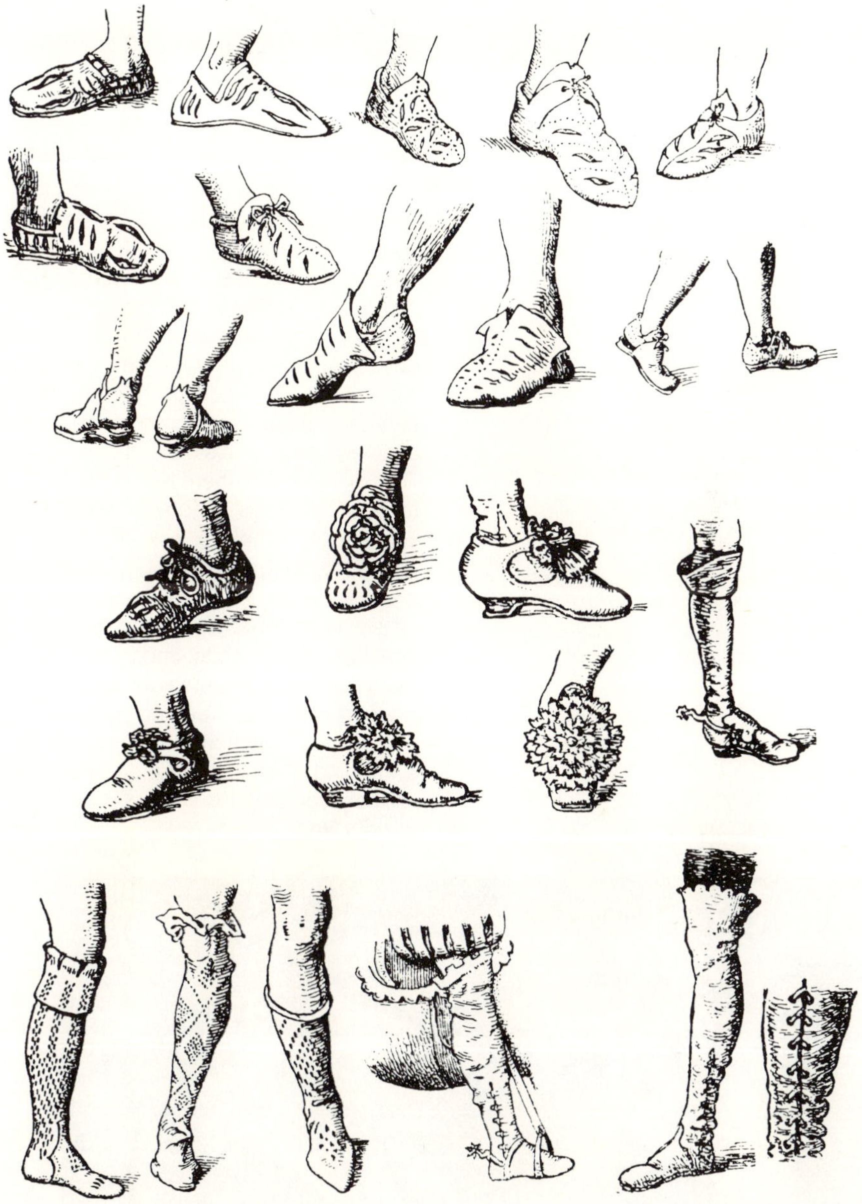

Find out how and why people have changed physically over the years. How has this affected the things we do in our lives?

Puberty Rites

In some cultures, special ceremonies called "puberty rites" mark the end of pubescence and the passage into puberty. The most spectacular and elaborate ceremonies involve the initiation of boys. The whole community celebrates the boy's growth from childhood to manhood.

One meaningful religious ceremony of this kind is the *Bar Mitzvah*. It symbolizes the beginning of maturity for the Jewish boy. The thirteen-year-old boy spends months in preparation for the synagogue service that marks the commencement of a new period in his life.

For many of you, there is no special recognition of this period of change in your life. Nonetheless, it should be regarded as a significant and pleasant change.

It is very important for you to develop sensible eating habits, and to ensure that you have between eight and ten hours of rest daily. Keeping yourself physically fit with activities such as swimming, skating, tennis, and dancing will help you develop skills you will enjoy all your life.

A Bar Mitzvah ceremony

adolescence
Bar Mitzvah
chronological age
facial proportion
growth spurt
physical change
puberty
puberty rites

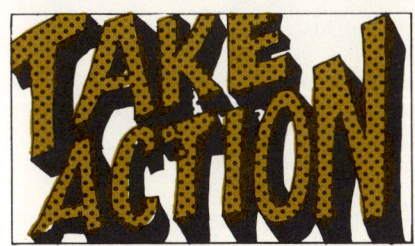

1. Write a short poem describing yourself entitled "Who Am I?"
2. **Just as the tadpole changes into a frog, or a caterpillar into a butterfly, so does the body of a child change into the new body of an adolescent.** Discuss this statement. List the characteristics of adolescent physical development.
3. Go to the library and read up on a puberty rite celebration. Report your findings to the class.
4. Do the type and number of hygiene and grooming practices change during puberty? Describe the routines you have developed that you didn't follow when you were in elementary school.
5. Discuss the part the family plays in helping you meet basic physical needs at this time. Do people outside the family also assist in meeting your basic needs?
6. What do you think it would be like to be "early" or "late" in physical development? Form a circle and answer in turn. The first person plays the role of an early developer and the next person of a late developer. Each person puts forward an advantage or a disadvantage for the person he or she is playing. Now, go around the circle once more and give a suggestion for coping with one of the advantages or disadvantages mentioned.
7. At mealtime discuss the "Who Am I?" exercise with your family. How do different members of your family identify themselves? In what areas are there similarities? In what areas are there unique qualities?

11

2 Adolescence

Childhood, adolescence, and adulthood are three very distinct periods in life. Each period is not only chronologically different, but is also accompanied by unique physical and psychological developments. Adolescence is a time of self-discovery leading to maturity. How would you describe adolescence? Here's what some adolescents have said:

"Sometimes I feel like a half-child, half grown-up."

"Adolescence could be called 'Teen-age Traumas.'"

"It was easier being a child. You could let your parents make all the decisions."

"There are so many changes to get used to."

"You are supposed to be responsible for your own actions. I can't blame anyone but myself. That's tough."

"Nobody really understands me."

Adolescence covers the years from age twelve to the early twenties. During this time span, most teenagers prefer relating to others of their own age or older.

Are you playing a waiting game? Are you always wishing you were a different age? Is there a perfect age? How would you fill in the blanks in the following statement?

I wish I were _____ because _____
(age)

Why are there specific age requirements in these organizations? What other chronological milestones can you think of?

Question I just met a good-looking boy at a party. We really enjoyed each other's company. Now I'm sick. I found out today that he's only twelve! I'll soon be fourteen. Do you think he's too young for me?

Answer Do you think he would be able to ignore all the razzing he'd get from the boys in his class? Would you be able to ignore all the razzing you'd get from the girls in your class? If the answers are "no," then you're both too young.

Question I am thirteen and want to join up for ski lessons at the Ski Club. The problem is that I have to choose between the ten to thirteen age group and the thirteen to sixteen age group. Group one meets on Saturday mornings, and group two on Tuesday evenings. I really want to join the second age group. However, there are two problems: this group costs more, and my parents worry about my taking a bus alone at night.

Answer Would the sixteen-year-olds really include the thirteen-year-olds? Would you be the only thirteen-year-old in group one? If your answers are "no" to these questions, then you probably realize which is the better choice.

Let's look at some of the things that will help you to understand the changes and concerns confronting you throughout the adolescent period.

Nutrition

Adolescence is a period of rapid growth. It is important for you to know what you need in the way of extra food and rest during this period. In chapter 1, you learned about the physical changes that occur in adolescence. You will cope better with these changes – and feel better – if you get a nutritious supply of food.

Do you always feel hungry? Could you eat all day long? This is not unnatural at your age. A fast-growing person may never feel that his or her appetite is satisfied. The stomach is often too small to hold as much food as the adolescent body needs, so you will feel the urge to eat at very frequent intervals. Do you find you eat the most readily available foods? Are these foods mainly snacks that are filling and sweet, but not necessarily of good food value? Typical snacks, such as potato chips, soft drinks, and candy, give you a quick supply of energy, but they are "empty calorie" foods, which means they contain lots of calories, but they don't contain the vitamins, minerals, and proteins required for growth and health. The result of too many calories is too much fat.

The "yo-yo" or "see-saw" method of reducing is very common. The failure here is due to an unbalanced diet and a return to former poor food habits. Where did this boy go wrong? What method of dieting would have helped him keep off that excess weight? The problem of being too heavy can create other emotional and physical problems for the adolescent.

Roxanne and Lynn decided to have a competition to help each other reduce. They were the only ones who thought they needed to reduce, but no one could convince them otherwise.

Roxanne decided to go on an egg and grapefruit diet. "Because, after all, eggs and grapefruit are both good for you," she said. Lynn chose to count carbohydrate grams, eating mostly meat, cheese, cream, a little salad and no bread or fruit. The first couple of days were great, because it was fun to have the will power to resist snack food and to dream about how their lives would change when they were model-slender.

They might have been enjoying this experience, but their friends and family found they were "touchy" and tended to be cranky. On the fifth day, Roxanne had terrible stomach cramps. She realized that the great quantities of grapefruit and egg were affecting her body. She also admitted, "If I eat one more egg today, I'm sure I'll start clucking."

Lynn decided to continue, and did so for a week. She really missed her juice in the morning and a piece of fruit with her lunch. The real problem was she began to have dizzy spells and often felt sick to her stomach. Lynn also decided to stop her fad diet and instead cut down on the amount of food she ate in her regular, well-balanced diet.

1. Why did Roxanne and Lynn go on diets? Do you think their reasons were good?
2. What was wrong with the diets?
3. Do you know anyone who has gone on a "fad" diet? What is wrong with such a diet?

When Cynthia arrived at the bus stop, there was a startled exclamation from Diane. "Do you ever look super! You're so slim! How did you do it?" Cynthia sat by Diane in the bus and explained that six months ago her doctor had recommended she see a nutritionist. The result of that interview was a well-balanced, low calorie diet which included a number of foods Cynthia liked. She also developed a better understanding of why she had to change some of her food habits.

Cynthia didn't mind telling Diane how insecure she used to feel around others, and of how for years she had been called "fatso." Clothes did not interest her, because once she put them on, all she noticed were the bulges. She tried to be jolly, but found it difficult since she didn't feel that way. Cynthia had always had good posture, and now her clothes really looked great on her – she said she felt great, too.

1. Why did Cynthia go on a diet?
2. Why was Cynthia's diet better than Roxanne's and Lynn's?

Guide to Good Eating...

A Recommended Daily Pattern

The recommended daily pattern provides the foundation for a nutritious, healthful diet.

The recommended servings from the Four Food Groups for adults supply about 1200 Calories. The chart below gives recommendations for the number and size of servings for several categories of people.

Food Group	Recommended Number of Servings				
	Child	Teenager	Adult	Pregnant Woman	Lactating Woman

Milk
1 cup milk, yogurt, OR
Calcium Equivalent:
  1½ slices (1½ oz) cheddar cheese*
  1 cup pudding
  1¾ cups ice cream
  2 cups cottage cheese*
	3	4	2	4	4

Meat
2 ounces cooked, lean meat, fish, poultry, OR
Protein Equivalent:
  2 eggs
  2 slices (2 oz) cheddar cheese*
  ½ cup cottage cheese*
  1 cup dried beans, peas
  4 tbsp peanut butter
	2	2	2	3	2

Fruit-Vegetable ½ cup cooked or juice 1 cup raw Portion commonly served such as a medium-size apple or banana	4	4	4	4	4

Grain, whole grain, fortified, enriched
  1 slice bread
  1 cup ready-to-eat cereal
  ½ cup cooked cereal, pasta, grits
	4	4	4	4	4

*Count cheese as serving of milk OR meat, not both simultaneously.

"**Others**" complement but do not replace foods from the Four Food Groups. Amounts should be determined by individual caloric needs.

Courtesy, Guide to Good Eating, National Dairy Council

In affluent societies there is a tendency to overfeed children and to overeat as adults. Although overeating doesn't have dangerous consequences for children, many fat boys and girls grow into fatter adults.

It's easy to find excuses for eating too much. Often people overeat when faced with a problem or during a period of stress. It is a good idea to recognize when you are "feeding" your problems and to look for positive ways of solving them.

Overeating, like other addictions, is a form of self-gratification: something you indulge in that makes you feel better – temporarily. Overeating is a result of conditioning: you become conditioned by the kinds of behavior you have learned.

Sleeping Habits

The ninth grade students went on a ski weekend to a resort in the mountains. The trip took nine hours, and it was midnight when they arrived at the hotel. The excitement continued as everyone ran back and forth checking on each other's rooms and chatting. Some people carried on until really late and were hard to wake up in the morning. Three girls locked their door and refused to go skiing. A couple of the boys who stayed up late were so miserable that no one would talk to them for fear of being snapped at.

Finally, the chaperone and a few students started discussing whether it was safe for those who were physically exhausted and not mentally alert to go skiing. The group decided they would go skiing only if they felt well enough rested. Those who had to catch up on their sleep could stay at the hotel and be picked up after lunch to go to the ski hills. The students decided to set their own curfew for the next night. Since they had raised the money through a group project, they didn't want to waste their time and money sleeping when they could be skiing.

1. How many hours of sleep do you require each night?
2. Does everyone in your family require the same amount of rest?
3. Are you a "morning person" or a "night hawk"?
4. Do you know anyone who gets extra rest by taking "cat naps"?
5. Can you describe how you react when you have gone without sleep? Do you get grouchy, quiet, irritable, giggly, or uncommunicative?
6. What happens to the other members of your family when they have had too little sleep and are overtired? How does lack of sleep affect your best friend?

Health Problems

Adolescents are relatively free from illnesses, but they do develop health problems such as acne, eye troubles, and tooth decay.

Difficulties with eyesight often occur at this age. Good eyesight is important for success both in and out of school. Wearing glasses upsets some people, but there are many attractive frames to choose from, or perhaps contact lenses might be a solution. When you have eye difficulties corrected, you'll never be accused of snubbing your friends because you literally couldn't see them!

Skin Problems

Acne is a skin ailment that troubles most adolescents at one time or another. It can be very disturbing because it interferes with the way you want to appear to others. Do you ever have the feeling that just before every big occasion your face breaks out? Don't spend hours fretting about the problem – *do* something. Seek the advice of your school nurse or a dermatologist. Since this is a major concern at your age, you could form a study group to consider complexion disorders, their causes and treatment.

Interview a cross-section of people. Ask them what causes their skin to break out. One person may break out the day after eating seafoods. A boy may break out from contact with his girlfriend's makeup. Some people find that planning a school event causes skin eruptions. Make a master list of skin problems and of some solutions to the problems. Remember that this exercise is to prevent skin disorders. Do not play "doctor" and diagnose treatment for acne.

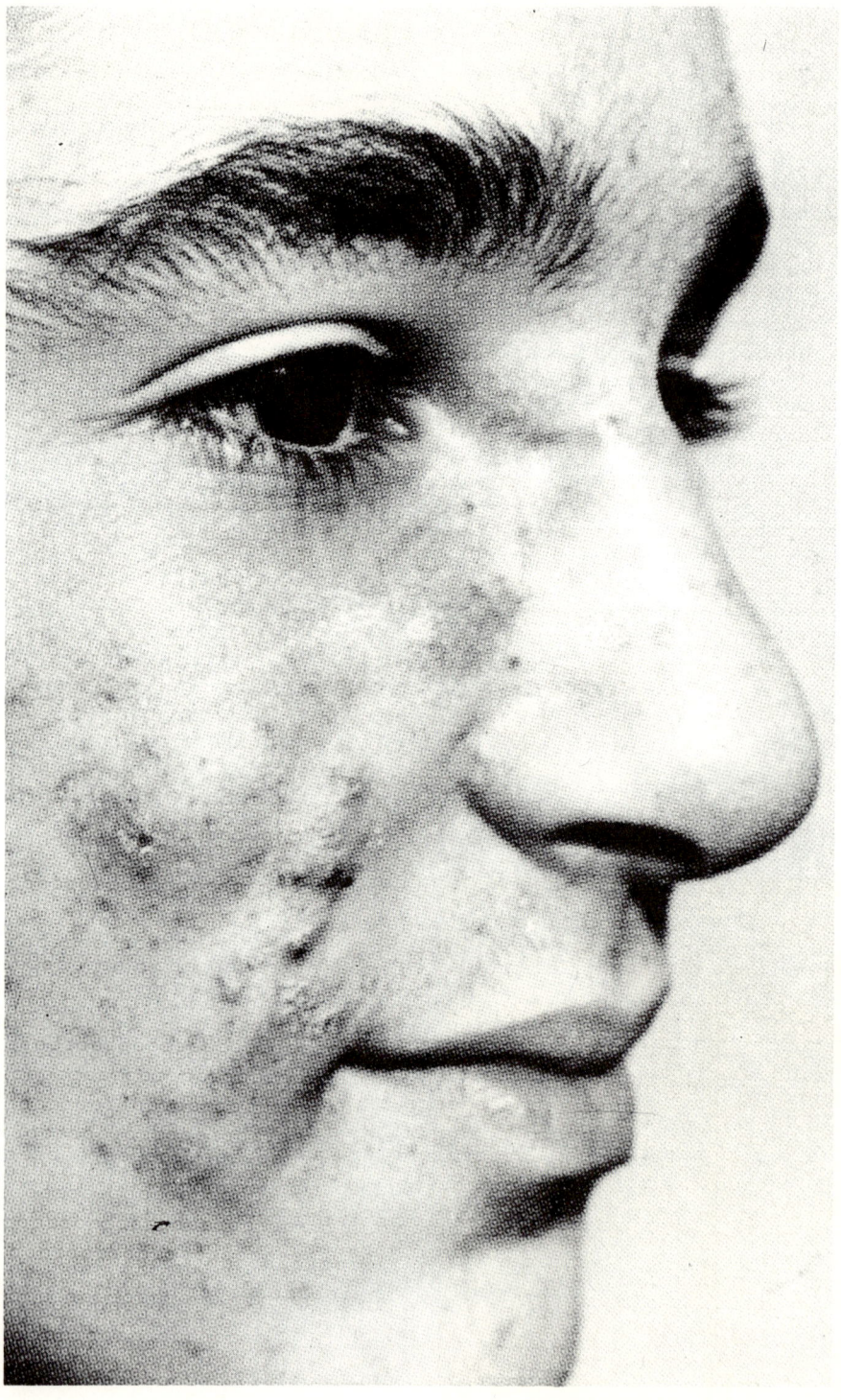

General Rules for Skin Care
- ☑ Wash the skin at least every morning and night.
- ☑ Be sure to rinse well after each washing, as soap residue will clog pores.
- ☑ Make sure your diet is well balanced.
- ☑ Avoid emotional stress.
- ☑ Use clean face cloths and towels.
- ☑ Keep your hands away from your face.
- ☑ Do not pick blemishes.

We had a lot of trouble finding a photo of someone with acne. Since acne is a common adolescent problem, why are there so few photos showing it?

Venereal Diseases

The most serious diseases threatening adolescents are venereal diseases. What are venereal diseases? Syphilis and gonorrhea are the two most common venereal diseases. They are both infectious.

What's the truth about V.D.? Can you catch V.D. in public washrooms, from drinking glasses, bed linens, or other items used by infected persons? The fact is that V.D. is almost exclusively contracted through sexual intercourse. V.D. germs die when in contact with air or soap and water. They require direct contact with the human body in order to survive and multiply.

What are the symptoms of V.D.? After the germs enter the body, a few symptoms occur. They are usually so minor they go unnoticed. Unusual soreness or discharge from the genital organs and contact with a person suspected of being infected should be brought to the immediate attention of a doctor.

Shame or embarrassment often stops young people from going to a doctor.

Most large hospitals have V.D. detection clinics. They are staffed by people concerned with fighting disease and not with passing judgments on a person's behavior. They can also be trusted to respect the privacy of patients.

Can you explain why V.D. is called the silent epidemic? Did you realize that next to the common cold V.D. is the most communicable disease? V.D. germs are present in the body for up to twenty years – multiplying and destroying body cells. Eventually disabilities result. This disease has reached epidemic proportions in the U.S. Statistics show that in the twenty-two-year period between 1957 and 1979, the incidence of gonorrhea increased from 214,496 to 1,003,958 reported cases. This was an increase of 368 percent.

It is important that all adolescents know the facts regarding the causes of venereal disease and understand the importance of immediate treatment.

Accidents

Accidents are responsible for the greatest number of deaths among adolescents. Adolescents have a great desire for independence and tend to be adventurous in their activities. So this is a very vulnerable period. Parents are very aware of the rate of accidents, and this is the basis for their concern about where you go and what you do.

Drugs, smoking, and alcohol are often experimented with at this stage. You will probably have to decide whether or not to indulge in these things. The use of these chemicals can cause both physical and mental health problems. You have a responsibility to yourself and to your future to learn about these chemicals so that you can make wise decisions about their use. Accidents often occur when young people are under the influence of alcohol or drugs.

CASES OF SYPHILIS AND GONORRHEA REPORTED BY STATE HEALTH DEPARTMENTS, 1969-1979
(Known Military Cases Excluded)

Year	Syphilis Cases	Gonorrhea Cases
1969	92,162	534,872
1970	91,382	600,072
1971	95,997	670,268
1972	91,149	767,215
1973	87,469	842,621
1974	83,771	906,121
1975	80,356	999,937
1976	71,761	1,001,994
1977	64,621	1,002,219
1978	64,875	1,013,436
1979	67,049	1,003,958

Source: STD Fact Sheet, Edition Thirty-Five, CDC-VDCD, Atlanta, GA 30340, 1980

Alcohol Pre-Test	True	False
Using a separate sheet of paper, respond to these statements by labeling each one either T (true) or F (false).		
1. Alcoholism is a major public health problem.		
2. For young people, the most immediate danger in drinking is intoxication.		
3. The number of female alcoholics is steadily increasing.		
4. Alcohol speeds up a driver's reaction time in the event of an emergency.		
5. AA is a national automobile association.		
6. Nutritional diseases, such as beriberi and pellagra, are often found among alcoholics.		
7. The average person with 0.5 percent of alcohol in the blood is in critical danger.		
8. Most alcoholics are found on skid row.		
9. One should be critical of alcohol and its effects, but should also have a positive understanding towards the alcoholic.		
10. Alcohol is a stimulant.		
11. Alcohol cures colds.		
12. Excessive drinking may produce serious physical and mental diseases.		
13. Alcohol causes feelings of inferiority.		
14. Alcoholics come from all social classes, professions, and backgrounds.		
15. Judgment, vision, and reaction time in the individual's performance are frequently impaired by a small amount of alcohol.		

Answers to Pre-Test

1. T 2. T 3. T 4. F 5. F 6. T 7. T 8. F
9. T 10. F 11. F 12. T 13. T 14. T 15. T

Why do people drink or take drugs? Is it because they feel more relaxed, are able to forget problems, believe that it increases their creativity, or because they like to experiment? List other possible reasons.

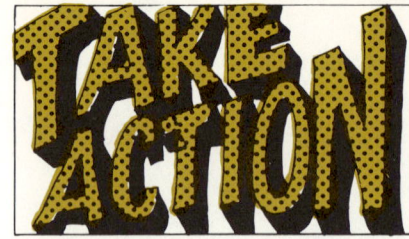

Discuss the following statements:
1. "Everything that is fun is dangerous."
2. "It's my body. I'll do what I want with it."
3. "Do as I say, not as I do."

Motor Coordination

A noted psychologist once said that throughout childhood there is a strong tendency to be active, but that as one matures, there is a strong inclination to sit down. Do you agree?

The quality of motor activity varies according to body build and rate of growth. In our society, the mature, capable, athletic person is admired.

Rapid growth, plus lack of self-confidence, often result in adolescent awkwardness. Different parts of the body grow at different rates and this also results in awkwardness. The feet, for example, grow to their full length before full body height is reached to accommodate them.

Do you feel like a clodhopper? Here are some ways to overcome clumsiness.

- ☑ Take up some activities that increase your control and balance. Bowling, dancing, yoga, gymnastics, tennis, and skating all contribute to smoothing your movements.
- ☑ If you don't care for athletics, try woodworking or guitar lessons.
- ☑ Practice walking. Copy the walk of someone who moves well. Remember to buy comfortable shoes that are not too clumsy and that don't throw you off balance.
- ☑ Remember that physical education classes and activities will definitely help you to improve your motor coordination.

Intellectual Development

Physical development is closely related to psychological, intellectual, social, and personality development. As you mature, your thought processes become more highly refined. You begin to use your resources – what you already know – as you interact with your environment.

Would you agree that your thinking is now becoming freer, and that you do not accept everything you hear? Do you consider all the available information and then make your own judgment about things?

Adolescent thinking has characteristics that distinguish it from the thought processes of children. You are now freer to move in any direction in your thoughts; you are beginning to be more flexible. You are not usually stuck with one perception or set of conclusions. You are beginning to control your thoughts. You can ignore distracting, irrelevant thoughts, gather pertinent information, keep it all in your head, organize your thoughts, relate them to the situation at hand, and come to conclusions. You have now developed the ability to think about your own thinking.

An elementary-school-age child is happy to describe something, but the adolescent wants to explain it. Description merely indicates how things are; explanation indicates why they are that way.

Story-Telling Activity

Ask some preschool children of different ages to tell you a story. You will quickly notice when the change occurs from a descriptive to an explanatory story. The interests of each age group differ too.

Two-year-olds vary in the size of their vocabulary and in their willingness to cooperate with your request. Mature two-year-olds can give a brief story in a series of short sentences – not necessarily related to each other in meaning. Their stories are about facts and what they have learned, and often relate to their homes. They usually like to tell "friendly" stories:

"That baby David. He's my friend. He goes burp. He goes goo goo. You like David? Can we get a baby too?"

Three-year-olds love to tell stories – and at this age the stories are longer, too! Violence predominates. One thought follows another, and one has no greater emphasis than the next. The only emphasis comes from the repetition of simple actions:

"See that dog . . . he's going to get hit. When he walks on the road, cars will hit him. Then another one – hit, HIT!"

Four-year-olds are becoming self-conscious. If they are feeling comfortable, they will rattle on and expand on an extremely violent theme. This is the high point for violence, fantasy, and far-from-home tales:

"Well, . . . you know the kids. Balloons blew up big and broke. The squirrels came in the chimney and ate up the house. They will bite your toes and you'll break your head off. Then the ambulance comes and takes you away. Your head will get stuck back on."

Five-year-olds prefer repeating familiar storybook tales to telling their own. Stories are realistic and often deal with family matters. Violence is still a big theme:

"The king lives in that funny house. His little girl has cats and a pretty dress and lots of toys. If she rips the books, her daddy will spank her and she will cry. Then they will live happily forever."

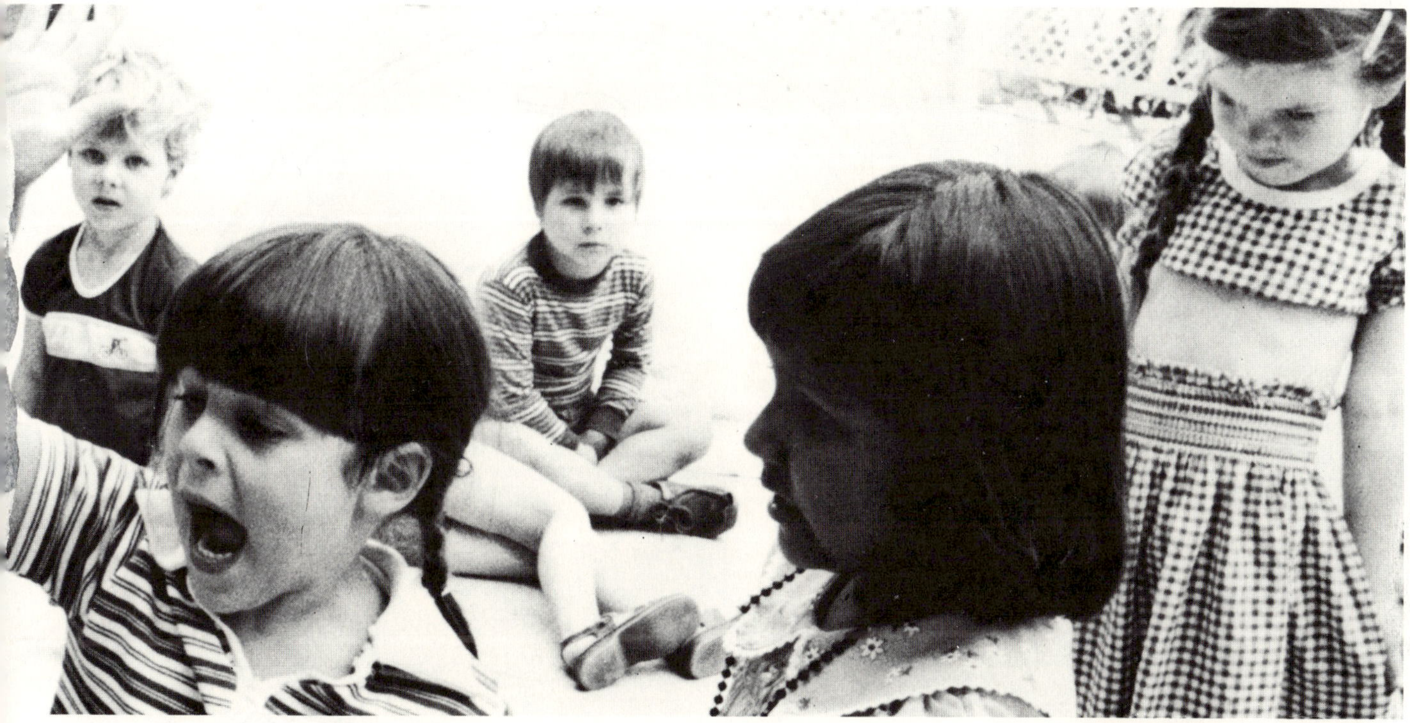

The adolescent begins to build theories, and can distinguish between "what is" and "what could be." The child tends to accept the first plausible explanation, and then decides the matter is settled. An adolescent will test and judge various hypotheses, reject some explanations, seek new evidence, discover a new possibility, and thus build up a system of thought.

Adolescents can move back and forth between fantasy and reality. Children lose themselves in situations. You can imagine yourself in a situation, then stand back and analyze it. Your creative thinking can result in new ideas, products, and solutions. Can you think of some examples to illustrate this new kind of thinking?

Schools are now including more activities and courses to encourage creative problem-solving and to promote creative behavior. Can you think of some school or home activities that are available to you in which you can exercise your creative talent?

acne
chronological differences
conditioning
empty calorie foods
energizer
fad diet
motor coordination
nutrition
poor eating cycle
self-gratification
venereal diseases

1. Interview people who have been on fad diets. List the ways these diets affected their bodies and their personalities.
2. Read *Go Ask Alice*, no author named (New York: Avon Books, 1972).
   (a) Explain the title.
   (b) What questions would you ask Alice?
   (c) How was the fifteen-year-old girl introduced to drugs? Do you think this was fair? Why or why not?
   (d) Give two reasons why Chris and the fifteen-year-old girl fitted the saying, "Birds of a feather flock together."
   (e) Why is it so difficult for the fifteen-year-old girl to stay "clean"?
   (f) What is the real purpose of this book?
3. *Blindfold Game*
   (a) Choose one person to be blindfolded. Appoint someone else as a recorder. Place an object in the blindfolded person's hand and ask the person to describe it. Record the description.
   (b) Repeat this exercise with a child. Did you discover that the older person both describes and explains what he or she feels, whereas the young child simply describes the object?
4. Try to solve this mystery and you will see how your thought processes are more advanced than they were in elementary school.

"Detective Dan," said Sue Scoop, "we have been asked to assist the local police force on a crime they find most baffling. Here are some of the details. Apparently a lady was brutally murdered by one of her employees. The victim employed the three women suspects to work for her consumer research company during the evening to telephone the general public to find out the success of their research program. The woman employees – Mrs. Katz, Mrs. McPerson, and Mrs. Peeper – had worked at their present jobs for years even though each had her own personal reasons to wish her employer dead. The women worked in separate little offices off the main office where their boss worked.

"The women were employed to start at 6:00 p.m., the time most people are home, and to phone until 9:20 p.m. This gave them enough time to make exactly one hundred phone calls each at the rate of one every two minutes. At 9:20 p.m. the women left their offices and returned to the main office to file their reports and leave the office by 9:30 p.m. On the night in question, the women left their offices as usual at 9:20 sharp and returned to the main office to find their boss sprawled on the floor, dead.

"The security guard at the main desk swears no one left or entered the building between 6:00 and 9:20. A thorough search of the building has turned up nothing. So one of the ladies must be the murderer, but, of course, none of them admits to any knowledge of the crime. Our problem is to find out who is lying."

"Let's go to the scene of the crime," said Detective Dan. "A good idea," Sue Scoop said.

Here are the important clues Sue Scoop and Detective Dan found.

(a) Any one of the three women could have committed the murder and returned to her office unseen.

(b) The murderer could have left any of the offices, committed the murder, and returned to her office in two minutes.

(c) The work sheets the ladies did that night reported the following: Mrs. Peeper – 41 people saw ad A, 40 people saw ad B, 50 people saw ad C, 7 people saw ads A and B, 8 people saw ads A and C, 6 people saw ads B and C, and 5 people saw ads A, B, and C.
Mrs. McPerson – 53 people saw ad A, 50 people saw ad B, 50 people saw ad C, 10 people saw ads A and B, 12 people saw ads A and C, 15 people saw ads B and C, and 8 people saw ads A, B, and C.
Mrs. Katz – 50 people saw ad A, 60 people saw ad B, 65 people saw ad C, 10 people saw ads A and B, 15 people saw ads A and C, 15 people saw ads B and C and 18 people saw ads A, B, and C.

"Well," said Detective Dan, "this is a dead end. These sheets just tell us how many people saw the different advertisements, not how many were phoned. What we need to know is which woman didn't make her hundred calls. The murderer must have missed at least one phone call."

Sue Scoop just muttered as she worked with her pen and notebook. "There," she said excitedly, "I know who did it. She only made ninety-nine phone calls."

27

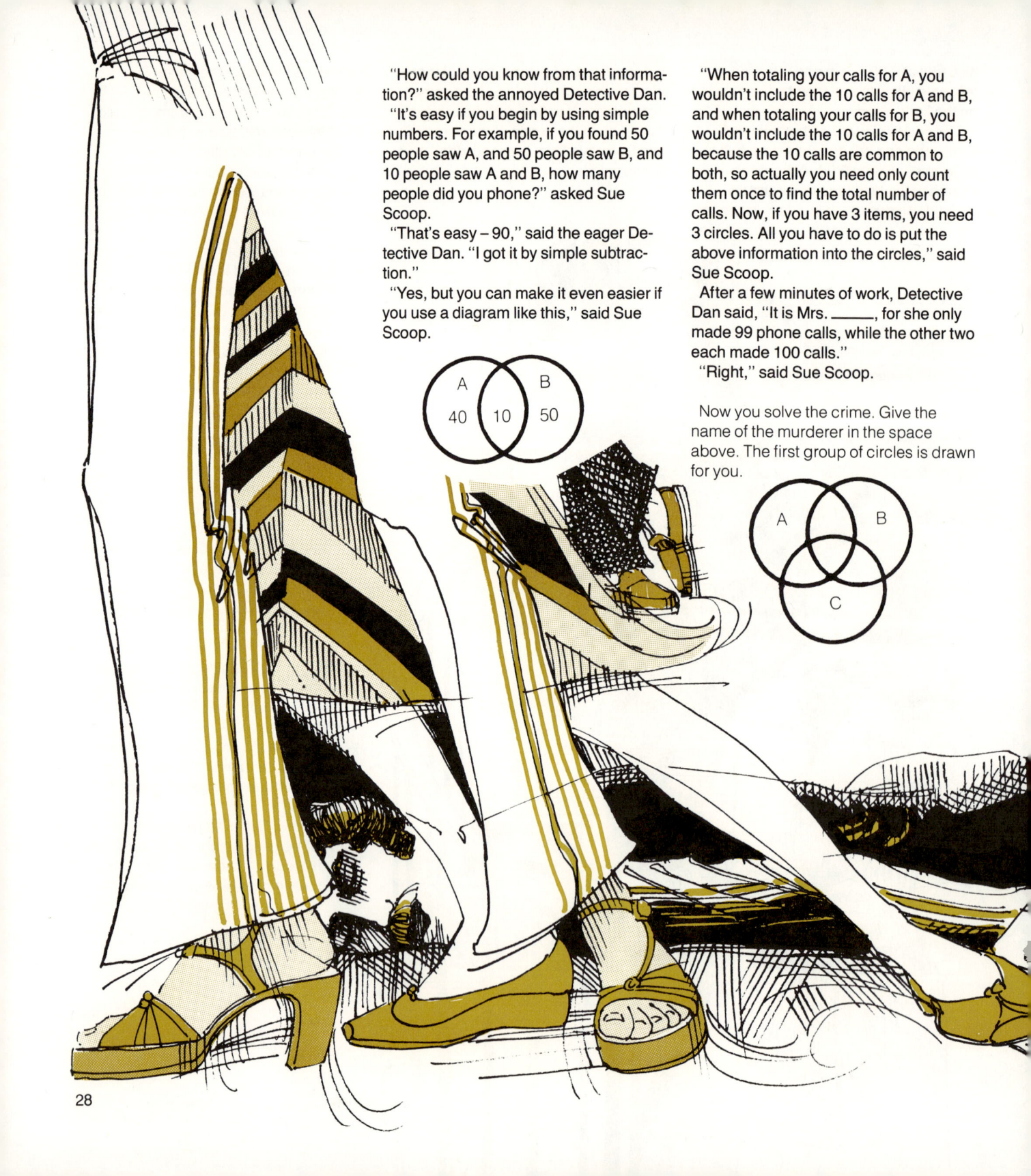

"How could you know from that information?" asked the annoyed Detective Dan.

"It's easy if you begin by using simple numbers. For example, if you found 50 people saw A, and 50 people saw B, and 10 people saw A and B, how many people did you phone?" asked Sue Scoop.

"That's easy – 90," said the eager Detective Dan. "I got it by simple subtraction."

"Yes, but you can make it even easier if you use a diagram like this," said Sue Scoop.

"When totaling your calls for A, you wouldn't include the 10 calls for A and B, and when totaling your calls for B, you wouldn't include the 10 calls for A and B, because the 10 calls are common to both, so actually you need only count them once to find the total number of calls. Now, if you have 3 items, you need 3 circles. All you have to do is put the above information into the circles," said Sue Scoop.

After a few minutes of work, Detective Dan said, "It is Mrs. _____, for she only made 99 phone calls, while the other two each made 100 calls."

"Right," said Sue Scoop.

Now you solve the crime. Give the name of the murderer in the space above. The first group of circles is drawn for you.

5. Your school has asked students to design new mini-courses which are to be taught in the next semester. Design a course to be called "Creativity." List activities that would help students to become more creative in their thinking; suggest activities for making actual objects and activities that make use of items that are often discarded.
6. Discuss lyrics from popular songs. What typical adolescent times do they talk about? Bring a current popular record to school and play it for the class. Discuss the lyrics.
7. A great deal of advertising is specifically directed to the general health of the public. People tend to ignore common sense and choose patent medicines to relieve their problems. Read this old ad and see how it tries to convince people of its cure-all abilities. Find a similar contemporary ad.
8. What common drugs are taken in your home? Are they abused? How could the observance of health rules and proper physical care prevent the need for these drugs? You might consider drugs such as caffeine, aspirin, diet pills, sleeping pills, and tranquilizers.

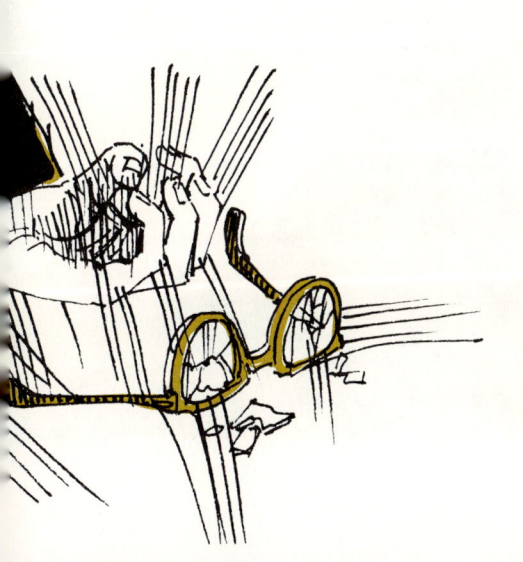

3 The Socialization of You

Cindy and Jim are playing with their two-month-old son, Timothy. They are amazed that he can already smile and babble at them and follow every move they make. Timothy also likes to watch the animal mobile moving in the breeze above his carriage. Every time Cindy and Jim call, he turns his head in their direction and gives a little smile and gurgle.

Timothy has already learned to respond to his parents and to objects around him. Do you think Timothy reacts this way naturally, through instinct, or has he learned to respond?

Children learn how to think, feel, and behave. They learn by watching, listening and imitating. Andrea and Barb are high school students who have been friends since they were four years old. Teachers and classmates often call them by each other's names because they laugh in the same way, use the same expressions, and have similar mannerisms. They have been influenced by each other.

Do you remember anyone saying, "You are exactly like your father" – or your best friend? You may not be conscious of it, but because you learn behavior from the people around you, your actions will be similar to theirs.

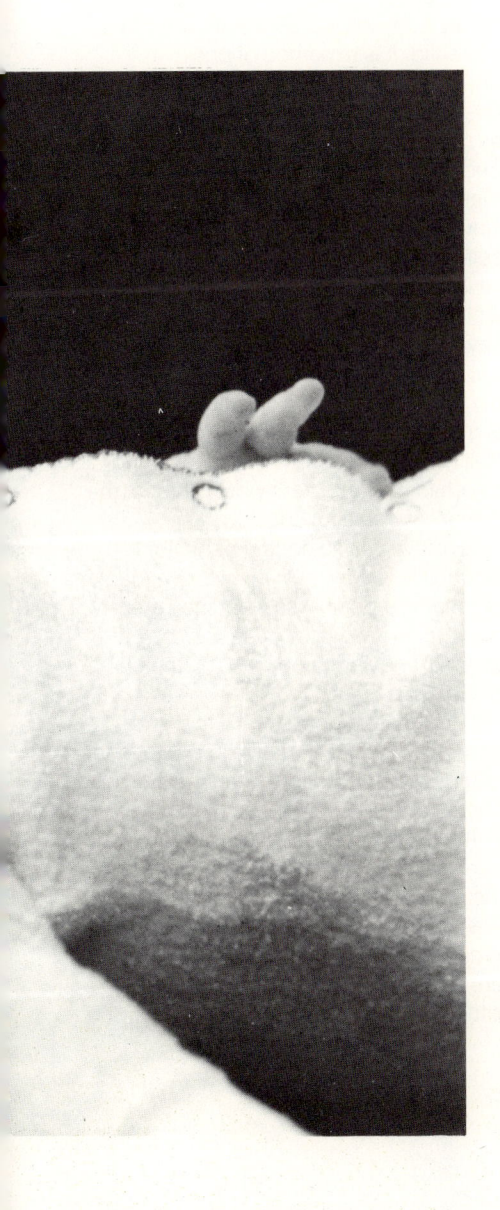

Social Learning

Infants listen to and copy the sounds around them: the human voice, a squeaky toy, or the family pet. They imitate the actions of their parents, sisters, and brothers. Children watch a wind-up toy, a frisky dog, or other children running and playing, and they pattern their behavior on the actions they observe. This process is called *social learning*. The behavior pattern learned in the first years of a child's life often determines the thoughts and actions this person will have as an adult.

Young children learn to do many things before they discriminate. They grasp at anything and everything that comes into reach and put everything into their mouths. When they demand attention, they expect immediate results. At first, parents will "child-proof" their world, until infants gradually learn what is safe and acceptable to touch and eat, and how to communicate with others. This learning is part of the *socialization* process that all infants go through. Socialization is the teaching done by parents, other members of the family, teachers, peers, and members of the community. These teaching models help children to evolve as individuals and to find a place in society where they can communicate and interact successfully with others.

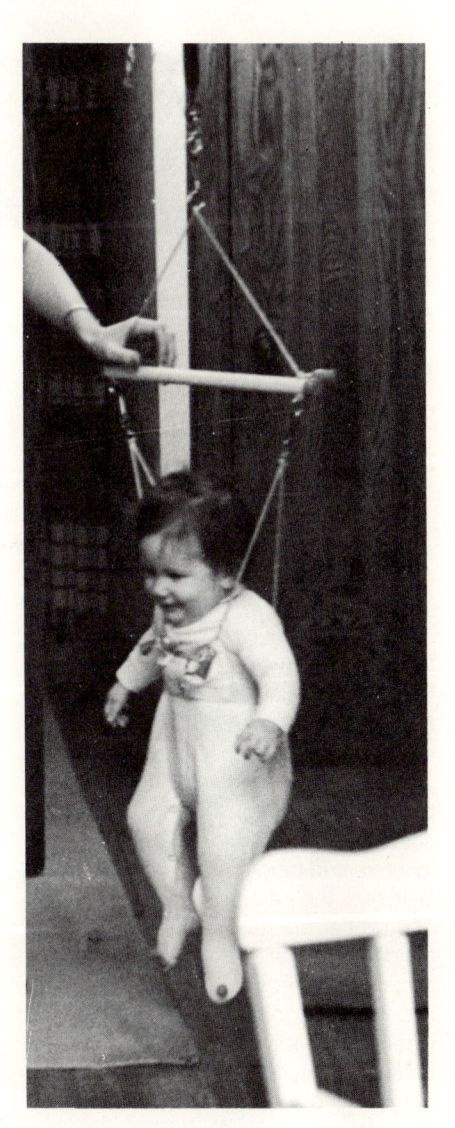

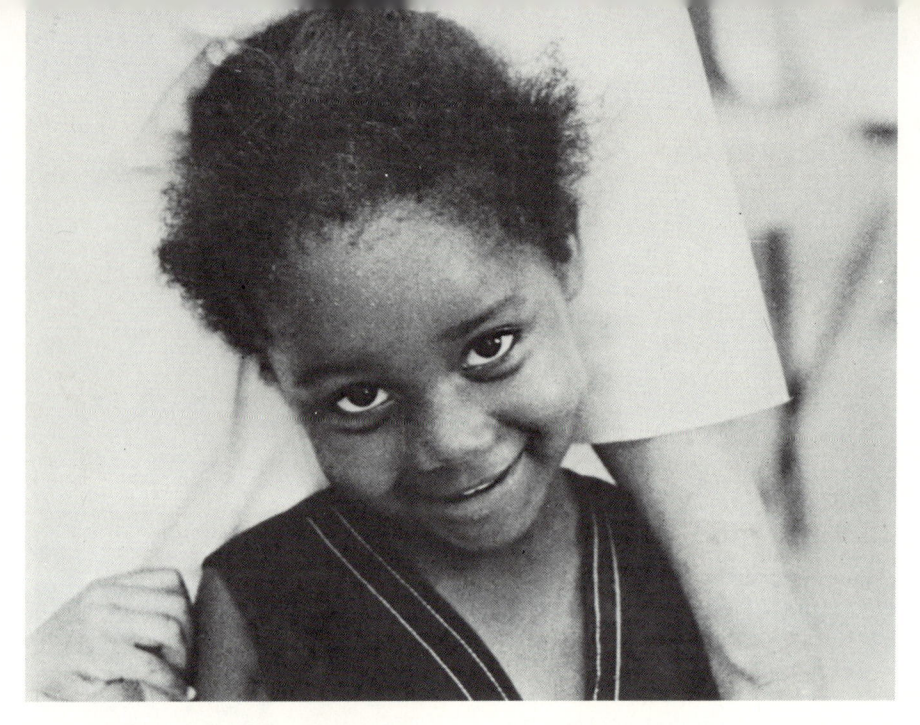

Socialization and Personality

The socialization experiences a person undergoes have an effect on personality development. If the experiences are good, the child develops into an adult with personality characteristics that make him or her compatible with the rest of society.

The way the young are socialized varies from society to society. In some societies, for example, toilet training is begun before the child's first birthday, while in others the child is left to learn to control himself or herself. Often, the older children teach the younger through shame and ridicule. When children are toilet trained before their first birthdays, it is, in fact, the parents who are "trained." They act as caretakers – getting the child to the toilet on time. Too much emphasis is frequently placed on toilet training. This goes back to the days when there were no modern conveniences – no automatic washing machines, no disposable diapers, and no indoor plumbing. In some cultures, the mother would want to rush toilet training, as the infant was carried on her back all day and she didn't want to get wet.

Stop and think of the many socialization demands that are made on a child between the ages of two and four – learning to talk correctly, learning table manners, adapting to a time schedule, learning to share with others, learning to speak the truth, and acquiring a whole set of habits related to food and cleanliness.

Does a child have to be disciplined in order to be socialized? In a sense, the answer to this question is "yes," but if the discipline takes the form of positive direction and guidance, it will achieve the goal of *self*-discipline and result in a happier human being.

Behavior Control

Let's think of some of the ways parents guide children. One method of guidance is to control a child's behavior with "things." A child may be denied treats or privileges if he or she is "bad" or bribed with things to encourage good behavior. Control may also be exercised through physical punishment. Another technique is to help the child see that the way people feel about him or her is important. What are your feelings about these methods?

The first two examples are negative ways of behavior control because they make a child feel shame and fear. The importance of the people-caring method is that it develops a sense of conscience in a child. It is a method of positive behavior control. Children who are guided in this way will want to act in an acceptable manner because it pleases people who are important to them and makes them feel good about themselves. This also helps them to become self-directed and self-disciplined.

It is harmful to withdraw your love from a child if the child is behaving badly. To say, "I won't love you anymore," or to bribe children by saying, "I will give you my time and attention if you do this . . ." is a threat. It may also make the child feel that he or she is not worthy of love and the child may constantly compete for the "favor" of being loved.

A positive way to control behavior is to let children know that you still love them, but that you do not like what they are doing. This method focuses on the children's behavior, rather than on the children themselves.

Children are guided best if they get both positive and negative expectations and direction. If children know what they should and should not do, they will be better informed and know which forms of behavior help them to interact best with the people in their lives. What guidelines have you received from your parents? What techniques do you use with brothers and sisters, or when you are babysitting?

Johnny was out for a walk with his mother one mild fall day. They kicked through the leaves, crunched over stones, peeked through bushes, and had a great time. When they stopped to talk to a neighbor, Johnny soon became anxious to move on and tugged impatiently at his mother's hand. When he saw this got little attention, he started making footprints in the muddy puddle at the side of the walk.

His mother's first reaction was to say, "Get out of the mud!" Since she understood that he was bored standing still and had found this way to entertain himself, she realized he needed a suggestion for an activity that was less messy. "Johnny," she said, "could you find some pretty stones beside the walk here that we could collect? Could you put them in a row and make a long train out of them?" "O.K. let's make a train," Johnny said gleefully.

Johnny was easily diverted to this activity which occupied him in a way he enjoyed. There were no hard feelings, his shoes would not become muddier, and his mother could continue her conversation with the neighbor.

1. Why did Johnny start to play in the mud?
2. Do you think his mother's reaction was a good one?
3. What would your reaction have been?
4. Socialization occurs throughout life. Parents do not imitate your behavior, but they do learn as you and your friends express your interests, thoughts, and feelings. Have you ever influenced your parents' choice of clothing, reading, or movies?

Ferals and Isolates

Let's look at some studies of children who were secluded from human contact. How do you think they would differ from you? What actions, thoughts, and feelings would these children exhibit?

Have you read the legend of Romulus and Remus? These children were abandoned by their parents and a she-wolf suckled and reared them until they could fend for themselves.

There is evidence of real children who have been reared by animals. The wolf-girls of India, Amala and Kamala, were found by a missionary, Reverend A. L. Singh. They were covered with great clumps of hair through which their faces could be seen and crawled and moved as wolf cubs did. Their eyes were bright and piercing like animals', but it was obvious they were human beings.

The chronological age of Kamala was guessed to be about eight, and Amala would be about one and a half. They had to be treated like infants as they couldn't speak. They had developed the natures of animals. It took hard work and a great deal of inconvenience to change their set habits. They ate salads with their teeth and not with the aid of forks. They drank water by lapping it up like dogs.

Amala died a year after her capture, but Kamala lived for nine years. In this period, she learned a vocabulary of only about forty words.

Individuals like Amala and Kamala are called *ferals*. Ferals, reared by wolves, bears, or other animals and thus deprived of human contact, do not develop the ability to interact with fellow human beings.

Unfortunately, there are cases of children raised by parents who have been given only a minimum of human interaction and attention. These children are called *isolates*, because they have been totally isolated from social, emotional, and physical contact with people. Here is a true case study of an isolate.

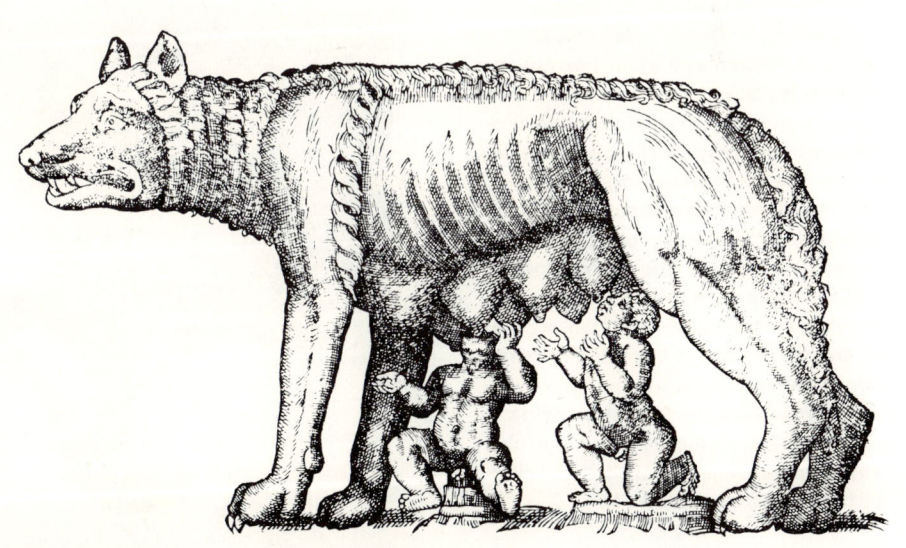

Romulus and Remus were two children raised by wolves. They are reputed to be the founders of the city of Rome.

Anna was an illegitimate child. Her mother lived with a stern widowed grandfather who strongly disapproved of his granddaughter's pregnancy. Anna was placed in various foster homes during the first five months of her life, but since her mother could not pay for her care (and no one was found to adopt her), she was brought to the grandfather's house and kept in a room on the second floor. Anna's mother was too afraid of the grandfather's anger to bring her downstairs, so Anna was left alone with only enough care to keep her alive. She was seldom moved, and her bedding and clothing were filthy.

At six, when Anna was found and removed from her grandfather's house, she could neither walk nor talk, and showed no signs of intelligence. She was badly undernourished, looked like a skeleton, and had a bloated stomach. She had been fed only on cow's milk during the period of time spent under her mother's care.

For the next two years, Anna was looked after in a country home where she progressed to walking, feeding herself, and understanding simple commands. She was then placed in a private home for retarded children where she lived until her death at ten and a half years of age. By the time of her death, Anna could follow simple directions, play with blocks, and string beads. She could also recognize some colors and make the distinction between pleasant and unpleasant pictures. Her favorite toy was a doll. She was very neat and continuously washed her hands and brushed her teeth. She could talk in phrases and repeated them often, trying to make conversation. She tried to help other children. Anna had a good sense of rhythm, walked well, and could run, although clumsily. She became easily excited, but all in all had a pleasing disposition.

1. Describe the changes that took place in Anna's behavior in this study.
2. Explain why Anna's behavior changed.
3. What do you think might account for the difference in development between Kamala and Anna?

We know that the socialization process can help a child develop from a totally dependent being to an independent, reasonable, well-balanced adult. We know that socialization is a teaching-learning process. We also know that children can become socialized more easily and more successfully if they receive guidance from parents.

Your socialization is helped by your family, your friends, and your experiences at school. You are not totally influenced by those around you, however, because you do experiment with what you see and hear. From your observations of others, you adopt, combine, and choose some forms of behavior and discard others. This process will continue throughout your life.

WORD POWER

behavior control
ferals
guidelines
imitation
isolates
self-discipline
socialization
social learning

TAKE ACTION

1. Observe a group of children at play. List the differences you see in children. (Children may be observed at home, in playgrounds, schoolyards, day-care centers, or in the homes of friends and relatives.)
2. Question your family about your activities when you were a preschooler.
   (a) How did you react to different socializing demands?
   (b) Did you enjoy imitating some of your parents' activities?
   (c) Were you a carbon copy of an older brother or sister?
3. What would it be like to live in a house without adults?
   Describe the day-to-day activities:
   (a) if the inhabitants of the house were three ten-year-olds;
   (b) if they were three fourteen-year-olds.
   What emphasis would be placed on housekeeping, meals, studying, leisure time, social activities, etc.? Would there be problems? If so, suggest what these would be and how they would be resolved.
4. Do you agree that:
   (a) dogs resemble their owners?
   (b) if a child grows up hearing classical music in the home, the child will develop an appreciation for classical music?
5. Personal Profile
   (a) Consider each of the characteristics in the diagram.
   (b) Copy the figure outline in your notebook and write in the characteristics that describe you.
   (c) Add some other characteristics that would give a more complete picture of your personality.
   (d) Try to determine what persons or situations have socialized you to become the person you are.
   (e) Share this profile with a friend to see if your friend would add other characteristics.
6. Read or recall a story about a person from a minority group or about someone living in a less fortunate environment than you. Is it possible that this child's socialization is different from yours? Could such a child be socialized to feel inferior to other people?
7. (a) Describe the way parents guided or guide the behavior of children in the following families:
   (i) a contemporary American family,
   (ii) an American family of an earlier generation,
   (iii) a traditional Chinese family,
   (iv) a contemporary Chinese family.
   (b) Discuss what the expectations were or are for children in each culture and how they were or are guided.
8. Interview parents or invite a panel of parents to the classroom and find out their experiences:
   (a) in being a model for the children in their lives; and
   (b) in learning from their children.

2 YOU AND YOURSELF

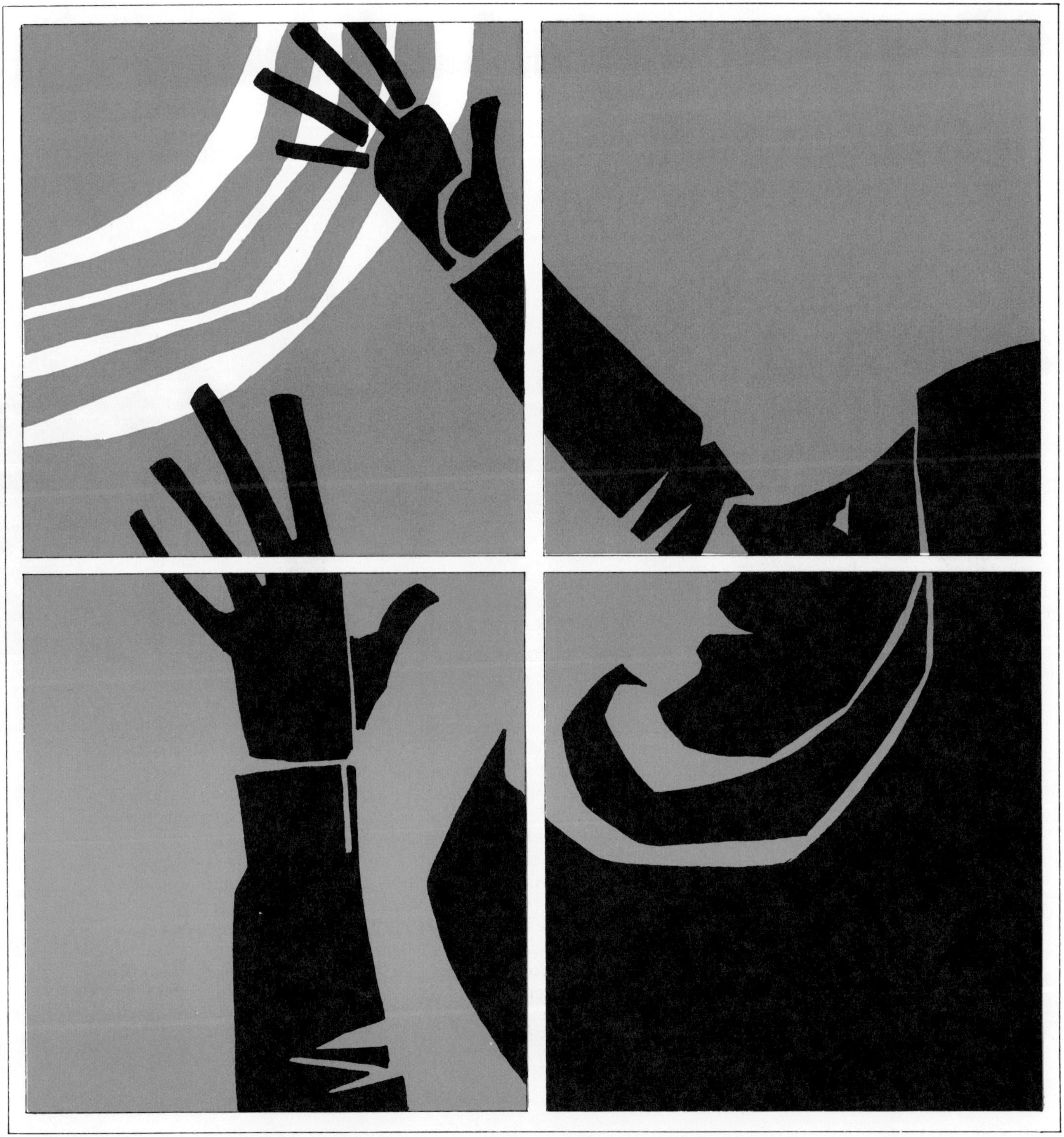

4 Developmental Tasks of Adolescence

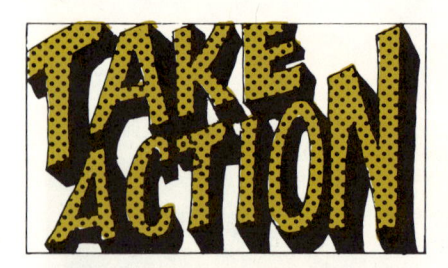

TAKE ACTION

Everyone follows a similar path from birth to death. Although you grow and develop in your own way, there are common principles of growth and development that each person follows. This common path is your lifeline.
1. Draw a line and mark all the significant happenings in your life on it. Start with your birth and add everything that has happened to you. Use the sample provided here as your pattern.
2. Compare your lifeline with those of your classmates. What similarities can you find? Do you think that a person's lifeline is predictable?

Lisa's Lifeline

Birth — Tomboy — New baby sister — Friends — Kindergarten

Along the road of life, you pass through a variety of stages of development. Each stage of development has its own developmental tasks. Developmental tasks are achievements, skills, knowledge, functions, and attitudes that you have to accomplish in order to be happy. Each task arises at a certain period of life. It is important to accomplish each task as it faces you in order to be successful with later tasks. You require personal effort, social awareness, and physical readiness to accomplish each task.

Think of an eight-month-old infant. Sucking is the infant's first method of obtaining food. As the infant grows and desires more food, he or she is introduced to solids. Have you observed a child eating his or her first fruit or cereal? It can be a very messy ordeal — usually more food is spit out than is taken in. Infants have to learn how to swallow. The task of swallowing strained foods must be accomplished before the child can learn to chew. Similarly, the task of progressing from the bottle to drinking from a cup takes a while to accomplish.

Can you describe the tasks a child has to accomplish when learning to walk?

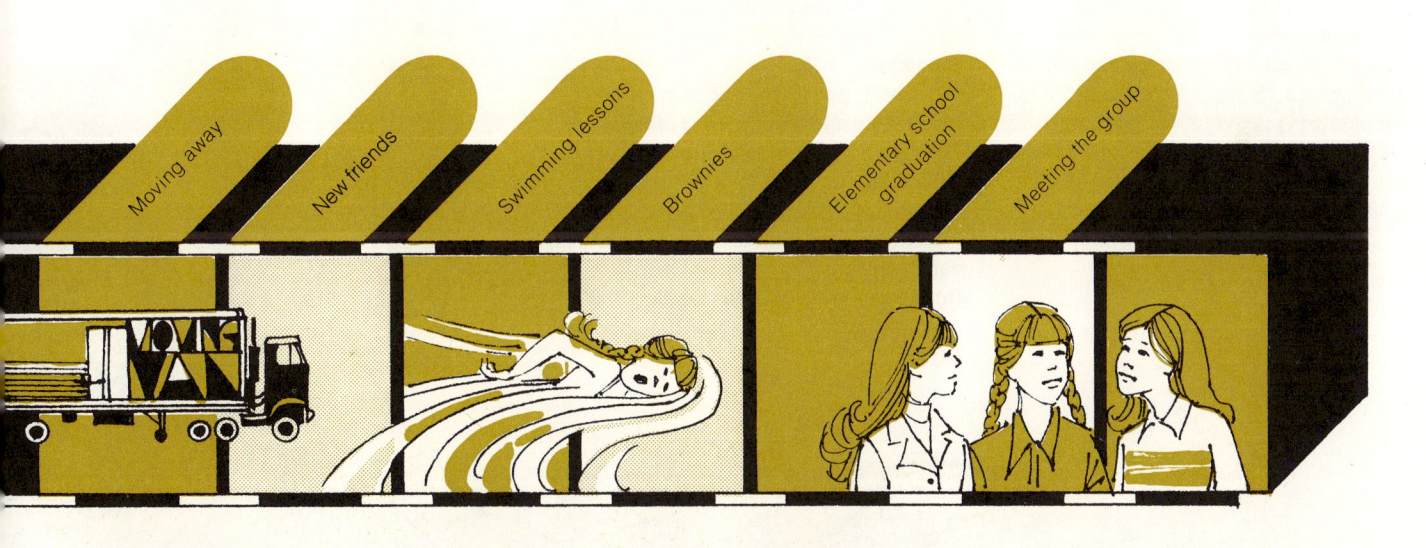

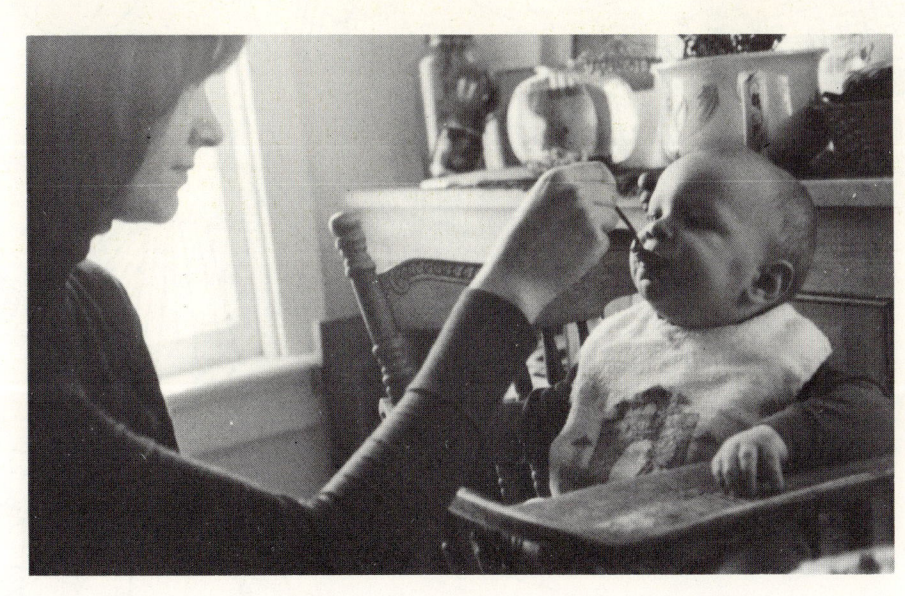

Moving away · New friends · Swimming lessons · Brownies · Elementary school graduation · Meeting the group

39

Developmental Tasks of Early Adolescence

1. Accepting and Adjusting to a Changing Body

Bill had always been the tallest boy in his class. He felt awkward and clumsy, and when he won a fight with someone else, he was always told to pick on someone his own size or to act his age. He hated his nickname "Tiny."

In ninth grade, Bill's feelings about himself changed. He was very good at broad-jumping and pole-vaulting. The girls liked his tall physique. He improved his posture and made an effort to look where he was going and not to bump into things.

Comment:

The approval Bill was receiving helped him to accept his physique.
(a) At what stage of development do most people learn to control and coordinate their bodies?
(b) How can rewards or punishments have an effect on Bill's acceptance of his physique?

2. Forming New Relations with Peers of Both Sexes

Brothers Sean and Kevin have no sister and have not been in the company of girls very often. Friends of their parents are going to spend the day at their home, and the boys must entertain the guests' thirteen-year-old daughter, Anne. They expect to have a boring day. To their surprise, Anne teams up with Kevin to play tennis against two older boys. Kevin and Anne win. Anne is pleased that she has changed Kevin's and Sean's opinion of girls.

Comment:

A stereotyped image had been influencing Kevin's and Sean's ideas of females. They felt they could really have fun only with males.
(a) What is the importance of having contact with friends of both sexes from an early age?
(b) Give an example of a situation that changed your opinion about the opposite sex.

3. Gaining Emotional Independence from Parents and Adults

Jennifer was extremely shy around adults. Whenever anyone came to visit, she tried to be busy in her room. At school, she avoided speaking up in class and only gave her opinion to a close friend. Jennifer's teacher realized that Jennifer had feelings of inadequacy. She praised Jennifer in class whenever the chance presented itself and gradually Jennifer built up confidence. Attention and understanding were really what she needed and wanted.

Comment:

In the past, Jennifer had failed in attempts to communicate with adults and she was letting negative feelings predominate. The teacher's attention and efforts helped Jennifer give of herself in situations where she had previously felt inadequate and this enabled her to feel more confident.
(a) How can a variety of experiences help a person gain independence?
(b) How can parents and adults help a young person feel more comfortable in an adult group?

4. Achieving Assurance of Economic Independence

Tom's goal for a long time had been to have a car of his own. He started saving most of his money from his paper route and watched his bank account grow. He enrolled in Driver's Education the day he was sixteen. There was a family agreement about the use of the car, and Tom enjoyed his turn to take the car. Tom got another part-time job to enable him to buy insurance and to help pay for all the other expenses he would have when he owned his own car. He took the auto shop course at school to learn about engines and how to make repairs himself.

Comment:

Tom's need to be economically independent is no different from anyone else's. His dream has come true now that he has his own money and can spend it on whatever he likes.
(a) Can giving a child a small allowance help the child to feel a little independent?
(b) What problems would people face if they never earned any money of their own?

5. Selecting and Preparing for an Occupation

Cathy wanted to become a family studies specialist. She had trouble in her science subjects and always scored her lowest mark in them. The school guidance counselors assured her she had to have chemistry in high school or she would not be accepted in family studies at the state university.

Comment:

Cathy was faced with the task of improving in her science subjects or of choosing another career.
(a) How can Cathy improve her skills in a subject that causes difficulty?
(b) How can Cathy learn about more careers so that she can choose a career she can succeed in?

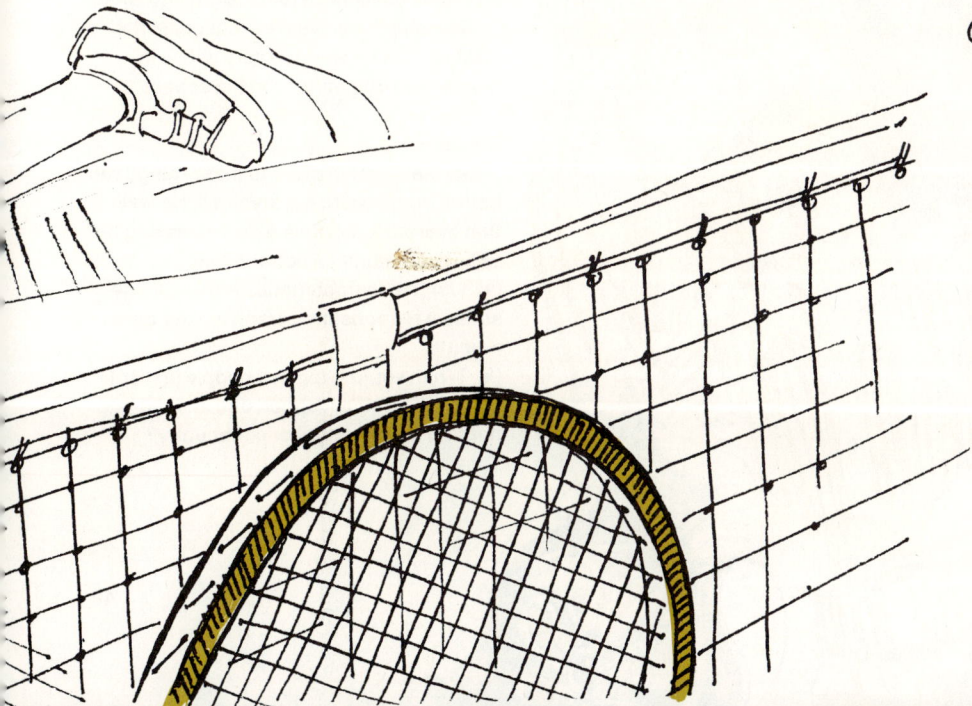

6. Discussing and Achieving Responsible Behavior

Peter's grandparents were staying with him and his brother and sister while his parents were on vacation. Peter had a bunch of kids over one night and things got kind of rowdy. Some of the kids started to eat up anything they found in the refrigerator and cupboards. By the time the grandparents discovered this, the house was in a shambles. Since Peter's grandparents were responsible for the house, they were really angry. They called all the kids and their parents over, even though it was 2:30 in the morning, and the kids had to clean up and work out a way to replace all the food by the next night before Peter's parents got back.

Comment:

Peter's grandparents felt responsible for looking after the family and the house. They let Peter have a party because they felt the kids would have some regard for other people's property.

(a) List some situations where young people have not shown responsible behavior when they are out socially. What solutions would you suggest?

(b) What would you do if you were Peter? the grandparents?

7. Preparing to Accept One's Future Role as a Responsible Citizen of the Community

In tenth grade, Michael was elected class president. He enjoyed student council meetings and realized that ideas could be worked through by such a group. In eleventh grade, he worked hard on committees and then decided to run for school president. Developing his platform, working with campaign committees, giving speeches, getting a lot of help from some people and having others who fell through on promises gave him a real insight into what "citizenship" involves. He lost out in the election, but he was still very active in helping the committees in the school.

Comment:

Mike feels that in order to make things run better, you have to get involved. He feels that everyone can take a part in making his or her community a better place.

(a) List the characteristics that would describe a responsible person in your community.

(b) What would happen if people just criticized everything, copped out, and did nothing in the school or community?

8. Formulating a Belief and Value System

Dawn was bored by the end of the summer because there was nothing for her to do. She thought about the birthday gift she had to get for her best friend and thought it would be a great joke to steal something from the department store. She didn't feel too upset about it because she figured the store had lots of money and wouldn't miss a small thing. When she gave Jill her gift of a record, Jill was thrilled, but Dawn was starting to worry Jill would find out it was stolen.

Comment:

Dawn felt a few pangs from her conscience because she knew Jill would not want to use a "hot" gift. Dawn is at the stage of developing a philosophy of life and an image of herself in relation to her world.

(a) What does shoplifting do to the price of goods in a store?
(b) What could happen to Dawn if she were caught?
(c) How would you feel about receiving a stolen gift?

Developmental Tasks of Adolescence

Developmental tasks	Early adolescence	Late adolescence
1. Accepting one's body and using it to its fullest potential.	Learning to be happy with, or at least tolerant of, one's body. Learning to use and protect one's body properly.	Learning appropriate sexual outlets. Learning new athletic and work skills.
2. Relating to others of both sexes. Some group activities need to include both sexes.	Learning to work and get along with others. Friendships are likely to be more lasting than they were in childhood.	Working towards a common goal with others and minimizing personal feelings and opinions.
3. Receiving and giving affection.	Realizing one is worthwhile and worthy of love.	Building strong affections with a possible partner.
4. Learning maleness and femaleness.	Forming strong identity with others of same sex. Learning to relate to the opposite sex.	Assessing characteristics of a future mate. Becoming "desirable" as a future mate. Becoming a responsible citizen in the community.
5. Achieving emotional independence and the beginnings of economic independence.	Needing adult approval. Resenting parental authority. Developing respect for other adults. Desire to earn personal money.	Establishing an independent pattern of deciding and doing things.
6. Selecting and preparing for an occupation.	Developing ability to learn and think. Exploring a variety of jobs one has the ability to do satisfactorily.	Discovering interests and abilities. Beginning to set up long-term goals for the future. Selecting and preparing for an occupation suited to one's ability.
7. Developing morals, standards, and a set of values.	Wanting to discuss, argue, or debate. Deciding what is right and wrong.	Resolving problems and contradictions in moral behavior in a responsible way. Will discuss, argue, and debate in order to arrive at a set of personal standards.

If you master each of these tasks, you will be well adjusted and able to master the harder tasks later in life. If you do not master them, you will lack stability, suffer anxiety and social disapproval, and will have difficulty with later tasks. The tasks are sequential — you must learn one before going on to the next. They must also be learned at a specific time or "teachable moment" in your life.

Look back at Lisa's lifeline at the beginning of this chapter. Her acceptance or rejection of a new baby sister would depend upon her achievement of the task of feeling, giving, and sharing affection. Lisa may have been a tomboy because her playmates were boys. Real friendships were probably developed when Lisa was able to interact happily with her peers and to establish a sense of belonging. Going to kindergarten is significant to a child. Lisa probably adjusted to kindergarten as she learned to depend less on her parents and to abide by new rules. Lisa's adjustment to each change in her life is a result of her ability to achieve each task at the right age.

You will have completed your lifeline up to the present day. Review the chart of developmental tasks from early adolescence to adulthood and determine where you are. What efforts could you make to achieve future tasks? How can your attitude have an effect on the achievement of each task?

WORD POWER

developmental tasks
economic independence
emotional independence
lifeline
responsible behavior
responsible citizen
value system

TAKE ACTION

1. Give a report, in story form, describing a task that you are undertaking at the present time. Refer to the tasks in the chart in this chapter.
   (a) Describe what progress you are making in this developmental task.
   (b) State how you are going to continue to progress further.
2. Explain how a student who did not learn to read well in elementary school is hindered in his or her high school program.
3. Do you remember when you tried to ride a bicycle? It looked so easy you thought you could just pedal away. What was your reaction after you first attempted to ride the bike?
4. Do adults have developmental tasks? Choose one of the seven areas in the chart and explain what you feel would be the developmental task for adulthood.
5. Illustrate how individuals develop from being completely dependent to acquiring independent personal behavior. Explain in what ways family members "interdepend" on each other.
6. Describe the characteristics of a person in your community and one in your school who would fit your impressions of a "good citizen."
7. One of the developmental tasks is relating to others. Describe some situations demonstrating a variety of acts of friendliness to people of different ages, sexes, and schools.

5 Heredity and Environment

We all have specific, unchangeable traits that we inherit from our parents, grandparents, or other ancestors. These include: physical appearance, color of hair and skin, resistance to diseases, blood type, mental characteristics, emotional tendencies, and intellectual abilities. These are hereditary influences.

Once we are conceived, the influence of our surroundings begins. The type of food and drugs and the quantity of cigarettes and alcohol consumed by the expectant mother, as well as her emotional health, all affect the environment of the unborn child. After birth, we are affected by such things as climate, geographical location, home and school settings, and the emotional, intellectual, and cultural atmosphere provided by the community and the people in our lives. These are environmental influences.

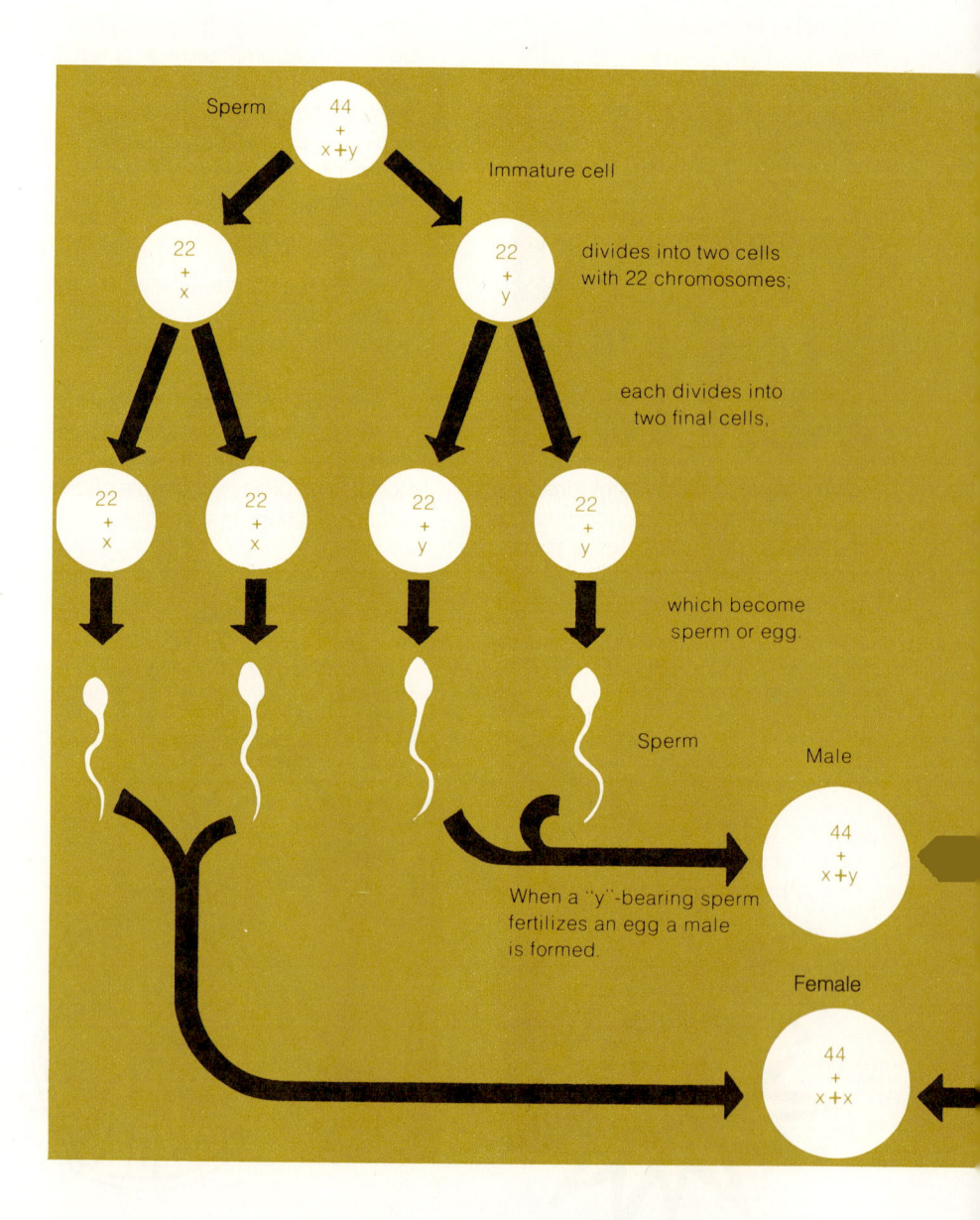

Sperm
44 + x+y
Immature cell
divides into two cells with 22 chromosomes;
each divides into two final cells,
which become sperm or egg.

When a "y"-bearing sperm fertilizes an egg a male is formed.

Male 44 + x+y
Female 44 + x+x

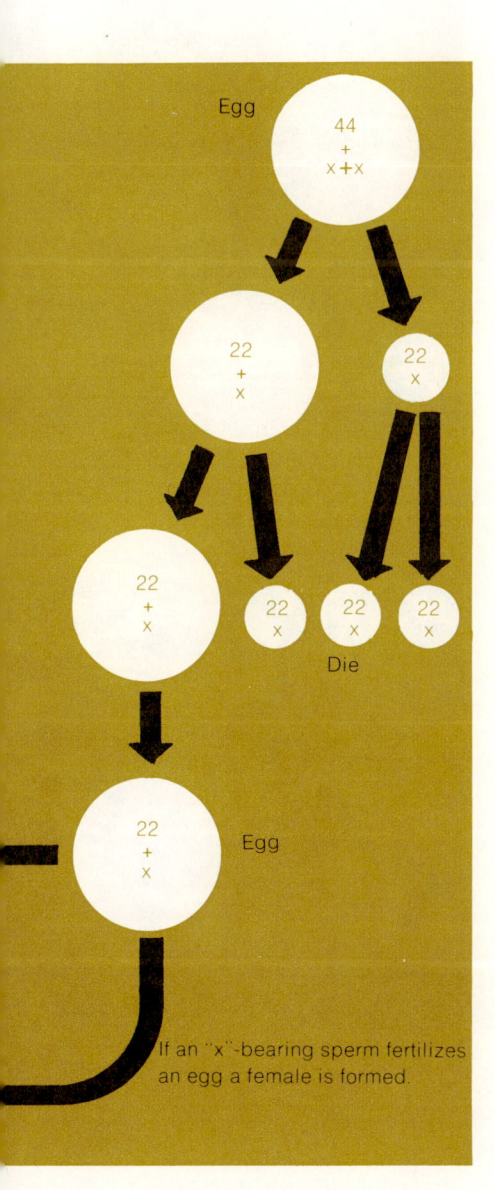

Heredity

This diagram will help you understand reproduction and how you receive your hereditary traits.

The male and female each contribute twenty-three chromosomes (one of which is a sex chromosome) to the new being. A new life begins when the *ovum* (female germ cell) is fertilized by the *spermatazoon* (male germ cell). Maleness or femaleness depends on the male chromosomes. Female chromosomes are labelled *x*. The male sperm contains either *x* or *y* chromosomes. If the male sperm, meeting the female egg, contains the *x* element, the child will be female. If it contains the *y* element, the child will be male. The sex of a child depends on the father's contribution.

We have discussed the biological process for a single birth. Now, let's look at the process that occurs in multiple births.

Identical Twins. Sometimes the egg cell divides into two ova, and each grows as a single unit. Thus, two embryos develop, and identical twins result. Are identical twins very similar in many characteristics? Why? Would they be the same if they were separated at birth and raised in different environments?

Siamese Twins. Siamese twins result when the first cell division is not complete. These babies will be joined at some part of their bodies. Today they are usually separated in infancy, whereas in the past they lived their lives attached to each other.

Fraternal Twins. Fraternal twins are the result of two eggs being fertilized at the same time by different sperms. These twins can be of the same or opposite sex and frequently are no more alike than ordinary brothers and sisters.

There are many interesting aspects of reproduction that you could research. Some of these topics are:
prenatal environment
dominant genes
birth defects
genetic counseling
recessive genes
triplets, quadruplets, etc.

Mental Inheritance

Can you think of any characteristics related to your intelligence or personality that you may have inherited from people in your family? Remember that strong characteristics will weaken if not practiced or strengthened by a positive environment and that weak characteristics can be strengthened with perseverance and a nurturing environment.

Do you know which characteristics of your intelligence and personality are inherited? Could you list some? See if you were right:

Intelligence. You inherit basic mental ability, which determines your capacity to learn. You may inherit special aptitudes in certain areas, such as music, mechanics, painting, or mathematics.

Personality. There is evidence that you will inherit these aspects of personality: expression of emotions, level of energy and activity, creativeness, ability to cope with stress, frankness in interpersonal relationships, ability to organize, and extroversion and introversion.

Environment

Environments are made up of living and material things. They are the settings in which you live and interact. Your environments are classified as the far environment (the whole world) and the near environment (your home, school, etc.). There are physical environments made up of material things. There are also human environments built on interpersonal relationships, that is, relationships between you and other humans.

Can you think of a group of people who make you feel uncomfortable? Each group of people provides an atmosphere or environment. A group that makes you feel you don't belong is setting up an unpleasant environment.

Environments that you inhabit, come in contact with, or observe affect you. They can contribute to your developmental growth or they can stunt it. Describe a home environment that could inhibit the growth of a child.

Now visualize the environment of a junkyard, an old car cemetery, or a campsite disposal dump that is being disturbed by hungry bears. Would you be uncomfortable in these surroundings? Think of the most pleasant environment with which you have been in contact. It might be a hiding spot used in childhood, a stretch of beach, or the privacy of a bedroom filled with the things that are special to you.

The quiz on the next page will provide you with interesting ways to explore your own environments.

Why do you think these environments are uncomfortable to some people? Find photographs of human and physical environments that make *you* feel uncomfortable.

Environment Quiz (Use a separate sheet of paper.)

1. (a) List five environments that are important to you in your life. Don't limit yourself.
   (b) How would you characterize your feelings when in these environments?
   (c) If you were free to change each of these environments, what changes would you make?
2. (a) Close your eyes and concentrate on sounds for a minute or two. How many *different* sounds do you hear? Are they clear, distant, pleasant, disturbing? List the sounds and rate them.
   (b) Zero in on the scents that surround you – ink on paper, a recently sharpened pencil, freshly brewed coffee, food! How many environments can you think of that have a characteristic scent? What are your reactions to each?
   (c) Take a "blind walk" around the room. Touch different surfaces. How many textures, shapes, and temperatures can you identify? What are your reactions to each?
   (d) Now take a good look at your environment. What do you like? What don't you like? What could you change in it? Why haven't you done something about it?
3. (a) How do you feel when someone sits very close to you and touches you during a conversation?
   (b) When you walk into a room, do you choose the chair nearest to or farthest from another person?
   (c) How do you feel if someone sits in your usual seat at the table where you eat?
   (d) Do any members of your family have an implied claim to a seat or area of the home?
   (e) If you were given the opportunity to have a room of your own, of any size, what size room would you choose and what would be your plans for the use of the space?
4. How would you describe your P.Q. (privacy quotient)? Consider the following questions:
   (a) How much privacy do you need?
   (b) How much would you like to have?
   (c) How do you fulfill your needs for privacy?
   (d) In what creative ways might privacy be arranged in your daily routine?
   (e) How many innovative ways can you think of to create privacy?
5. Complete the following statements:
   (a) The environment that inspires me to be myself is . . .
   (b) Areas around my home or school that I consider my territory are . . .
   (c) One ritual or tradition I like because it links me with my past is . . .
   (d) An object or article I feel I would always want with me wherever I go is . . .
   (e) If I could plan an ideal environment for myself, I would include . . .
   (f) If I could plan an ideal school environment, this is what I would do . . .

Courtesy of the J.C. Penney Co., Inc.

Let's Compare Heredity and Environment

Comment on the following statements:
- If heredity is "nature," then environment is "nurture."
- Heredity is thought of as "God-given" and environment is created by people, although the natural world (climate, wildlife) is also part of the environment.
- People, including family, friends, and neighbors are part of environment too.
- Culture is also part of your environment: the ideas, beliefs, values, customs, institutions, educational system, religion, and government of your culture provide a specific environment that affects the way you develop.

You are given your hereditary traits at conception in much the same way as you are dealt a hand of cards in a card game. Each card is a different trait, and the whole hand of cards (or traits) are the raw materials you have to work with. They include physical traits, such as body size, hair color and texture, blood type, sex, and eye shape and color; and mental traits, such as intelligence, temperament, creativity, and special abilities.

These hereditary traits are the "what" of your existence. Environmental traits are the "how" of your existence. Environment determines how you use the raw materials you have inherited. In the card-game analogy, environmental traits are like the cards you draw from the pack. Each card could represent a specific value, such as love, your attitude towards people, beauty, health, freedom, and so on. How has each environmental trait that you see in yourself developed or affected your hereditary traits?

Quiz
(Use a separate sheet of paper.)

Beside each statement mark "H" if heredity is the major factor, "E" if environment is the major factor, or "HE" if both are involved.
1. _____ John likes candied sweet potatoes in orange sauce.
2. _____ Fred has blue eyes and stands 180 cm [72 in.] tall.
3. _____ Mary has a large skeletal frame and therefore tends to be heavier than other girls her age.
4. _____ Ted and his brothers are reckless drivers like their father.
5. _____ Debby resembles her mother physically; they both have many habits and interests in common.
6. _____ German shepherd dogs can be trained to be either vicious or gentle and loyal.
7. _____ Herb likes to square dance.
8. _____ Ed is a good conversationalist.
9. _____ Andy's temper gets him into a lot of trouble.
10. _____ Marge speaks slowly and haltingly whenever boys are around.

A good human environment can influence behavior and development in very positive ways. There are many environments in which you perform your everyday functions. These include physical and social setups – home, school, a seat on a bus, a city street, a store, or a desk. It is important for your well-being and development that these environments be people-oriented or designed to meet the needs of the people who occupy these spaces.

Characteristics often develop in response to your environment. Different children thrive in different ways in identical environments because each child has unique potentialities. Both heredity and environment affect what you become, but you can control environment because you can change what you do. You can learn from books, experiences, and other people. All of these can help you develop to your fullest potential.

Did you realize that:

☑ Each individual, on the average, will move into fourteen different environments in a lifetime?

☑ Adults not actively participating in a child's environment can cause children to feel indifferent, antagonistic, and alienated?

☑ An environment in which families eat together is fading? The average person eats only one meal per day with the family.

☑ It is very important that daycare and preschool centers provide a nurturing environment, as 62 percent of children under six years of age go to these centers each day?

☑ A noisy environment causes damage to the unborn child, as it affects the ears and the nervous system?

☑ A crowded home environment can cause members to go outside the home for privacy and peace?

☑ Environments that do not provide outlets for creative activities can cause mental and emotional disorders?

Answers to Quiz

1. E
2. H
3. H
4. E
5. HE
6. HE
7. E
8. HE
9. HE
10. E

TAKE ACTION

1. (a) Describe a pleasant physical environment and a pleasant human environment. Describe an unpleasant physical environment and an unpleasant human environment. Analyze how each of the four environments created a pleasant or unpleasant atmosphere.
   (b) Make a picture scrapbook of a variety of environments and state what kinds of feelings or development an individual in each environment might have.
2. Each child in the family has a unique environment. Explain how the environment differs in the case of the oldest child, middle child, and the youngest child in a family.
3. Suggest books for your classmates to read about people who come from a variety of environments. A few examples are:
   Bugs in Your Ears, Betty Bates (New York: Pocket Books, 1979);
   Come to the Edge, Julia Cunningham (New York: Avon Books, 1978);
   A Prairie Boy's Summer, William Kurelek (Boston: Houghton Mifflin, 1975);
   M.C. Higgins the Great, Virginia Hamilton (New York: Dell Publishing, 1976).
4. Comment on these statements:
   (a) "He is a born loser."
   (b) "You can lead a horse to water, but you can't make him drink."
   (c) "You can't teach an old dog new tricks."
5. Have you ever visited a new town or home or been in a group setting that gave you the feeling that you had been there before? Describe the setting and why you felt so familiar there.
6. Here is Melanie's footprint. Why do so many hospitals take footprints of babies? Compare your fingerprints with those of your classmates to show how each differs. Note also the difference in length and shape of your fingers.
7. Read a book on palmistry. Find out why some cultures rely on this method to determine the hereditary characteristics and the possible future of an individual.
8. Here is an idea of an interesting art activity. Make an art fingerprint. Place your thumb and any number of fingers on an ink stamp pad. Make an interesting arrangement of your fingerprints on a sheet of paper. You can combine them into a variety of shapes such as animals, fruit, trees, and people.
9. Describe the characteristics of the hospital environment that a child enters immediately after birth.

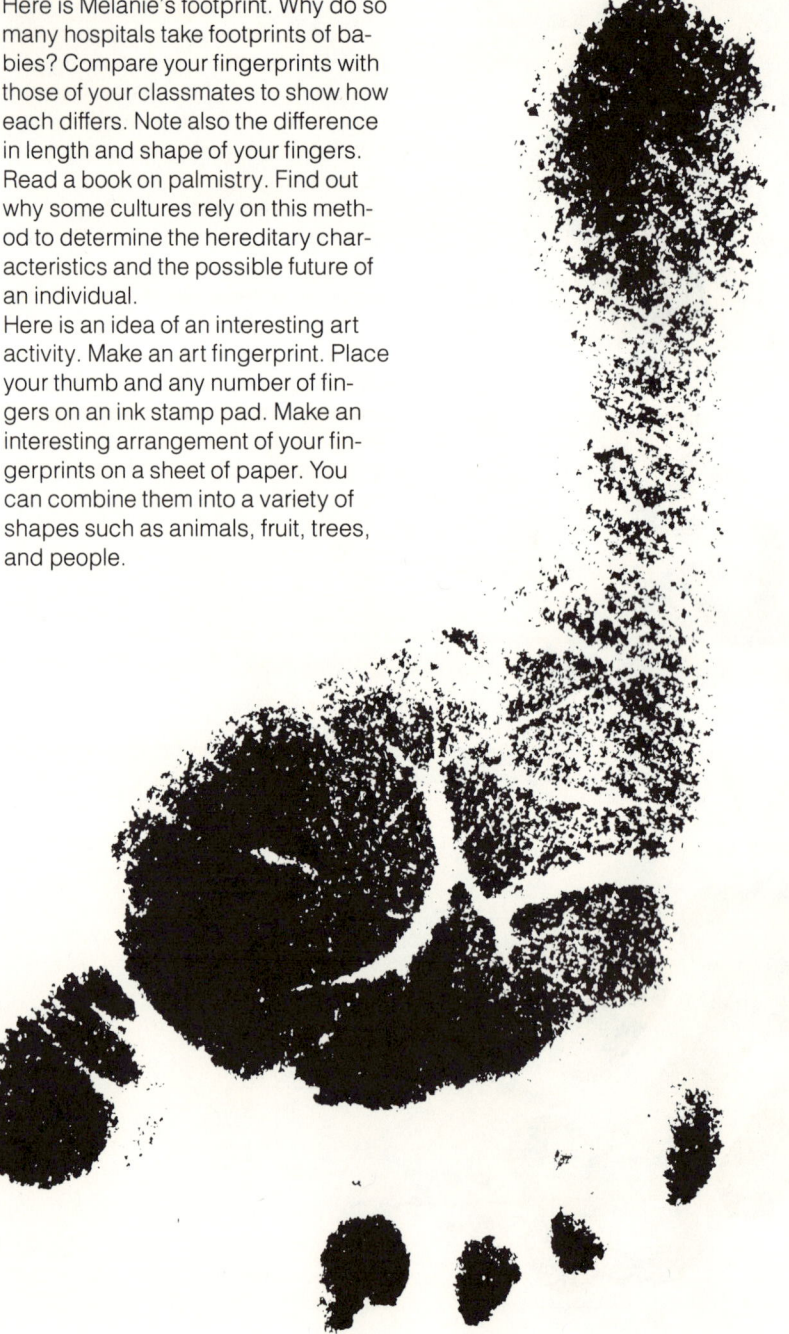

PEOPLE POWER

culture
environment
heredity
interpersonal relationships
multiple births
nurture
temperament
traits

53

6 The Parts You Play

All the world's a stage,
And all the men and women merely players:
They have their exits and their entrances,
And one man in his time plays many parts. . . .
As You Like It, William Shakespeare

  Did you ever think that life was like trying out for a play? Did you ever think about the many roles each of us plays in life? A group of teenagers made up the checklist on pages 56 and 57 of the roles of the people in their families. Discuss them in class to see if you agree.

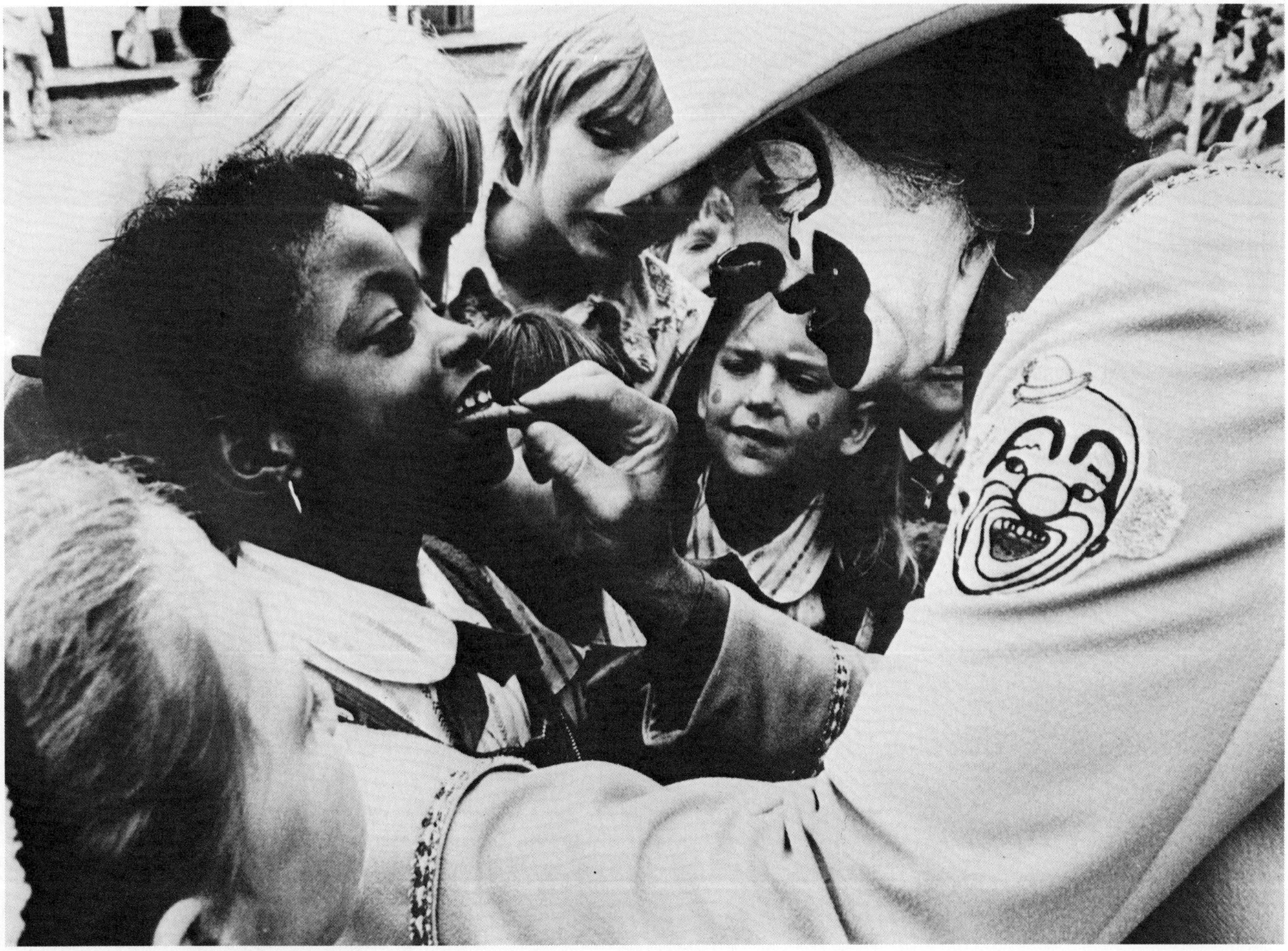

Role of Parents

- ☑ To set guidelines and rules.
- ☑ To care for and love children.
- ☑ To set reasonable limits.
- ☑ To raise children in an acceptable way.
- ☑ To provide a good, relaxed home atmosphere.
- ☑ To set a good example for children to follow.
- ☑ To open their children's eyes to things they may not want to see.
- ☑ To help children so that when they leave home they can set up their own guidelines.
- ☑ To keep order in the home.
- ☑ To show trust in and love for the family members.
- ☑ To make children feel secure by knowing they can count on their parents.
- ☑ To try and find time to be a friend as well as a parent.
- ☑ To recognize each child as an individual and to treat each differently.
- ☑ To be close to their children, so that the children can come to them with their problems and be able to discuss these problems knowing that parents will try to do the best for them.
- ☑ To be there when their children need them and to relate to their children whether they are happy and in a good mood, or whether they are sad and depressed.
- ☑ To raise a child to become a responsible person having self-pride and a feeling of ambition with compassion.

Role of Daughter or Son

- ☑ To help with younger children.
- ☑ To obey guidelines – if they are reasonable!
- ☑ To help with housework.
- ☑ To respect parents.
- ☑ To be responsible and trustworthy.
- ☑ To make parents satisfied by showing them they've done a good job of bringing you up.
- ☑ To make everyone feel better when something goes wrong.
- ☑ To listen to and try to understand parents.
- ☑ To be a friend to mother and father.
- ☑ To take part in family activities.
- ☑ Not to let the family down.

Role of Older Brothers and Sisters

- ☑ To help younger brothers and sisters with problems parents wouldn't understand.
- ☑ To be a companion for younger brothers and sisters.
- ☑ To set an example for younger brothers and sisters in their future lives.
- ☑ To pass on the benefit of their experience.
- ☑ To be someone who gives advice and on whom the family can lean.
- ☑ To stand up for younger brothers and sisters.

Role of Younger Brothers and Sisters

- ☑ To share with.
- ☑ To be a bother to older brothers and sisters.
- ☑ To help around the house.
- ☑ To follow in the footsteps of older brothers and sisters.

Now, using a separate sheet of paper, complete the following checklist and find out how *you* see a father, a mother, and an adolescent. These statements are the impressions of a number of fathers, mothers, and adolescents who answered the question, "What are the things a good father, mother, and adolescent do?" Can you guess which statements were made by adolescents? by fathers? by mothers?

Father

1. Helps provide a harmonious home by building family relationships.
2. Teaches the children right and wrong.
3. Provides good advice.
4. Takes an interest in the children's activities.
5. Attends community and school functions in which the children are participating.
6. Is active in his religion and provides a religious background for the children.
7. Provides enough money for family comforts.
8. Encourages the children's education.
9. Considers the children's problems as seriously as his own.
10. Doesn't teach by fear, threats, or distrust.
11. Does his share of household tasks.
12. Helps to care for children.
13. Cultivates children as pals.
14. Sets a good moral example.
15. Builds a close relationship with mother and children.

Mother

16. Educates children to think for themselves.
17. Keeps up with current trends and ideas.
18. Is a good cook and household manager.
19. Teaches children manners for every social situation.
20. Tries to understand the children and their needs.
21. Shares and cooperates with the children.
22. Has outside interests.

Agree   Disagree

	Agree	Disagree

23. Teaches children right from wrong.
24. Teaches children homemaking skills.
25. Teaches religious values.
26. Respects children's feelings and is a good listener.
27. Provides children with plenty of love and affection.
28. Sets a good moral example.
29. Combines family needs and welfare with her own career and intellectual needs.
30. Shares family discussion with father and children.

Adolescent
31. Learns to do own thinking.
32. Takes active interest in family group activities.
33. Learns to respect parents.
34. Takes school seriously in order to get good grades.
35. Shares joys and sorrows with family.
36. Attends and takes part in religious activities.
37. Takes part in household responsibilities.
38. Avoids doing things that displease parents.
39. Learns to develop personality.
40. Helps rather than hinders siblings in their social adjustment.
41. Considers and weighs the advice and experience of family and others.
42. Develops spirit of give and take.
43. Is polite and mannerly.
44. Is always truthful and honest.
45. Lives within the moral standards of the family.

This checklist will help you determine whether your ideas about roles tend to be traditional or progressive. The *traditional* statements are numbers 2, 3, 6, 7, 8, 14, 18, 19, 23, 24, 25, 26, 28, 33, 34, 36, 37, 38, 43, 44, and 45. The *progressive* statements are numbers 1, 4, 5, 9, 10, 11, 12, 13, 15, 16, 17, 20, 21, 22, 26, 27, 29, 30, 31, 32, 35, 39, 40, 41, and 42. The statements made by *fathers* are numbers 1, 2, 3, 5, 6, 12, 13, 16, 18, 22, 24, 25, 30, 31, 34, 36, 39, 41, and 44. The statements made by *mothers* are numbers 1, 4, 8, 14, 19, 20, 21, 28, 29, 35, 38, and 42. The statements made by *adolescents* are numbers 7, 9, 10, 11, 15, 17, 23, 26, 27, 32, 33, 37, 40, 43, and 45.

Role-Playing

Can you define a role? Roles are the parts you play in the different situations in your life. A role consists of a sequence of accepted acts that help you interact in specific social groups or situations. You learn the behavior that is appropriate to your position in a group. You learn this from others who hold beliefs about what your "normal" role should be and reward or punish you according to how you perform your role.

People also choose not to conform to groups, but to speak, act, and appear as they wish. This may be to get attention, or because they do not feel a need to behave in the way a group expects.

It was the first day of school, and the Clothing 1 class was taking a look at the sewing machines, the fabric samples draped on the bulletin boards, and checking out their figure types against those on the wall charts and dressmaking dummies.
"Ginny Bruce?"
"Here."
"Lorraine Grabnik?"
"Present."
"Gerry Burton? . . . Does anyone know if she is coming today?"
Just then the door opened and a tall, athletic-looking boy rushed in.
"Sorry I'm late. I'm Gerry Burton," he said as he anxiously checked all the girls in the room. "Is Jim Druwe here? We signed up together for this course."
"I just got a withdrawal slip this morning, so I guess he changed his mind," said Mrs. Andrew.
"Checked out, eh?" Gerry said nervously. "Well, I guess . . ."
"Tell me, Gerry," said Mrs. Andrew, "why did you decide to sign up for the course in the first place?"
"I guess I got the idea from my sister. She saved money making her own clothes. I didn't see why I couldn't make some pants and T-shirts and stuff. I figure if she can do it, why can't I? But . . . I don't know how I feel now that Jim's not here."

Although Gerry feels uncomfortable being the only boy in the class, he feels the benefits of the course outweigh the difficulty of giving an explanation for being in a situation unusual for a male. Can you think of other situations in which your choice of role has to be explained?

You are role-playing when you act assigned roles and fulfill your commitments in a group or situation. As you learn roles through interaction with others, you also acquire expectations of how others in the group will behave. The actor in a play or movie must be able to predict what others expect of him, and how they will react to him, in order to perform his role successfully.

"Hi, Cindy. What happened to your brother? He sure looks great! I hope you don't mind my saying that, but I've never seen him out from under his car, or in anything but those greasy clothes."
"I know. If I have to say so myself, Bob does look pretty good," said Jennifer. "He signed up for a special child study course where he gets to work with children in primary grades. Well, the day before he was to meet these little kids, he got his hair cut and put on some of those clothes Mom has been harping about because they were collecting dust in his closet. We were all so shocked when he arrived for dinner! He mumbled something about the kids might think he was weird and wouldn't want to learn from him."

Bob was playing the role he felt was suited to the commitment he was making as a teacher-assistant. Bob was predicting what the children would expect of his appearance, and he wanted them to react favorably to him. Think of times when you made such assumptions of what people would expect of you. Do you think your assumptions were accurate or false in each case?

Roles may be stereotyped or unique. Certain roles are traditional. These are the roles that you automatically acquire because of your sex and the kinship bonds in your family. Each of these relationships carries certain role expectations. Traditionally, for example, a daughter and son may be expected to be loyal, responsible, communicative, and willing to share. Grandparents and parents expect you to understand the family's values. In all family relationships, everyone is expected to compromise in order to get along with each other.

Many roles a person plays are played unconsciously. You may not be aware that you are carrying out some of the roles you play.

What parts or roles do you play? From this diagram, figure out your own role cluster. A role cluster is a set of roles that you play at one time. How large is your role cluster?

What different roles do you play in your life?

Experiment with the following situations and see if it helps you to understand your roles and those of others better.

Role-Making: The Creation of and Changes to Existing Roles

"Grandma can't understand why Mom wants to go out and work. She feels Mom could keep herself busy at home – making bread, preserving, or making our clothes." How have the roles of mothers changed from Grandma's time? *Hints:* modern conveniences; job opportunities; change from a producers' society to a consumers' society.

Role-Making: Swapping Roles

Joan and Grant were both furious! They had yelled all night at each other about how to spend their savings. Grant was reading up on all the handyman ideas, and he wanted a set of power tools. Joan felt that after six months of marriage, it was time they had their own sofa instead of the one they had salvaged at a garage sale! When they calmed down, Joan recalled the technique they had been shown at their marriage preparation class. They were told to swap roles and try to understand how the other felt. Joan took Grant's role and argued for the tools, and Grant explained why he felt Joan would want a new sofa. What do you think was their final solution?

Role-Making: A Series of Roles a Person Plays during the Life Cycle

List all the roles you will likely play during your life cycle.

Many people act out roles because they feel most comfortable taking on the role of a group. Others feel better about "doing their own thing." As people mature, they learn to enjoy the person they are and have less of a need to role-play.

In family situations, some people choose to work on a partnership arrangement – sharing tasks and decisions and roles. Other families enjoy and prefer a more traditional relationship. The most important thing is that each family chooses those roles that work best for the whole family, and that each member is comfortable with the roles he or she plays.

WORD POWER

developmental role
role
role cluster
role-making
role-playing
stereotyped role
traditional role

TAKE ACTION

1. Consider the following situation and explain how Carlo is modifying his role or creating a new one.

   Carlo and Carmel are twins. They have grown up in an isolated farm community and have just recently moved to the city. They have been best friends to each other and have enjoyed many of the same activities. Carmel has joined the touch football team, and Carlo, having never played football, thought he'd like to break into this new sport by first playing touch football. Some team members thought this funny, but said O.K. Some parents, on the other hand, felt Carlo was spoiling the girls' fun.

   What do you feel? Why do people find it difficult to accept a male on a female team?

2. Two people act out the following situation while the rest of the class watches and reacts. Recall what you discovered about swapping roles and changing positions. Try to work out a solution to the problem.

   Janice had a holiday because of a Teachers' Institute day. She planned to go downtown with a friend to see a movie. Her mother felt that because it was really a school day, she should finish up a school project, and maybe help with her little sister.

3. Write a poem or a short story about "Terry the Typical Teenager." Describe all the roles the teenager is struggling to fit into and the roles that others try to impose on the teenager. Describe how Terry feels in these conflicting role situations.

4. (a) Do a survey asking people to list the characteristics of the following roles: police officer, druggist, swimming instructor, custodian, cafeteria food specialist, student council member, health inspector, welfare department clerk, etc.
   (b) Remove the words that identify the people in (a) and list only the role characteristics you collected. See if class members can identify each person by the characteristics given.
   (c) Discuss the reasons for incorrect guesses. Discuss role expectations and how conflicts develop when individuals or groups view their roles differently from those with whom they interact.

5. Develop a skit in which the father of a family decides to change roles. He is to be the househusband while his wife goes out and pursues her career. Consider in what ways his role change will cause role changes in other family members.

6. Discuss the word *stereotype*. Relate situations where you have been embarrassed because you viewed a situation according to a set of stereotypes.

7. Divide the class into "families." Each family can decide on its own make-up and the kind of family it will represent. Each member chooses a specific role (mother, grandfather, etc.) and discusses the function of that member within the role he or she is playing.

8. Role-play a family situation such as:
   (a) dividing up the jobs to be done in the house,
   (b) deciding what to do about one family member who is rebelling,
   (c) choosing a special birthday gift for Dad.

What are the roles of the family members in this photo?
How have the roles of family members changed since this photo was taken?

65

7 Self-Concept

Think of the day the class pictures arrive at the school. What are some of the reactions of your classmates? Do you hear people say: "It doesn't look like me at all!" or "I can't stand the expression on my face," "What a sick smile," "You can't see, it's so terrible," "That's not what I look like," "You always say that yours never turns out," "I'm getting a retake"?

It comes as a shock to realize that the way we see ourselves is not always as others see us. The way you see or perceive yourself (your *self-concept*) is based on the beliefs you have about yourself and your behavior, your likes and dislikes, aptitudes, interests, habits, ability to get along with others, and strengths and weaknesses. Your self-concept is formed not only by your own beliefs about yourself and your characteristics, but also by the way other people react to you and the way you want others to view you. The way you think you should be, or the way you would like to be, also influences your self-concept.

67

Let's Discover Your Self-Concept

Using a separate sheet of paper, complete this chart. Rate yourself. Be objective about yourself and find out which are your good qualities and which ones you can improve upon.

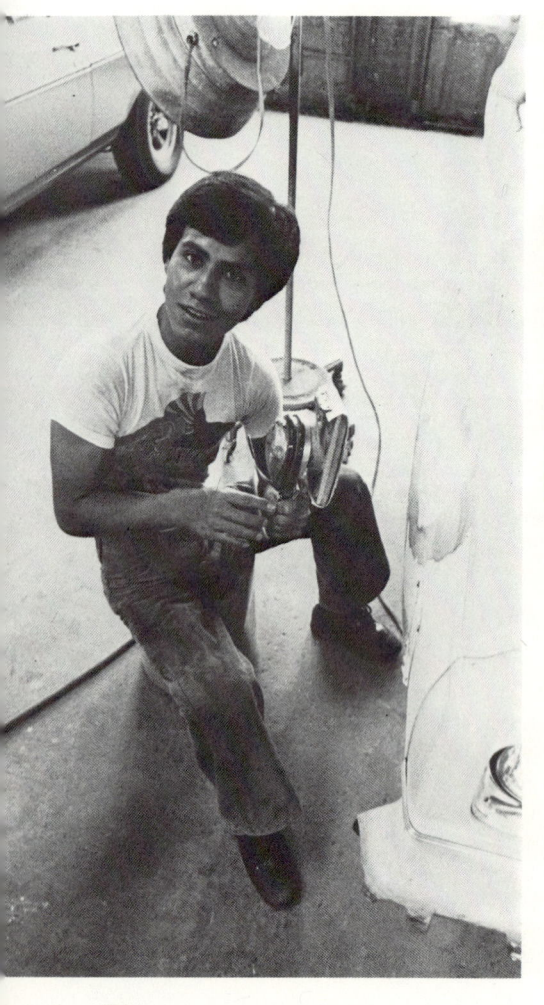

Trait	Very Good	Good	Average	Fair
Ability to listen				
Alertness				
Cheerfulness				
Conversational skill				
Cooperativeness				
Enthusiasm				
Expression of ideas				
Facial expression				
Friendliness				
Honesty				
Leadership qualities				
Manners				
Personal appearance				
Physical fitness				
Self-confidence				
Sense of humor				
Sincerity				
Study habits				
Understanding of others				
Unselfishness				

If you answered "good" or "very good" to most of these, you think of yourself in positive terms — you have a *positive self-concept*. If you rated yourself as largely "average" or "fair," your self-concept could be strengthened. Think about ways in which you could improve in these average or fair areas. This will help you develop a more positive self-concept.

A house of mirrors gives a distorted picture of people.
Is your image of yourself more realistic than this mirror image?

How Do Others See You?

Do you often ask yourself, "I wonder what he/she thinks of me?" or "Does he/she know what I really think about him/her?" Which thoughts are really yours, which do you imagine, and which thoughts really belong to others? As you learn to distinguish your thoughts and feelings from what you imagine are the thoughts and feelings of others, you become more realistic about how others really think and feel. You will discover that they have similar thoughts to yours and are worried about what you think of them.

TAKE ACTION

1. View yourself in a full-length mirror. In one column list your physical characteristics. In the next column list your personality characteristics as you see them.
2. In class, each student receives pieces of paper to equal the number of students in the room. On one side of each piece of paper, write the name of a classmate. On the other side, write a *positive* characteristic that describes that person. Repeat this for each member of your class. At the front of the room there will be an envelope for each person in the class. Place your comment for each person in that person's envelope.

Now you have feedback about your best characteristics and you have a better idea of how your peers view you. Now ask a parent or other adult to give a list of how they view your physical and personality characteristics. How do other people's ideas of you compare with your own?

Some of the comments of students who did this exercise were:

"I'm very shy with people I'm not sure of. I'm very glad people find me friendly and usually either smiling or laughing. Some of the remarks I received would bring tears to my eyes privately. Yes, they did differ from what I thought. What I'd like to say is THANKS to all my friends."

"People think that I am very nice and that I am shy. I thought that people thought I was stupid and not very nice at all – that I was shy. I thought that no one thought I was nice because I have a boyfriend."

"I found that some feel I have a sense of humor which I felt I was lacking. Though I felt I was outspoken, a few think I'm shy. Yes, it does differ from my own feelings about myself, although most people agreed with some of my ideas about myself."

"Everyone said: nice, funny, easy to talk to, honest, kind. I was shocked because I didn't think I was actually like that. But I know I get along with people because that is what I always try to do."

3. Divide into groups of four. Each group is to describe the personality, characteristics, and interests of a person everyone in the class knows. Each group then presents their description of this person to the class. Have the class determine the sex, occupation or interests, age, and physical appearance of this person. Did everyone in the class guess the right person in each description? Would you have described any of the people differently? How might this exercise demonstrate the different images people project?

4. Record the conversation of the class at a time when the class is not conscious of being recorded. Another day, play back the tape and try to identify the voices. Could you identify your own voice? Did others recognize your voice? Does the way you sound match your perception of your voice tones and inflections?

At this stage in life, you will often feel that you are the focus of attention. You will regard your feelings as quite unique. Have you ever stood in front of your mirror and acted out a situation with an imaginary audience? You set your own scene and mood, and also imagine the reactions of the "audience." If you are critical of yourself, the audience will be critical, too. Since the imaginary audience knows all about you, it knows how to pick out your strengths and weaknesses. The problem with personal fables like this is that it leads you to feel that most people know your weaknesses and strengths and thus judge you. In fact, most people do not see you as critically as you do yourself.

Maureen said, "I found out that people think of me as a very carefree person and one who is never worried – which is wrong – I *always* worry. They think that I am outgoing – I think I am very shy; that I have a good singing voice – which I don't agree with."

On the other hand, a personal fable may lead to a self-admiring situation. A boy blow-drying his hair may imagine fighting off all the girls at the school dance. A girl with a new shirt may imagine herself as being the most popular girl at the dance. Both the boy and girl are more concerned about how they are observed than with being observers in the group.

Gaining a Positive Self-Concept

Everyone has basic needs. If these basic human needs are met by others — individuals and society — and if you yourself work towards satisfying these needs, you will be more likely to have a positive self-concept.

Some of these basic needs are purely physical: the need for sleep, food, air, exercise, and so on. These are called *maintenance* needs. Maintenance needs must be met to keep you fit, and to enable you to satisfy other needs.

You cannot feel secure if you don't feel physically safe. A sense of security reduces worry and gives you a feeling of well-being that enables you to do the things you want to do.

All people need love and the feeling that they belong to other groups. Love and a sense of belonging give you the warm, comfortable feeling that you are accepted. Love, and the ability to give love, will make you more sure of yourself and will add to your positive self-concept. We all have the need to gain approval and to approve of ourselves. If you and others approve of your feelings and actions, you will feel you are worthwhile and will have self-respect. If you feel that you are able to do many things in at least an average way, you will feel a sense of worth. By developing the ability to solve some of your problems and make your own decisions, you will also gain self-respect. You need to feel that you continue to change, grow, and develop into a better person. The need for self-fulfillment is satisfied as you increase your talents, interests, and experience in life.

You will feel happier, have a better self-concept, and be able to face life better if you work towards satisfying all of these basic needs.

Steps towards a Positive Self-Concept

- Self-fulfillment
- Sense of worth and self-respect
- Feeling of love and belonging
- Safety
- Body needs

What Is a Self-Concept?

Are you aware of the three factors that interrelate to form your self-concept?

The *personal self* is the way you see yourself physically, mentally, and socially. It is the image you are aware of through your beliefs, values, feelings, and sensations. The personal image may not necessarily be based on realistic facts.

A plain person who is appreciated and rewarded with praise will feel accepted and act like an attractive person. Often you will hear a family member describe his or her family something like this:

"Janie is not much to look at, but she sure is smart. Doug has all the looks in the family, but Dad says he'll never amount to anything with his attitude, and I guess you'd say my oldest brother is the athlete because he can play every game in the books."

The members of this family will develop in the ways that they expect of themselves. Sometimes people get put into roles that are not very accurate. If people repeatedly hear the same statements or "prophesies" about themselves, they begin to live up to them and begin to believe them.

The *social self* is built on the impressions, attitudes, and feelings you have about yourself when relating to other people – the acceptance and approval you feel you get from others. Your social image is based on your perception of how others judge you, and how you feel about these judgments. All people react to you in some form. You will develop a *reference group* of people to whom you will refer for feedback about your social self. In most cases you will tend to choose reference groups that respond positively to your behavior.

The *ideal self* is based on what you would like to become, or on what you believe you should be like. Your desires, strivings, positive feelings, and goals are all important to your ideal self.

For mental health and maturity, it is necessary to combine these three selves. To become a satisfied person, you need to have the same feelings and attitudes about your personal self as you do about your social self. Your view of your ideal self should be realistic, so that what you wish to become is within your physical, mental, and social capabilities.

Check Your Self-Concept

How do you feel about yourself and others? (Do not write in this book.)
- ☐ I feel most comfortable when I make the decisions.
- ☐ I have to be recognized and noticed.
- ☐ I exist to share and give to others.
- ☐ I believe people are basically good.
- ☐ I am not too concerned about how others feel.
- ☐ It is better to be like other people.
- ☐ I enjoy being different and developing new ideas.
- ☐ I obtain great pleasure from looking as good as I can.
- ☐ Outward looks are not as important as the essential me which comes from within.
- ☐ Life is competitive. You have to fight for what you get.
- ☐ I am alone.
- ☐ I need to have someone around me.
- ☐ If I were in love, I could live on less than I am used to.

This exercise has no right or wrong answers. However, the more you are aware of your feelings, the better you are able to form a realistic concept of yourself and to use your abilities more effectively. You are a little like a lot of people, and sometimes like one particular person, but in many respects you are like nobody else. The more you are aware of the facts about yourself, the better able you will be to form a realistic self-concept.

Word Power

ideal self
maintenance needs
personal fable
personal self
personality characteristics
reference group
self-concept
self-respect
social self

Take Action

1. Complete these sentences:
   What people like most about me is _____.
   I think of myself as _____.
   I'd like to have my picture taken when _____.
   People think of me as _____.
   I think that in my future I will _____.
   When I first walk into a room, people think _____.
   When people notice me, _____.
2. Describe a person who is respected and liked, who doesn't seem to be concerned about what other people think of him or her. What might be the reason for this unconcern?
3. Describe some annoying characteristics that a person might have, such as being a bully, a loudmouth, conceited, critical, argumentative. Explain how these characteristics may be a reflection of a negative self-concept.
4. Give examples of how a weak self-concept may cause problems for an individual when:
   (a) conversing with others,
   (b) admitting she/he is wrong,
   (c) expressing feelings,
   (d) accepting constructive criticism,
   (e) expressing ideas that differ from other people's.
5. You will find it helpful to understand yourself better if you describe your self-concept. Without a great deal of analysis, write down your self-concept based on what you feel is your personal self, social self, and ideal self.

6. As a class, discuss the self-concept of a character in a novel or play you are reading in English. Decide what has contributed to his or her self-concept and how this self-concept affects the character's behavior.
7. Imagine you have to meet a person at an inter-school event to pass on some information about your school. Divide the class into pairs to act out the situation. Imagine you are talking on the phone with the person from the other school, setting up the time and place to meet. You would need to describe yourself to each other. Allow each person two minutes. Discuss how your self-concept determines how you describe yourself to others.
8. What's in a name? What does a name say about a person? Do you like your name? How do you feel if people forget it? What nickname do you have? What name would you have given yourself?
9. Consider some important people in your life (reference group). Describe the ways they help or hinder your self-concept.
10. Look at this illustration and consider the two images each person has of himself or herself. Could these images represent each person's ideal self and real self? How do these images affect a person's self-concept?

8 Values

Do you know anything about values? Can you define values? Do you have any? Do you have the same values as your friend, brother, or grandmother? Values are hard to describe. You can't see them, touch them, or smell them, but they are with you all the time. Let's try to understand values.

Identifying Values

Can you identify some of your values? Identifying values helps to explain your actions, emotions, and decisions. If you can identify your values, then it is easy to explain them to others. By explaining your values to others, you help them to understand you, your individuality, and your reactions to experiences in life. The more you clarify what your values are, the easier it is to relate to other people. By identifying others' values, you will discover what makes others tick, and it will enable you to understand them.

It is helpful to appraise your values – to find out whether or not they are worth defending. Do they need revising or changing to help you feel better about yourself? Sometimes people may *say* they value something but they really don't indicate the value by their actions. Clarifying values can help you to determine what is meaningful to you and what you want to achieve in life. It will help you to determine the type of world you want to live in, and to work towards the life-style you desire.

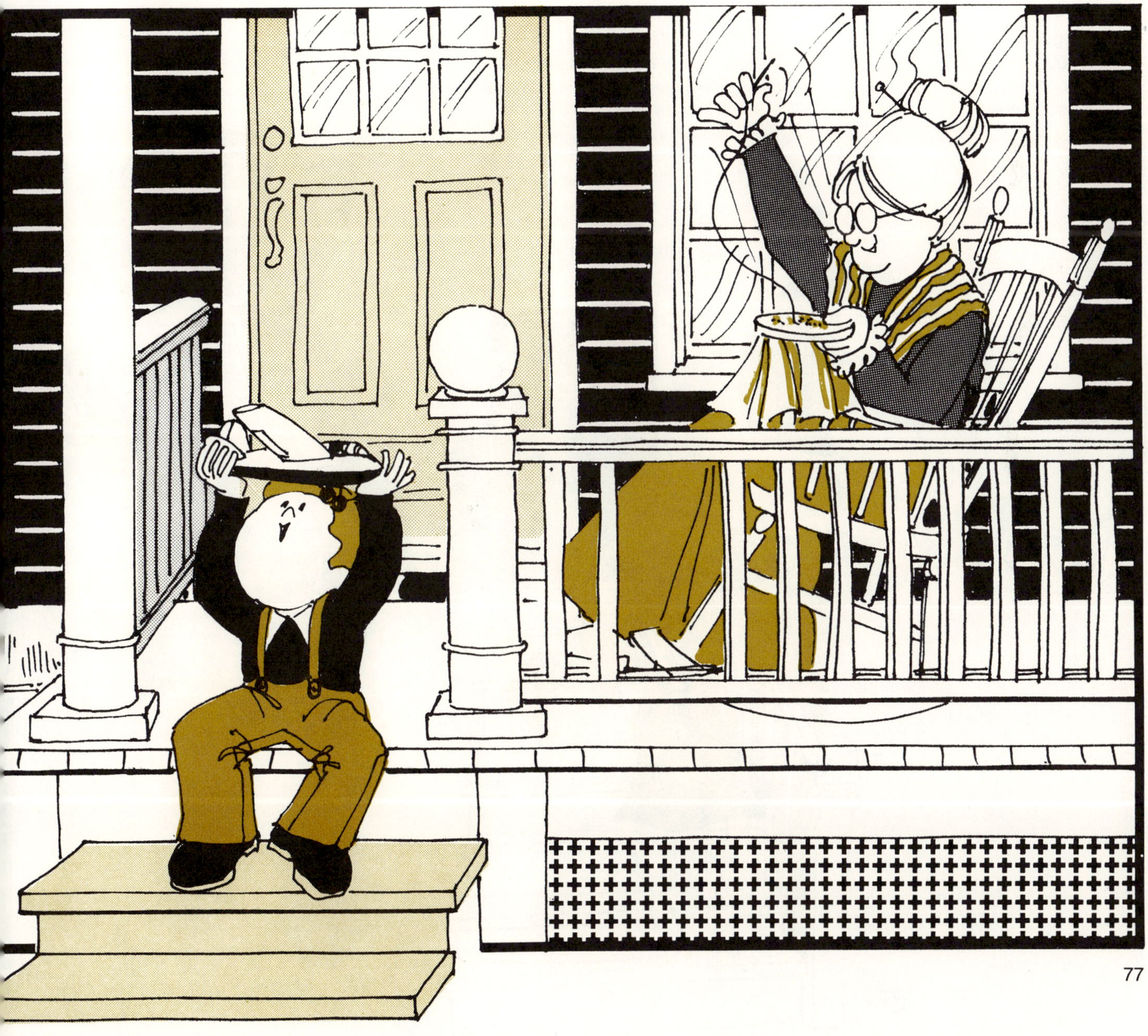

TAKE ACTION

Number the completions of each of the following statements in your order of preference:

1. I feel a good friend should be
   ☐ a good listener
   ☐ a good adviser
   ☐ a good sport

2. I feel the time to come in on the weekend should be
   ☐ decided by me
   ☐ decided by my parents
   ☐ decided by me and my friends with our parents

3. It would be most difficult to accept
   ☐ losing my weekly allowance
   ☐ losing my weekend privileges
   ☐ losing my regular baby-sitting job

4. I least like a person who
   ☐ plays practical jokes
   ☐ tells everyone what I do
   ☐ gossips about everyone

5. The best neighbor to have would be
   ☐ a boy my age
   ☐ a girl my age
   ☐ owners of a swimming pool

6. It is most difficult for me to
   ☐ keep quiet
   ☐ talk to adults
   ☐ talk to the opposite sex

7. I would be happy if I got
   ☐ all A's on my report card
   ☐ to go on a class exchange trip
   ☐ more school holidays

8. If I got a gift of ten dollars, I would
   ☐ put it in the bank
   ☐ buy some clothing
   ☐ spend it on movies and snacks

9. I mostly spend my spare time
   ☐ with friends
   ☐ reading
   ☐ watching TV

Values are ideals, beliefs, and traditions that people feel are worthwhile. Values direct the course and action of your life. They are reflected in your behavior and in what you say. Because we have only a limited amount of time, we tend to spend it doing those things we value most.

Tom believes in spending his time and energy playing hockey. He values being part of a team and practicing his skill on skates. His friend values music. He feels a sense of accomplishment when playing a tune on his guitar.

How do you spend your after-school time?

Which of your values are reflected by your after-school activities?

A value is the quality or worth of things that are desirable or useful. Articles you purchase have a monetary or material value. They are marked a specific price. The quality or usefulness of an article is your guideline for determining its value to you. The activities you are involved in have a personal or social value for you and for your community.

Universal values include the following:

Acceptance	Health
Achievement	Honesty
Beauty	Justice
Cleanliness	Love
Education	Maturity
Family harmony	People
Freedom	Responsibility
Friendship	Security
Happiness	Truth

Joanne and Dick were curious about the parade of trucks carrying trees down the street they traveled to get to school. This tree-transport seemed to go on for days. On Saturday, Joanne and her mother were driving out to a brand-new shopping center that had just opened on the other side of the city and happened to get behind a truck carrying two Benjamin fig trees. It turned out that the cavalcade of trees was headed for the new shopping center where they were being transplanted – both outside and inside the high-ceilinged meeting center of the mall. They especially liked the idea of having the outdoors brought inside, as the trees made the huge concrete spaces more attractive and gave a feeling of summer on the very cold winter days.

What values are reflected in this story?

What values are reflected in this picture?

Aesthetic values reflect appreciation. Values are a measure of what you treasure. Aesthetic values are reflected in your feelings about what is beautiful in nature and life. These values help you appreciate the way things look, sound, feel, taste, and smell. Recognizing beauty and good design in clothing, in music, and even in a clump of weeds is a result of your aesthetic value system.

Cathy values a locket passed down from generation to generation. A family heirloom like this is priceless because of its association with people in the past. It also may have a design not crafted today. Because it cannot be duplicated, it is a real treasure and of great value to Cathy.

Do you like to see trees in a shopping mall? Is it worth the great expense?

How Do Values Develop?

Values develop from family and friends, and from your religious experiences. Children imitate others. Through socialization, children adopt family values as their own. When children begin school, they begin to consider other people's values. They appraise, evaluate, and adopt values of people they respect. Family values generally give direction to the wishes and behavior of family members.

TAKE ACTION

Design a family ring. Instead of a birthstone for each family member, draw a simple picture to represent a value for each family member.

Andrea was working with a group of third grade children at the community recreation center. The group wanted to plan a special Christmas project. They discussed and listed the family traditions that they most valued:

- **stringing popcorn for the tree**
- **making a gift for everyone in the family**
- **buying gifts for under a dollar**
- **making pull taffy**
- **collecting toys and clothing for needy families**
- **taking homemade cookies to older people**
- **going to the country to cut down a Christmas tree**
- **inviting a foreign student for Christmas dinner**

Which values do you think are expressed in these traditions? Did you think of: sharing family work and fun, remembering those less fortunate than yourself, appreciating another's faith, being thrifty or being creative? Which traditions do you most value?

Values result from your experiences and from your reactions to these experiences. You live in many environments. Your home, school, community, and society all present different experiences. Your personality, aptitudes, experiences, and the nature of the environment you are interacting with cause you to react in your own way. You will develop your own personal values from these experiences.

Think of two children growing up in the same family. One may drop out of school and drift from job to job, while the other may study and go through college. They have lived in the same environment and have been exposed to similar values. Because of different experiences, personal abilities, personal reactions, and friends, they have different values in life.

Find out how Christmas is and was celebrated around the world and at different points in history. Try to identify how values are different from place to place and from one time to another.

TAKE ACTION

1. You are shopping for jeans with a good friend. Your friend decides to wear the new jeans under his or her old pair, and leave the store.
   (a) Would you tell the salesclerk?
   (b) Would you try to explain the dangers of shoplifting?
   (c) Would you leave without your friend?
   (d) What would be some other solutions?
2. You are at a party with a group of friends. A little before the time your parents had told you to be home, the gang decides to go for pizza. If you go home now, that person you really want to impress will think you are a real drag.
   (a) Would you go home?
   (b) Would you stay and face the fireworks when you got home?
   (c) Would you phone your parents and ask to stay out? What would you do if they said no?

Values arise from your reaction to rules and regulations. Schools have rules, and society sets down principles of behavior. Your family sets guidelines, and even traffic lights tell us to stop or walk! Life is full of rules that are made mostly to give life order and to protect us. Your reactions to these rules and to people with authority influence your value system.

Try to analyze the importance of and the need for rules and regulations that you are expected to obey. It's easy to understand the rules of games and situations you think important.

Give some examples of family rules that are of real value to the well-being of the whole family. List and discuss the value of regulations in a school, on the roads, in a hospital, or in a fire drill.

Moral Values

Personal moral development occurs when a person realizes the difference between right and wrong. During adolescence, you begin to make your own moral decisions. These are influenced by yours parents' moral values as well as those of your peers. In the end you have to decide your own framework of what is right and wrong and in this way you form your own moral judgments.

The class was discussing the fact that Penny and Darlene had been suspended from school because they had accepted money from a wallet one of the boys had stolen out of a locker during gym.

When Penny and Darlene returned to school, they explained that their parents had come to the school and that the suspension was lifted now that their parents had been told.

Darlene told the group what really happened and how embarrassed she was. Her story goes like this:

"Everybody thinks Mark is a creep. He's always shoving people around and he's a loud mouth. Anyway, Neil took his wallet and there were four dollars in it. Neil told Penny and me that he had found the wallet and didn't know whose it was, so we took a dollar each and he took one and gave one to Wally. When we found out it was "hot," we gave it back and somehow Penny ended up with all four dollars. I went and told the vice-principal yesterday afternoon and we got suspended until our parents came at lunch today." Everyone started firing questions at the girls.

"Why did you take it in the first place?" asked one girl.

"Because I really thought he just found the money and didn't know who it belonged to."

"Oh well," said another student, "Mark is a real pain; he deserved it."

"I was lucky my parents were so understanding and believed me," said Penny.

"My dad said I was stupid to report it. I should have kept the money and no one would have been in trouble," said Darlene.

What are the moral issues involved in this situation? Analyze the decisions of each person involved in this incident.

Sexual Values

A very real concern at this age is the problem of sexuality and sexual behavior. Where did you learn the "facts of life"? From your mother? father? big brother? friends? or a group leader?

You may not realize it, but much of your sexual understanding and feelings come from your family. You learn from the way adults react to each other. They may be considerate and openly affectionate, or hostile and uncaring. You pick up information and attitudes from what you see.

Do you feel you should get more of "the facts" at home?

Discussion in the home about sex may not occur because parents and adolescents are so emotionally close that they both tend to avoid the subject. This is changing as both families and young people are presented with more sexual information. With increased knowledge and awareness, it is easier for both parents and adolescents to communicate on this topic.

The attitude of people towards sex alters and tends to go in cycles. Some people use the swinging pendulum to describe changes which take place in society.

TAKE ACTION

Choose two "eras" from your study of history which had widely different sexual morals. Research could be done on Rome when Nero was Emperor, France in Marie Antoinette's time, Chicago in the 1920's, Victorian England, the Puritan era, or today's life-styles. Conclude your report with your own thoughts on sexual morals.

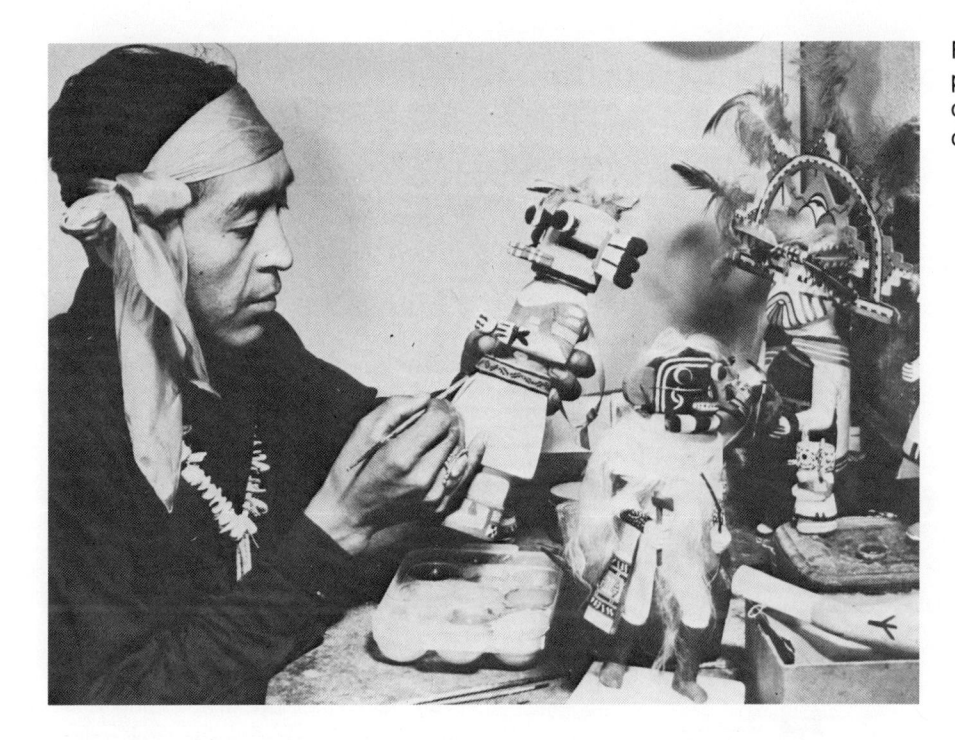

Find out more about the values of the people in these photos. Why do values change from one era to another or from one culture to another?

85

Religious Values

Parents' religious values often influence their answers to questions like these:
"What does God look like?"
"What does God mean?"
"You won't die before me, will you?"
Response to these and similar questions is one way the religious values of parents are passed down to their children. Young children usually accept their parents' values without criticism, whereas, in adolescence, these values are questioned.

Many young people are beginning to question traditional religious values. It is during adolescence that you begin to come to terms with your beliefs – and they may not be the same as your parents'. Religious values are often part of a family heritage and can be the basis of your moral development.

Religious institutions often have youth groups associated with them. These youth groups give everyone an equal opportunity for social acceptance and for building relationships. They give you a feeling of self-worth you may not gain through school or at home. Your association with other group members is significant also in that it helps you develop social skills.

Social Values

Imagine yourself in these situations. What would you do?
- You are the Administrator of our country's Environmental Protection Agency. What would you do to solve pollution problems?
- It is the year 2050, and you are in the midst of a population explosion. What would you do about this situation?
- You have an opportunity to evaluate all the new scientific inventions. Say which ones you feel are beneficial to mankind and which ones you would destroy.
- During a depression, money and goods are in short supply. List the things you would not like to give up.

Many changes occur in life that cause us to develop and change our values. Inflation and the rise of prices make us evaluate our methods of spending. Pollution problems have increased the desire for a clean environment. This concern may have caused you to recycle bottles, paper, and clothing. It may have helped you to value your environment more and to stop littering. World food problems make us more aware of the worth of human beings. They may cause you to value your life more and to be less wasteful of food.

Cultural Values

The values of any culture may be true of that group alone. Values may also be held in common by many cultures. For some groups, certain core values are the bonds that unite them. This is true of the Eskimos of North America. These people respect and value the dignity of the individual. Their values include the importance of cooperation and harmony with others. A person's "success" in life may be judged by his or her ability to work well with others. People are valued over things. Sharing is another value. Everything is shared by the community rather than being stored away for individual use.

Children are encouraged to listen to the wisdom of their elders and to seek their counsel, but also to be independent, to stand on their own two feet and make their own decisions, and to live and learn by those decisions. Children are afforded the same respect as persons that adults are.

The Eskimos are not clock watchers. Time is looked upon as a continuum, with no beginning and no end. This does not mean that they do not care about time; rather, things are done as needed.

Time values differ from person to person and place to place. You may have friends who can never seem to get anywhere on time. They move at their own pace and let everyone else wait for them. How do you feel about waiting for someone else? Do you mind if they have to wait for you? What does this tell you about consideration for other people?

Many things influence use of time. In some agricultural communities, schools have vacation time during the winter or late fall to allow students to help harvest crops. Does your perception and use of time differ from that of your friends, parents, and people in other communities?

What Can Values Do?

Your values will affect what you think, say, and do. If you value people, you will treat them with respect and dignity. The way you spend your time will reflect your values. The value you place on money will be expressed in the way you use money. Listen to people talking on a bus and try to determine their values.

Values influence a person's behavior, interests, and decisions. What values do you feel are important to each of these characters? Fill in their words, so that what they say reflects their interests, actions, and decisions.

Values influence your interests. If you value being alone, your main interest may be reading or working on a hobby. If you value being creative, you may build something or take a crafts course. People often talk about their interests: if they act on them, it indicates that they truly value these interests.

Values can influence your decisions. When Mary asked the group what they should do on Saturday, the replies were:
"Let's go to the roller rink."
"Let's go swimming."
"Let's make something to wear to the school dance."
"I'm going to fix my bike."
"Let's go downtown."
"I'm going to baby-sit."
"I'm going to deliver papers."

Each of these activities indicates a different value. Each value involves a different use of time, money, effort, and group involvement. What are the values expressed by the people in the group?

Values can affect human relationships. Some of your values are similar to other people's and some are different. If you don't understand someone's values, it can affect your relationship with that person. The more you understand what values influence decisions and actions, the more you can appreciate another person.

Values can reflect your individuality. Sometimes you like to be exactly like your friends; in the clothes you wear, the expressions you use, and the things you do. Are there times when you like to express your individuality? It is your differences in values that cause you to make different decisions and to pursue different interests. These different values also make you unique. It feels secure to have something in common with friends, but no one wants to be a carbon copy of someone else.

Don't get trapped by other people's values. Decide which of your friends' values to avoid. Don't get trapped by values that need to be appraised and suited to changes in your life.

LET'S MAKE SOMETHING TO WEAR TO THE SCHOOL DANCE.

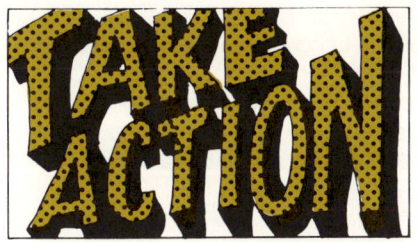

TAKE ACTION

1. Put yourself in someone else's shoes. Complete the following statements in a way that expresses a value that you do not possess. Put yourself in the other person's shoes and try to explain the value of each statement you have made.
   (a) I prefer to live in the _____ (country, suburbs, center of the city, on a farm).
   (b) I study _____ (one hour, zero hours, two hours, ten hours) each week.
   (c) I read the whole newspaper _____ (never, only on Saturday, I only read comics, every day).
2. Draw a comic strip depicting you and the ten most important values in your life. The whole class could make up a comic strip that would help you understand the class values that are similar, to appreciate each other, and to clarify or express your values.

89

Changing Values

How many times have you heard the expression, "When I was your age . . ."? Do a survey and find out what your parents or other adults valued when they were your age. List these values and determine how many of them you hold too. Did they mostly value things that did not cost money? Did they value doing things in large groups? Did they value family activities? Try to understand why their values were different from yours and to appreciate the similarities.

How might your values change if:
- you were newly married?
- you could vote?
- you worked in a foreign country?
- you lived by yourself?
- you moved to another city?
- you became a parent?

Do values change? Let's look at a few facts.

Fact 1: Values are affected by the people in your life.

Fact 2: Values are affected by your experience and your reaction to these experiences.

Fact 3: Values are different among people of different ages.

Fact 4: Values are different in different cultures, countries, and different parts of the same country.

Fact 5: Values are affected by the world situation and economic and environmental changes.

Considering these facts, you could conclude that, "Yes, your values change when any of these situations change." As you get older and more mature, your experience widens as does your contact with people. Maturity results in your ability to appraise values and adjust to changes in life. Some of your values will change, while other universal values – like honesty and loyalty – may stay with you all your life.

Ask someone of a different age, sex, culture, or country to react to these statements. Determine how their comments support the fact that values change.
- Women should fight beside men in a war.
- A couple should have to take a year's course and be counseled before being allowed to marry.
- Students should treat school like a job, attending for fifty weeks with a two-week vacation.
- Parents should pick out their children's marriage partners.
- A chaperone should accompany you on all your dates.

Do values change?

What Did You Learn about Values?

Values are:
- ideals, beliefs, and traditions
- the quality or worth of something
- based on knowledge and appreciation
- a measure of what you treasure

Values come from:
- family and friends and religious experience
- lifetime experiences
- reaction to rules
- changes in world situations

Values can:
- affect the way you act
- influence interests
- influence decisions
- affect human relationships
- change with maturity

WORD POWER

aesthetic values
appraise
cultural values
environmental values
monetary values
moral values
pollution
religious values
sexual values
social values
universal values
value clarification

TAKE ACTION

1. You are going to do these activities: attend a school dance, go baby-sitting, go camping, go to a bridal shower, and go downtown. What would you wear and what would you take with you? How do these choices reflect your values?
2. Make up a bingo card with one free space in the center and eight other empty spaces. Put the names of eight people in your class in these spaces. Go to each of these persons in turn and ask each person a question, such as, "How do you spend your time?" or "How do you spend your money?" Write the reply in the box under the person's name. When everyone in the class has filled in the eight squares, return to your seats. The teacher calls out the names of students at random from a complete class list. If a name is called that appears on your bingo card, cover that name. The first person with one line of names covered calls "bingo." This person then relates the values he or she feels are reflected by the persons named in the covered squares. If, for example, Bill says he spends his money on records, it might mean he values music, hearing the latest sounds, or having an up-to-date record collection. The person named can agree or disagree.
3. Look at some illustrations of a variety of rooms. You might clip these illustrations from magazines. Try to determine the values of the owners by the furnishings and articles of interest in the room.
4. Recall the books you are studying in your English class. What values are held by each character? Do these values come into conflict with other characters' values? How might these conflicts affect the characters' lives?
5. Take a stand. Make large posters labeled "agree," "strongly agree," "disagree," and "strongly disagree." Place these posters at different points in the room. This exercise will aid the group in clarifying and sharing values. Make up a question or statement that you feel each class member will consider important enough to take a stand on. These statements should be placed in a box and drawn out one at a time. When a statement is read, each class member should move to the poster that best expresses his or her feeling. The group at each poster can determine which values support their feelings. Some statements might be:

- All children playing in a hockey league should wear helmets and face masks.
- All junk foods should be banned from vending machines in schools and recreation centers.
- Women are not capable of filling most men's jobs.
- All businesses should provide day-care services for working mothers.

Value	1	2	3	4	5
Acceptance, belonging					
Achievement					
Beauty					
Change, new experiences					
Cleanliness, good grooming					
Comfort, convenience					
Courage, determination					
Education, knowledge					
Efficiency					
Family harmony					
Freedom					
Friendship					
Fulfillment, deep satisfaction					
Fun					
Happiness					
Health					
Honesty					
Inner peace, serenity					
Justice					
Love					
Maturity					
People					
Responsibility					
Security					
Truth					

6. Using a separate sheet of paper, complete this chart. Check off the values in order of importance to you. Number 1 is of highest importance, number 3 is of average importance, and number 5 is least important.

7. Use a separate sheet of paper and complete these statements individually, or with three other people with whom you want to share your values.
   (a) If I won one million dollars, I _____.
   (b) If I could have a hotline to anyone I wanted, _____.
   (c) If I could be granted three wishes, _____.
   (d) If I could only have one machine or appliance, _____.
   (e) If I could have any job in the world, _____.
   (f) If I could give children only one piece of advice, _____.
   (g) If I could give adults only one piece of advice, _____.
   (h) If I had to choose a flower to represent me, _____.
   (i) If I had to choose an animal to represent me, _____.
   (j) If I were in real trouble, I would turn to _____.
   (k) If I felt really low, I would _____.
   (l) If I could meet any famous person of my choice, _____.
   (m) If I could get into a time machine, I would travel to _____.
   (n) If I could change one condition in the world, _____.

9 Emotions

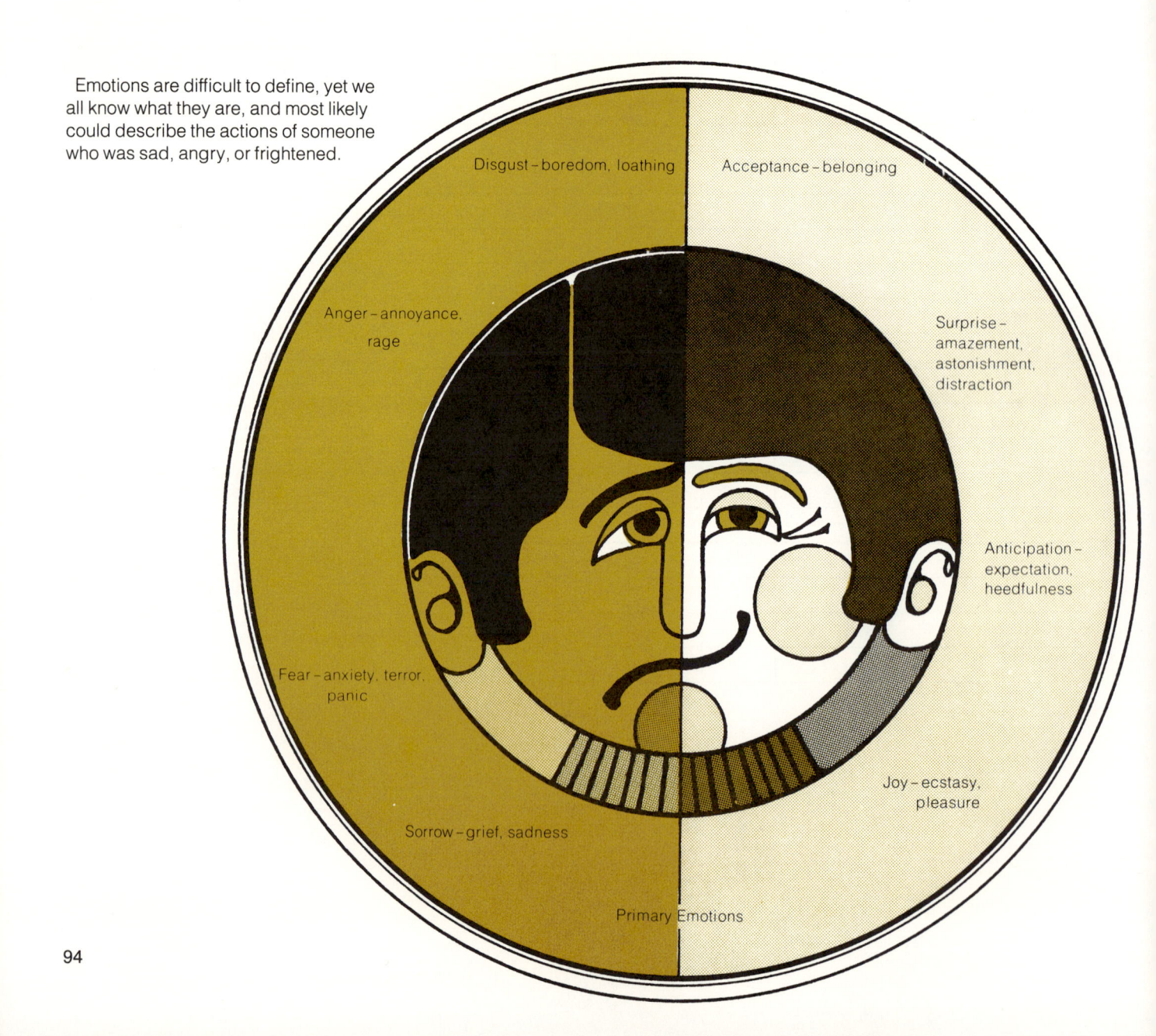

Emotions are difficult to define, yet we all know what they are, and most likely could describe the actions of someone who was sad, angry, or frightened.

Disgust – boredom, loathing

Acceptance – belonging

Anger – annoyance, rage

Surprise – amazement, astonishment, distraction

Anticipation – expectation, heedfulness

Fear – anxiety, terror, panic

Joy – ecstasy, pleasure

Sorrow – grief, sadness

Primary Emotions

94

Positive and Negative Emotions

Emotions involve feelings, ideas, beliefs, attitudes, and impulsive actions. The way you perceive or interpret something determines (1) the mildness or intensity of your feelings, and (2) your action in response to the situation. Think of the different ways people feel and respond when there is a thunderstorm. Some watch it and find it beautiful or exciting. Others hide in windowless rooms and shake with fright.

Emotions are positive when they motivate or stimulate your energy and bring satisfaction to your life. Emotions are negative when they cause you to be disorganized or confused, and result in unpleasant feelings and situations.

Emotions like joy and sympathy draw you to others, whereas emotions like anger, sadness, and boredom separate you. Negative emotions like fear, anger, and anxiety often occur when you feel ill, threatened, or insecure. Positive emotions like joy and acceptance occur when you feel good about yourself in relation to others and when life is going well for you. Positive emotions give you energy to do bigger and better things.

Craig was really crazy about Judy, who was the first girl he had taken out. She was very popular and he was the quiet, sit-in-the-background type. He wanted to be with her every minute of the day because he liked her so much and also because he was afraid someone else might step in on him. His grades started to drop and he was almost cut from the soccer team because he missed so many practices. He didn't care about anything else but being with Judy.

This is an example of how a pleasant or positive emotion (joy or pleasure) can have a negative effect. Instead of being motivated or energized, Craig is disorganized and not able to perform in his usual manner. Craig is letting one emotion control and dictate all his actions. What solutions can you suggest to solve Craig's problem?

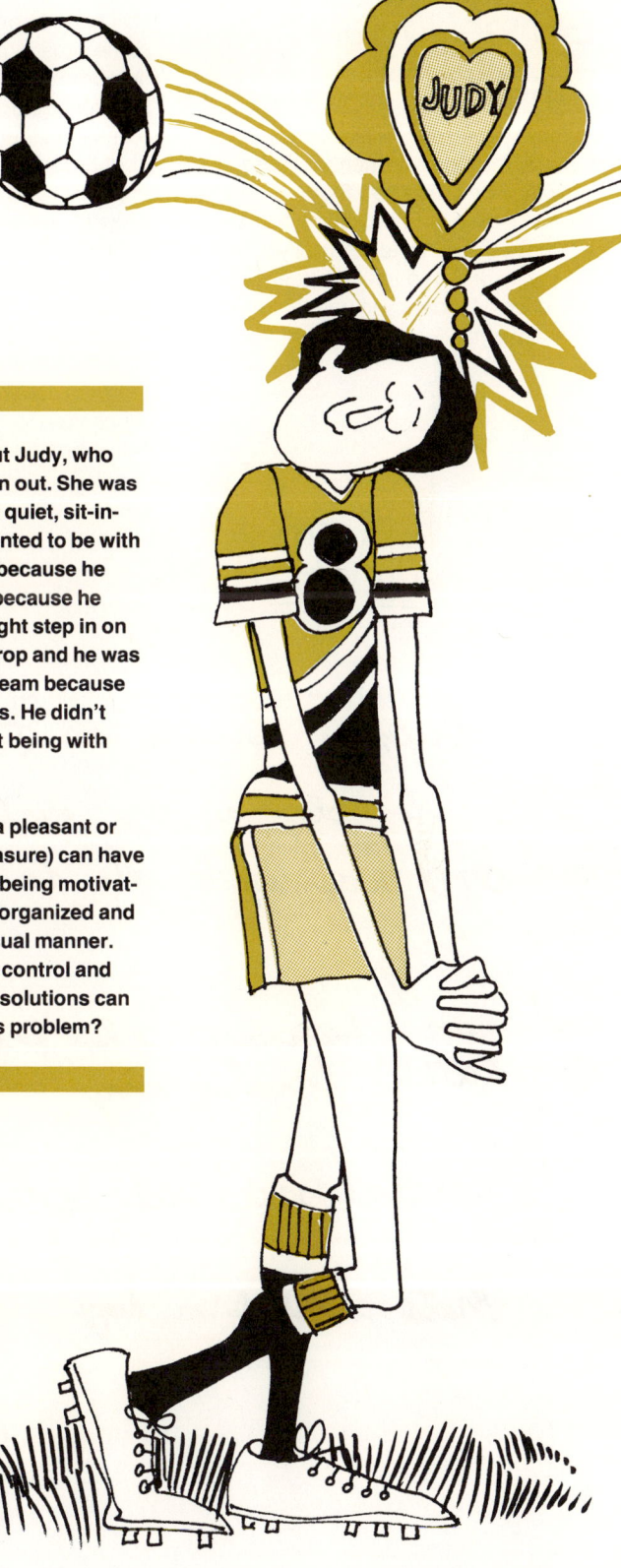

Expression of Emotions

Verbal expression of emotions is learned through experience. These drawings describe how fourth grade students felt one Friday afternoon. Do you have the same feelings at your age? Do you express yourself as freely, or do you have a tendency to conceal your true feelings?

Different people react differently to the same situation: something that seems humorous to you may seem silly to someone else. You may get angry at something that a friend feels indifferent about. Understanding your emotions and reactions will help your emotional growth towards maturity. Remember that your whole body is involved in emotions. Your body movements, glands, and organs are all affected by an emotion.

Try this "Zen morning laugh" tomorrow morning. It's a great way to start a day. When you get up in the morning, stand with your hands on the back part of your hips, with your palms facing upwards. Begin to laugh and keep laughing. Let your laughter grow and propel itself through your body and out. You will probably bend and move with your laughter. Continue for a few minutes laughing fully and completely. When it feels comfortable, stop laughing. Now you are ready for anything. Which parts of the body and mind did this expression of a joyous emotion affect?

HAPPY

I'm happy because on Friday I get to sleep at my aunt's house And on Saturday I get to play all day long and on Sunday the best day of year because my Grandma is coming

Thats why I'm happy

I Am feeling
SuPer because
I am going
to the Lake
with my friends
I feel like
Jumping out
of my chair
and Screaming

I feel mad because,
I have a cast on
and I am missing all my
BASESBALL GAMES
The end
TOBIN

Emotional Development

Each of us grows up physically, mentally, and emotionally at our own speed. Emotional needs are closely linked to physical needs. Babies feel physically and emotionally secure when they are fed, but they also feel joy and happiness if they are cuddled at the same time. If these needs are not met, babies will cry.

Let's consider the emotions of joy, affection, and love and follow their development in an individual from birth to adulthood.

5. Love as a parent

4. Love of opposite sex

Selfish love → Emotional development → Selfless love

3. Love of same sex

2. Love of mother, father, family

1. Love of self

Stage 1

Learning experiences and physical and mental maturity have an effect on a person's emotional development. Infants love only themselves. Their world is entirely self-centered. Soon babies learn to love mother, father, and siblings. They move from selfish love and learn to trust and love others.

Stage 2

Toddlers develop a deep love for their mothers, not just because mothers satisfy physical needs, but because children have a great emotional need for love and attention. Toddlers gain emotional security from their mother's attention and approval.

Mrs. Brown was trying to carry on a conversation with a couple of neighborhood mothers, but was constantly being interrupted by Jamie. First he dashed onto the road, then he kept bumping into his mother's leg with his tricycle, and finally he just kept yelling "Mommy, Mommy" at the top of his lungs. Mrs. Brown finally said, "Well, I guess this ends our conversation. Jamie will do anything to get attention these days."

1. Why is Jamie craving attention?
2. What specific family situation could cause Jamie to have a lack of emotional security?
3. Compare Mrs. Brown's reaction to Jamie with Johnny's mother's reaction to Johnny on page 33. Which solution do you prefer? Why?

The next development in this stage is a real interest in and love for father. This presents the problem of sharing love with two people at the same time. When emotional development is immature, a child can only love one person, so this love shifts back and forth from mother to father.

99

Grandma remarked that Julie was certainly her "father's child" because she had to go everywhere with him and even had to sit on his knee while they ate dinner. Julie's mother replied, "Julie will do anything for her father, but I might as well be invisible."

1. Are there specific ages when girls are more aware of their fathers than at other times?
2. What are some activities you and your father both enjoy?
3. What activities do you enjoy with your mother?

In a loving environment, children learn that they can love both parents and that they can also love relatives and friends. Children will not feel torn or that they must divide affection among everyone in such an environment. You would think that loving both parents is automatic, but in fact this is learned and it is a difficult step towards emotional growth. The ability to share affection is very important in order to build other friendships and loving relationships.

Margie called Noreen to go to the park. They were all set to leave for the afternoon when Tina phoned and asked if she could play. Margie was really upset because she knew Tina didn't like sharing and would be rude to Noreen. She finally had to say she was sorry she couldn't, but made arrangements to see Tina after supper. Margie said to her Mom, "I feel like a pie. I have to cut up my time in so many pieces so that I don't upset anyone. Why can't everyone get along?"

Have you ever experienced a problem like this? What did you do?

Stage 3

Emotional interest from early school years to early adolescence is centered on people of the same sex. This is a time of deep involvements and very intense emotions. Everything seems to be terrific or dreadfully miserable. There doesn't seem to be an in-between. This is a time when you develop secret or "out in the open" crushes. This is a time of hero-worship of book characters, movie stars, rock stars, and so on.

Learning appropriate ways to gain attention and affection is a slow process. At first you may be clumsy and gushy in hopes of winning attention. A crush is very deep and short-lived. Later you learn control and how to get your feelings in the right balance. Crushes at this stage are always on people of the same sex – first older people (teachers, grandparents, or older sisters), then peers. Through knowledge of ways to win the friendship and attention of people you idolize and respect, you gain confidence and complete this third step towards emotional growth.

Stage 4

The fourth step – learning to appreciate the opposite sex – begins at puberty. As your body changes into an adult one, you will develop new needs and emotions. Besides the many physical changes, mental and social changes also occur. Emotional adjustment is difficult, as your biological changes often upset the emotional control you were beginning to develop.

"I don't know what's wrong with me," said Christy. "I either want to cry all day or laugh hysterically. If someone looks at me a little oddly, I burst into tears. I don't want to, but the tears just seem to gush out. I'm so afraid I'll do this when I'm out somewhere."

1. Why does Christy react this way?
2. Do you ever feel like Christy? Discuss some of your experiences with your classmates.

Crushes are natural at this stage, too. These trial and error experiences help you to learn how to love the opposite sex. Often the opposite sex is just an object of curiosity. Young people often choose friends that have the same values and standards as their parent of the opposite sex. This parent's appreciation or lack of appreciation has an effect on the friends and future partner you may choose. Think of your own situation. Is the opinion of your parent of the opposite sex important to your choice of friends?

A series of "puppy loves" and deep friendships are the stepping stones towards meaningful relationships. Those who have few friends, or poor relationships with their parent of the opposite sex, tend to get more deeply involved, then marry too early and often for the wrong reasons. All the developmental tasks for adolescents listed in chapter 4 must be achieved in order to accept changes and make the sacrifices necessary in selfless love.

With maturity, your expectations of another person change. Your romantic tendencies to judge a person by his or her looks, dancing or athletic ability will alter. You will look for someone who is considerate, has interests and values, and is willing to make changes with you to build a successful relationship.

Stage 5

The achievement of selfless love and/or love as a parent is the completion of the development of the emotion of love. Mature people continue to change and grow emotionally. Love deepens and takes on a different importance. Mature adults learn to manage their emotions so that they can solve problems and lead happy lives. As parents, they can pass on approval and love. They can set a loving example and be approving parents so their children's emotional growth is balanced. They can exhibit unselfish feelings and change their mothering and fathering so that adolescents may develop economic and personal independence.

Feelings Quiz

Directions: Complete this quiz on a separate sheet of paper, on which you have written the numbers 1 – 27. For each of the following statements that you think is true, or more true than false, write "T" beside its number. For each of the following statements that you think is false, or more false than true, write "F" beside its number.

1. I try to be optimistic and happy.
2. I am easily moved to laughter.
3. I cry over trifles.
4. I almost never get extremely excited.
5. I experience rather frequent pleasant and unpleasant moods.
6. I usually prefer to keep my feelings to myself.
7. I am shy and retiring.
8. I tend to do things on impulse.
9. Sometimes I have trouble getting to sleep because I have become so emotional.
10. I have become so angry I have felt like throwing things or pounding something.
11. My feelings are easily hurt.
12. I tend to be aggressive and seek attention.
13. I compliment others on their success.
14. I have a tendency to make alibis for myself.
15. I am reliable and keep promises.
16. I have strong likes and dislikes.
17. I can be a good loser.
18. I can sympathize with other people's problems.
19. It takes me quite a while to make up my mind how I feel about a person.
20. I am more interested in the future than the present.
21. I enjoy setting myself goals and accomplishing them.
22. I believe in getting as much fun as I can out of life.
23. I like to plan carefully before I do things.
24. Daydreams are an important part of my life.
25. I can deal much better with practical situations than with ideas.
26. I would rather listen to a story than tell one.
27. I am easily embarrassed.

After you have assessed your feelings, write a paragraph describing your emotional makeup. List three emotions that you wish you could change and determine ways by which you could control them to your satisfaction. Observe and listen to others to see how they handle their emotions.

Management of Emotional Problems

Think back to one of your childhood fears. Describe the fear to the class. Describe also the practical ways you developed to deal with this fearful situation. Did adults help you in any way to relieve your anxiety and concern?

Fears	Managing Emotions
Dogs – your experience?	People should not be forced to pat dogs, but whenever possible, be encouraged to be around friendly dogs. If you still feel afraid, why not acquire a dog as a family pet?
Thunder, lightning – your experience?	People should be taught to "respect" lightning, or to know what situations are dangerous. You can be aware of dangers without being afraid of this phenomenon. Talk about the situation when lightning occurs and keep calm in a rain storm.
Water and swimming – your experience?	Swimming instructors are trained to help a child overcome a fear of water. Everyone should learn to swim – if you do not know how, take lessons. Free or inexpensive classes and booklets are offered by the American Red Cross local chapters and many local Y.M.C.A. chapters. Knowledge of safety rules and of how to rescue yourself or others can eliminate this fear.
Failure – your experience?	Don't set unrealistic goals. If you are having real difficulty with a subject, seek remedial help early and it will be possible to be successful or at least make satisfactory progress in that subject. Next year you may decide to change your options and courses to ones that you are capable of successfully completing.
Humiliation – your experience?	Threats can be very humiliating. Parents may be the cause and not realize how you feel. A teacher can also be the cause, as can friends who make sarcastic comments. Maybe you have frequent feelings of inadequacy. Talk your problem over with a counselor or adult who can guide you in the situation. Try to analyze each situation so you know what type of comments and situations humiliate you. Work them out or avoid these situations.

There is a wide range of individual differences in emotional behavior. Everyone needs opportunities for self-expression to reveal, explore, and clarify feelings. Emotional energy needs to be used wisely. For example, how can anger be dealt with? Here are some suggestions:

- ☑ Do not let your anger build up.
  (a) Wisdom from the past can be used here. Count to ten. This gives you time to think about the situation and your spontaneous outburst may be dissolved.
  (b) Release your energy by walking slowly around the room before you speak. This gives you time to think through the emotion and postpone the discussion until you have cooled down.
- ☑ Avoid situations that annoy you whenever possible and don't become involved in needless arguments.
- ☑ Use creative outlets for emotional energy. A job you like to do can give you satisfaction and be a good emotional outlet. Has washing the car or really cleaning and polishing it given you an outlet for some frustrations? Perhaps emptying out your desk drawers and throwing out unwanted items has helped release energy as you gain a new outlook on a problem.
- ☑ If you become annoyed at someone not "coming through" with a job, spend your flood of feeling by doing the job yourself.
- ☑ A physical activity such as tennis, playing the piano, or riding your bicycle can help you get over a problem.

Brainstorming
On a separate sheet of paper, write your suggestions for ways to manage these emotions:

	Situation	Possible Solution
Frustration		
Hostility		
Sorrow		
Depression		
Boredom		

- ☑ If you feel like striking out, make a punching bag or go to a room by yourself and punch some pillows.
- ☑ When you feel tense and angry, finding time for a warm, relaxing shower also has a calming influence.
- ☑ You can control your anger by sitting down and writing a letter to the person with whom you are angry. You let out all your feelings and then tear up the letter. The next day you can review the situation and then decide what to do.

WORD POWER

anxiety
emotional development
emotional expression
emotional problems
love for opposite sex
love for parents
love for same sex
positive and negative emotions
primary emotions
selfish love
selfless love

TAKE ACTION

1. Look up the meaning of "empathy." Describe a situation in which you have had the feeling of empathy.
2. Sum up what you have learned about your own emotions and your increased understanding of the emotions of others in a poem or short essay. Draw a picture to illustrate your poem or essay similar to the ones done by the fourth grade students in this chapter.
3. "We only get mad at people we care about." Explain why you may or may not agree with this statement.
4. Inventory of Feelings:

lonely	shy
loved	repulsed
hated	impatient
hopeful	anxious
trusting	happy
inferior	bored
rejected	frustrated
nervous	insecure
angry	sympathetic
jealous	tense
calm	joyful
confident	afraid
protective	humiliated
content	silly
excited	superior
sad	awed
ashamed	thrilled
hurt	

   Using some of the feelings from this inventory, make a collage or bulletin board display of pictures and objects that express these feelings.
5. Listen to a variety of music and describe the emotions from the inventory of feelings that this music produces in you.
6. Most people prefer to laugh and be happy. Can you then explain why people say really sad books and movies are enjoyable?
7. Mood Boxes: Use a shoe box, or any box without a lid, to create a mood or feeling. Fill the box with objects, colors, textures, designs, or pictures that will create a mood or a certain feeling.
8. Experiment with different lighting in a room and describe the mood it creates. For example, bright lights in a shopping center, fluorescent lights, purple lights, strobe lights, pink-toned lights, yellow lights, or green lights.

10 Coping with Change

People have always lived with change. Some periods of history have shown little change, while others have changed at a tremendous rate. During this century, there have been more changes than there were in the previous 3000 years. Automation, population increases, computers, poverty, war, and pollution are some of the things that tend to cause changes and make people feel unsettled, and perhaps frightened. What changes are worrying you? Ask your parents what changes have bothered them over the years.

It is generally the unknown that is frightening. Resentment of change or the attitude of "ignore it and it will go away" will make you incapable of adapting to or coping with changes. Changes are easier to deal with if you learn about them and try to understand them so that you may use them to your advantage. Can you think of a situation when you had to change plans?

Some people suffer emotional upset if an established custom is altered. Some people believe that if a routine is set, it should never be changed. Even a slight change in a custom or routine is considered unnecessary. The ability to make adjustments to old ways and practices often indicates growth. Old ways should not be changed just because they are old, or are done by older people. They should be analyzed and changed only if there is a better, more satisfying alternative.

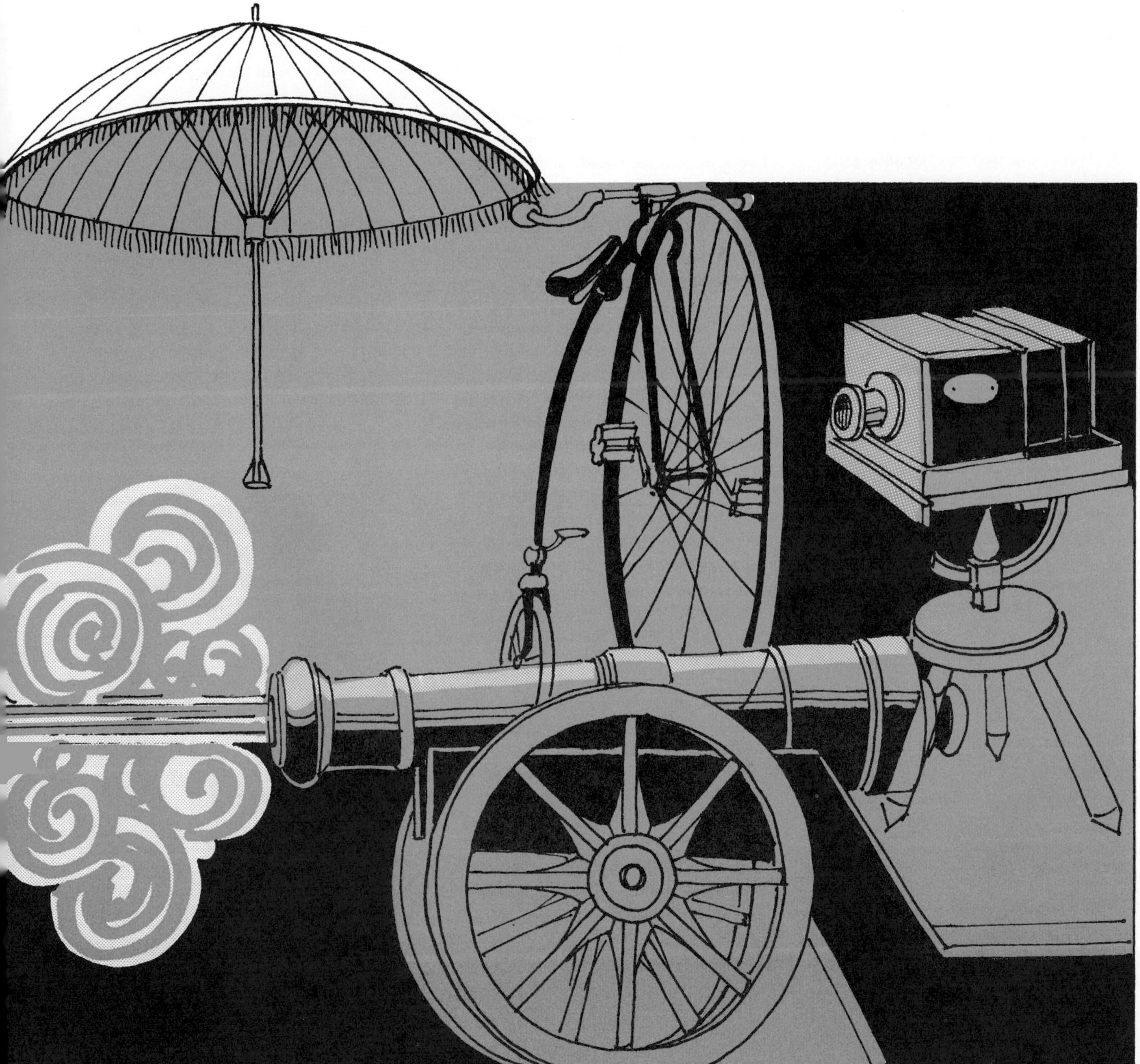

"When I first got married, I sure did some pretty dumb things," said Helen. "I remember having to give up my mother's special pea soup recipe because I couldn't do it exactly the same way. Somehow the ham bone would never fit into my soup pot. My husband offered to cut it up, but I said he couldn't. He laughed and asked why, and I said because my mother never cut it up. I didn't realize that perhaps her soup pot was bigger, or that the ham bone I used was too large for the pot. I didn't even stop to think that the soup would taste just as good if I cut the bone in half. Really dumb, eh?"

1. Why did Helen give up her mother's recipe?
2. (a) Have you ever had a similar experience?
   (b) If yes, describe it to your classmates and discuss it in class.

Bruce had a summer job helping out at the local bakery. He was responsible for preparing the peanut butter cookies. He really felt useless at first, but soon could roll out the dough, cut out the cookies, and get them into the oven quickly. It became pretty routine after a while, and he figured there must be a faster way. He decided to roll out the cookie dough on the flat cookie sheets, cut out the cookie shapes and then remove the extra pieces of dough from around the cookies. It saved him a lot of time and prevented breakage because he didn't have to transfer the cookies from the rolling board to the cookie sheets.

Bruce suggested the change to the baker's assistant, and received the answer, "What's wrong with the way I showed you to do it? Shaped cookies have always been made that way." But when the baker saw how many extra cookies could be made in the same amount of time, he was impressed and adopted this method. Bruce told his mother and she said, "I guess that's why I never have really enjoyed making shaped cookies. They always seemed to take so much extra effort and time. It's a great idea. I'll use it from now on. Why don't you make us a batch of cookies, since you're the cookie monster in this family."

1. Why did the baker's assistant object to Bruce's new method of making shaped cookies?
2. Have you or anyone you know ever reacted in this way to a new way of doing something? Why?
3. Make a study of change in your world. Document your own case studies to show how change can be resisted even if it is for the better.

Types of Change

Have you thought about the many changes in your life? Could you list what has changed in your life since you were in elementary school? Could you list some changes you expect to occur this year? Let's look at some types of changes.

Body Changes

We have discussed the changes in your physical development. You will be experiencing or beginning to experience the changes that provide you with an adult body. You may develop a change in eyesight. You may lose your baby fat, or all of a sudden change from being clumsy to being well coordinated. What changes have you noticed in yourself already? What other changes have you noticed in your friends?

Social Change

Jill overheard her mother talking to a friend on the phone. "Jill has a party to go to on Friday and she isn't sure what to wear. You know, it's really difficult for kids today because almost anything goes. The only problem is they still want to feel like part of the gang, so they don't want to be the only one in dress pants when everyone else is in jeans. Remember when we knew exactly what outfit was appropriate for each function? Mind you, you really needed a varied wardrobe, and really felt out of it if you didn't arrive with the correct outfit. It seemed a little easier for us because we had an unwritten rule book and always knew what was acceptable and what wasn't."

1. Ask your parents to tell you about some of the things they said and did as teenagers. Make a comparison of their adolescence and yours.
    (a) What things have changed?
    (b) What has remained the same?
2. Are teenagers better or worse today than they were in your parents' day? (Ask your parents if you're not sure.) Are the things teenagers find important today the same or different from the things your parents valued?

Complete these statements about change:
1. I really loved growing up in a large family with three brothers and a sister, but _____.
2. I have just finished an essay on child battering and am convinced that _____.
3. Last year's fad was _____.
4. My idea of a good vacation has changed from _____ to _____.
5. I feel the person who smokes must _____.
6. The laws about drugs should be _____.
7. My ideas of marriage differ from my parents' in that I _____.
8. When I look at a back issue of *Seventeen* (five years old), the most striking change is _____.
9. My favorite hit song has changed from _____ to _____.
10. When I look at the family photo album, _____.

Identify the trends related to each of these changes.

109

Changes in Expectations

Today young people make many more choices in their lives than did their parents. Just think of all the choices you have that your parents didn't have, or how your choices differ from those of an older brother or sister.

With these choices comes a change in people's expectations of you. People are all of a sudden expecting a lot from you. You are in a sort of no-man's land. You aren't fully protected as you were as a child, nor do you have the full rights of an adult. One minute you may be treated like a child, and the next reprimanded for not acting as an adult. It is difficult to know what is expected of you as you struggle to become an adult. Can you list a few of the things that are expected of you?

You and Your Response to Change

Quiz
(Use a separate sheet of paper.)

How do you respond to change? Give yourself 5 points for each "yes" answer, 2 points for each "sometimes," and 0 for each "no." How do you score?

_____ 1. Looked up the meaning of a word in the dictionary this week.
_____ 2. Used a new word this week.
_____ 3. Tried a new food or a different way of preparing food this month.
_____ 4. Aware of the current youth interest such as dance, craft, etc.
_____ 5. Read parts of the food page of the newspaper every day.
_____ 6. Watched a documentary or special newscast at least twice in the past month.
_____ 7. Participated in a class discussion on a current event.
_____ 8. Read a book (not on the curriculum).
_____ 9. Used your creative talents in some way this past week.
_____10. Are involved or willing to become involved in an action project which will aid your community, school, or society.

40 to 50 – Very aware of changes
20 to 30 – Average
below 20 – Try to improve

Coping Behavior

How can you feel more comfortable about the changes in your life? How can you adapt to and cope with changes? Here are some objectives that will help you deal with change:

- Become aware of the changes that are taking place and will occur in your near future.
- Gather knowledge that will help you live satisfactorily with future changes.
- Recognize that you can have a voice in future changes.
- Learn ways of adapting to and coping with changes.

Awareness about changes might be achieved by reading about and rehearsing situations that could occur in the future. A knowledge about the physical and emotional changes at your stage of development will help you live more comfortably with yourself. Recognizing that others are going through similar changes and sharing your ideas will help you to learn to adjust. By observing, and by analyzing and using facts, you can choose between constructive and destructive changes. To look at things openly without bias and prejudice can lead to an easy acceptance of change.

Adaptation is the ability to change your behavior to suit a changed situation. In adapting you show flexibility. Just like trees have to have some give to prevent breakage in a wind storm, people must be flexible so that they don't crack up under stress.

Flexibility is important in reactions to change in people, places, friendships, family situations, and circumstances. It will be easier for you to prepare for and adapt to change than to be forced into it. The changes that bug us are those we haven't anticipated. If you know about changes in advance and think about what you might do about them, you will be better armed against upsets when the changes occur. Old methods and practices do not have to be discarded. They are still useful for giving us some guidelines. They can be revised to fit the changing situation. Gradual revisions can help you avoid a crisis. If you have to change schools or a homeroom class, look at the pros and cons of each situation and the advantages in the change. Thinking positively will help you accept the change.

Coping behavior is the behavior you exhibit in responding to stress and crisis. Coping behavior usually means a struggle with a stressful situation. It also suggests a behavior that will help you handle the crisis situation with some measure of satisfaction or success.

Facts about Coping

- ☑ As you succeed in more and more developmental tasks, you will find your ability to cope will increase.
- ☑ Studies show that people handle stress situations differently. Some people will automatically go towards a stress situation and help out. Others will avoid anything – an argument, discussion, or small accident – that even slightly resembles a stress situation.
- ☑ The more experience people have with actual stress situations or of analyzing ways of behavior in simulated stress situations (e.g., fire drills), the more able they are to cope in any succeeding incidents.
- ☑ The way you cope is a result of family influence, your personality and emotional makeup, and the stresses you have experienced in your life.
- ☑ Remember that stress is normal and that there is often more than one solution.
- ☑ Initially a crisis might cause you to become immobilized for a while, but this will not correct the situation. The positive belief that there is a way to improve or cope with the situation is necessary.
- ☑ You also need to accept the responsibility of doing something about a crisis.
- ☑ Studies have shown that those who can talk about their concern or upset and not be afraid of their initial emotional reaction are better able to resolve the situation.
- ☑ Coping with stress can result in personal growth and self-confidence in handling future problems.
- ☑ Success in coping through developing your own personal positive coping behavior will aid your independence. It will free you from having to call on others unnecessarily and will also make you aware of who and what your best supports are during the time of stress.

adaptation
coping
coping behavior
established custom
fad
flexibility
social change
stress

TAKE ACTION

1. Form a 5–5–5 group. Five people get five minutes to write their reactions to five common expressions:
   "A change is as good as a rest."
   "Change for the sake of change."
   "You can't teach an old dog new tricks."
   "Subject to change without notice."
   "Time and tide wait for no one."
2. Set up a hot-line radio show. Have an announcer and a panel of guests speak on a topic such as – "Rapid changes in society have changed people's traditions and values." Have the remaining members of the class phone in and react or role-play reactions they might have heard stated by someone else.
3. Make a character sketch of each individual who would make the following statements:
   "But we've always done it this way."
   "Now is the time . . ."
   "In my younger days . . ."
   "Mission Impossible"
   "Time is marching on."
4. Prepare skits to illustrate how these social situations affect the family:
   (a) commuting workers,
   (b) prolonged adolescence,
   (c) premium placed on youthfulness,
   (d) shorter work week,
   (e) unemployed breadwinners,
   (f) zero population growth,
   (g) communication gap,
   (h) divorce or separation.
5. Write about any changes under the titles "Compare and Contrast" or "An Old Woman Remembers."
6. "The mind has a great wide door, through which gossip and rumor can rush in with ease, but a new idea can hardly get in without a set of burglar tools." How does this statement reflect individuals' acceptance or rejection of change?
7. Your ability to cope can be improved through practice. The following situations have been set up to allow you to fill the shoes of different people in different sets of circumstances. Each situation has two characters, and you can work them out in groups of two or in front of the whole class. Only the outline is given. It is up to you to determine what will happen in each case. Before beginning, consider the following checklist:

☑ Gather information about the situation by reading or getting firsthand information from people who have experienced the situation in real life.
☑ Imagine what would happen in each situation.
☑ Visualize how you and others will feel.
☑ Figure out where you could get help to solve each problem.
☑ Choose some possible solutions to the problems.
☑ List the possible consequences of these solutions.
☑ Determine whether your solution is acceptable to the other people involved.

After each situation has been acted out, ask questions to find out how each person "felt" in the role. Did he or she listen to the other person's problems? Was an alternative decision or compromise suggested? Did the situation help you understand a point of view different from your own? Would you feel confident coping with a similar situation? Now role-play the situations.

(a) Bites, Bites, and More Bites

Citizen: You are plagued by mosquitoes. You can't go outside for a minute without being covered with them. The City Clean Environment Committee continues with the ban of all spraying even though this is an exceptionally bad year for mosquitoes. You go to city hall with a petition signed by hundreds in the community.

Chairperson: You are the chairperson of the Clean Environment Committee. You are very aware of the evidence of progress (such as the return of birds) since the spraying ban went into effect three years ago.

(b) Rights of the Individual

Citizen 1: You are a homeowner in a segregated neighborhood (all black, all white, all Polish, or whatever). You want to sell your home to someone of a different ethnic background. Neighbors are complaining to you about your decisions.

Citizen 2: You are the neighborhood representative. A petition has been signed to keep the neighborhood ethnically pure. You pay a visit to the person now selling the house.

(c) Search for Meaning

Teacher: You are a teacher who uses new approaches to teaching. You have sent the students out of school for half a day to interview people on the street. They asked, "What is the way to happiness?" You get a visit from a parent.

Parent: You are a concerned parent and want your child to learn the basics of education, not all this nonsense that goes on about human relationships.

What are these people concerned about and what are they doing about it? Find other photographs showing people coping in different ways with troublesome situations.

(d) A Little Talk

Mother: You and your husband have finally decided divorce is the only solution. You have to tell your daughter.

Daughter: You have listened to your parents' arguments and sensed things were seriously wrong. When your mother calls you into her room for a little talk, you already know what her words will be.

(e) Death

Father: You have finally realized that your ten-year-old daughter is terminally ill. Her last heart operation, the only medical hope, was unsuccessful. Your young son needs an explanation as to why Tracy is so weak and should not be expected to always show a response to his enthusiasm.

Tim: You are a kindergarten pupil. You go to your father to ask questions about why your mother spends so much time with Tracy. Sometimes Tracy doesn't notice the rocks and things you bring to her, and she used to love to listen to your stories.

(f) Freedom and Responsibility Hassles

Hassled Parent: Your fifteen-year-old son/daughter is forever discussing the restrictions you put on him/her as to dating during the week, and the time he/she has to be in.

Hassled Adolescent: You are a son/daughter trying to get more freedom and independence and a chance to show you are responsible.

3 YOU AND YOUR FAMILY

117

11 Family Facts

What Is a Family?

Fill in your family tree with the names of the members of your family. If you wish, extend the tree to include more members of your family. Underneath each name, write a word or a number of words that you associate with this family member. Some of the words you might use are helpful, loving, strict, understanding, traditional, sharing, disciplinarian, or informative.

Do you think some of the words you have listed would help you to define a family? A family can be more formally defined as a group that provides for the basic needs of its members. There are many combinations that make up a family:

A family is a unit composed not only of children but of men, women, an occasional animal, and the common cold.

Ogden Nash

118

This family lives in different houses on the same farm.

Jim and Jane live in a city far away from their families.

119

Did you know?
- ☑ In Imperial China, a family lived in a large compound including as many as a thousand people.
- ☑ In some cultures, a family may be headed by a man with several wives or, in a few cases, by a woman with several husbands.

Is there one single description that fits all families? When you think about the families you know, does each have different kinds of relationships and forms?

What do you think a family is:
- two or more people who live together?
- people committed to each other?
- people who share their resources and abilities?
- a group of people who build customs and roots?
- intimacy?

The Responsibilities of a Family

Each family has the responsibility of developing its members socially, emotionally, physically, and spiritually. Families give their members a sense of security, trust, recognition, and self-worth. They pass on traditions, values, and attitudes. Families help their younger members to develop into responsible adults capable of making their own way in the community.

Your family is similar in many ways to the families of other members of your class, but in some respects it may differ widely. Different families often enjoy different kinds of activities and perpetuate different customs.

These photographs show people participating in various activities.
- Which of these activities does your family enjoy?
- What customs are portrayed in the pictures?
- What other traditions or customs could you include?

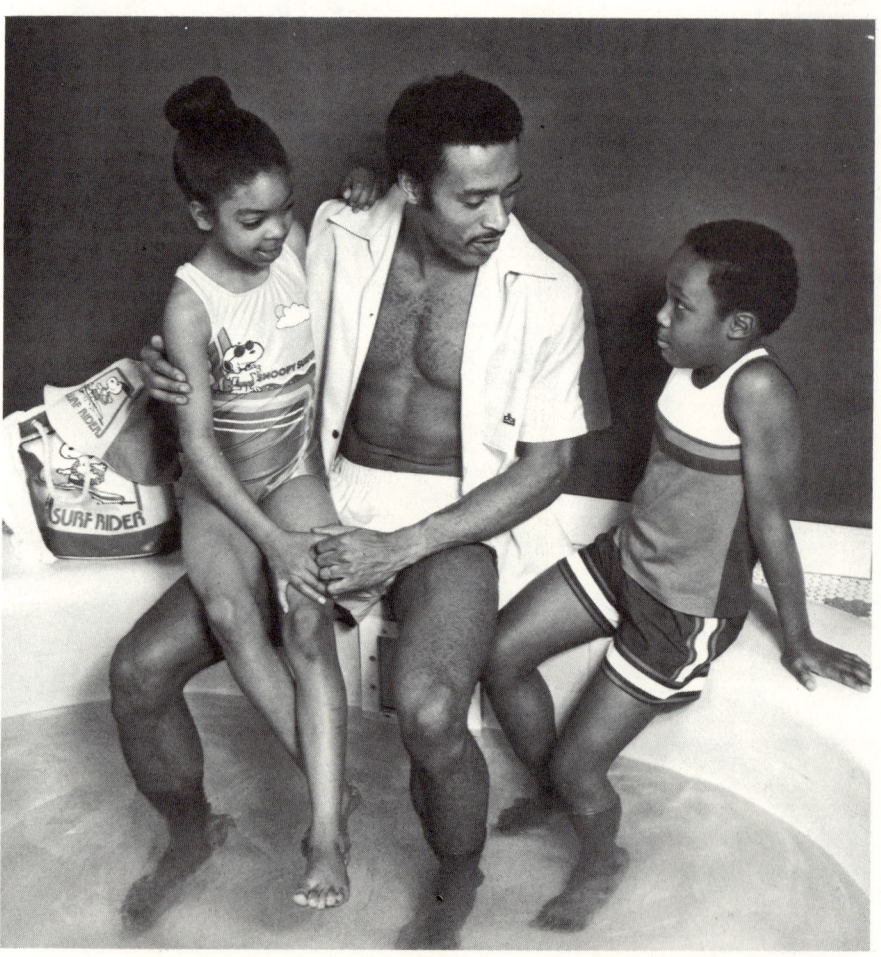

Margaret Mead, a widely known and respected anthropologist, said the family is the "toughest institution" we have. She meant by this that it is our strongest institution. Bringing children up in a family is the best way to help them become responsible adults who are able to marry and bring up their own children.

Can you list some of the functions of the family? Here are a few that you probably thought about: The family provides *physical care*, such as shelter, clothing, food, and everything needed for health care. The family *provides and shares resources*. It provides material goods, affection, authority, and space to meet the members' needs. The family provides for *sexual expression*. It is still considered the most socially accepted place for adult members to express sexual drives. It is the most suitable environment for reproduction. After bearing or adopting children, the family protects and cares for them.

We have already discussed the fact that the family provides for the socialization of its members in order that they may become comfortable members in society. The family also teaches cooperation. It operates on the basis of *division of labor* among its members – each member is responsible for specific jobs in the household, such as providing an income and day-to-day care of family members. It is this cooperation that binds the family closely together.

The family also *maintains order* among its members. It provides opportunities for interacting with people, for developing communication skills, and for giving and receiving affection. The family *motivates and encourages* its members and also helps in times of difficulty or crisis. Because the family does fulfill so many functions, it is an important unit in all societies.

Life Patterns

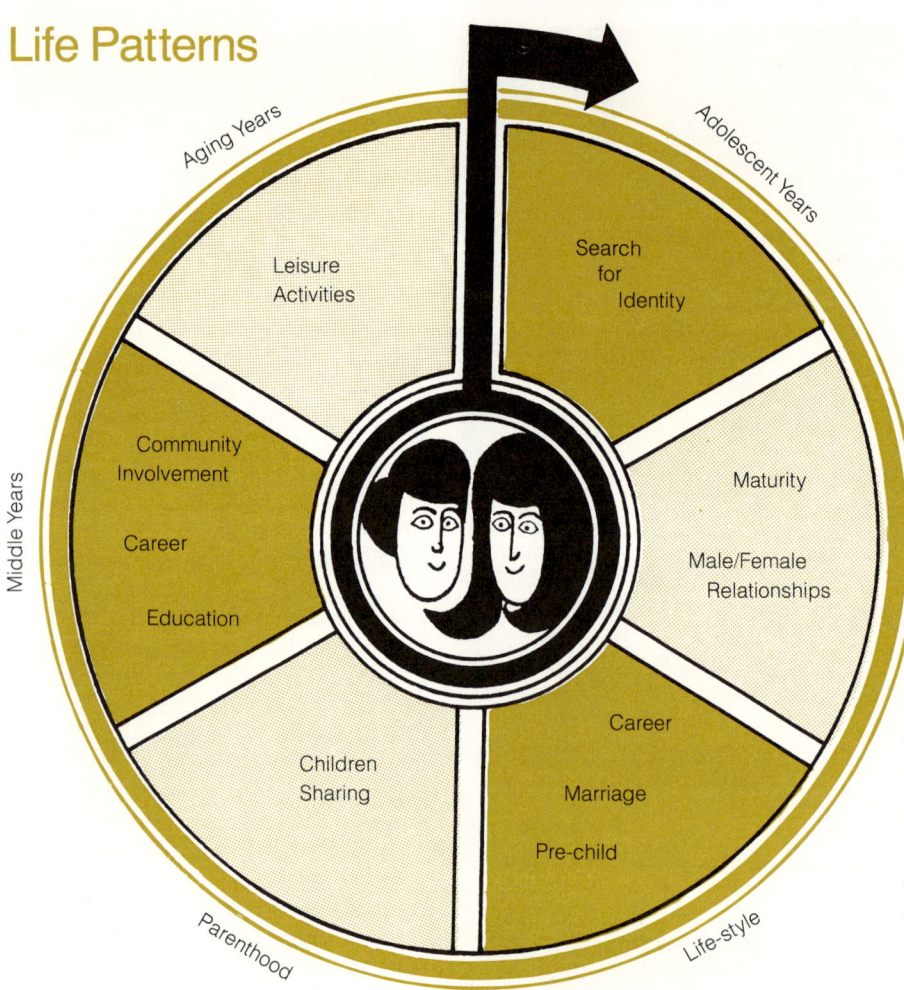

(Wheel diagram with stages around the circle:)

- Aging Years — Leisure Activities
- Adolescent Years — Search for Identity
- Launching Years — Maturity, Male/Female Relationships
- Life-style — Career, Marriage, Pre-child
- Parenthood — Children Sharing
- Middle Years — Community Involvement, Career, Education

Can you predict what your future life-style will be? Is there one particular pattern that most people follow? You probably won't be able to foresee every detail in your future, but there is a predictable cycle in life. Your family will pass through several stages of development and change. All families follow this cycle to some extent, but each family is unique in the choices it makes and in how the changes affect it at each stage of the cycle. You have choices to make in each of these stages. You have the opportunity to find or shape a life-style to suit yourself.

You and your family are now in the *adolescent stage*. This is a time in which you are developing physically, emotionally, socially, and are discovering your identity. Do you think you will ever become a parent? Try to imagine what it is like to be the parents of adolescent children. List specific ways in which parents can help in the development of children at this stage. Have you included some positive ways to strengthen family relationships? Why not discuss these positive ways with your family and try to work out a harmonious relationship?

The *launching stage* of the family is so called because this is the period when the children are ready to launch into a career, or further education, or to lead independent lives on their own. At this point, you will be maturing into a young adult, dating, and perhaps forming a steady relationship with someone of the opposite sex. You'll be making choices about the life-style you want when you have completed this stage.

- ☑ You may get married at twenty.
- ☑ You could stay single.
- ☑ You could have children or choose not to have any.
- ☑ You may live alone or have a roommate.
- ☑ You may live with a group.
- ☑ You may choose one career and then change to another.
- ☑ You could stay single and adopt a child.
- ☑ Now add two other suggestions that you can make choices about at this stage of the life cycle.

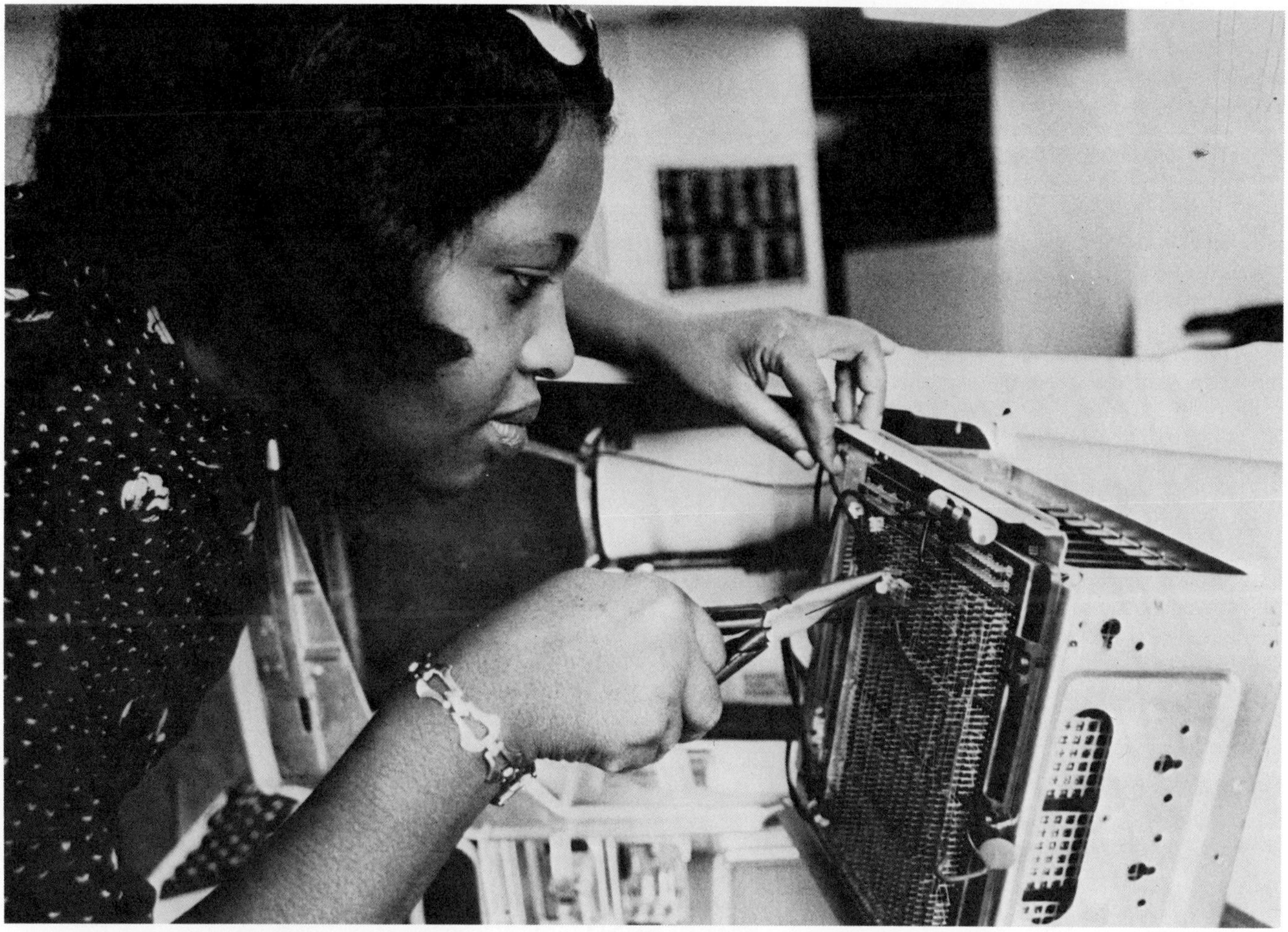

The marriage, pre-child stage is a time to develop a career and a relationship with another person.

The *parenting stage* is often referred to as the crowded years. The house seems crowded, and nobody ever seems to have enough energy, time, money, or privacy. Some people feel they have very little freedom at this stage. But this is the time when you can have pleasure in sharing activities as a family and in building close family relationships.

The *middle years* are ones in which most people have fewer family responsibilities and can spend more time pursuing personal interests. It is often a time of community involvement and helping people outside the home.

People in the *aging years* usually do not have daily job responsibilities and have a good deal of time for leisure activities and special hobbies.

Try to visualize yourself in each of the following stages of the life cycle. What decisions would you make about each area listed on this chart? Use a separate sheet of paper to write down your decisions.

Life stages	Adolescent years	Launching years	Marriage pre-child years	Parenthood	Middle years	Aging years
1. Money						
2. Time						
3. Recreation						
4. Responsibilities						
5. Greatest wish						

What Do You Think?

Your attitude towards your family, and what you expect from a family, will have an influence on your future life-style. Give your opinions on each of the following statements.

1. It is desirable for the whole family to plan hobbies and recreational activities.
2. Communes and experimental families are doomed to fail.
3. Women should be satisfied with being homemakers.
4. Holidays and birthdays should be big family events.
5. Family matters are best settled by one person, the head of the family.
6. Families benefit from the experience of moving from place to place.
7. Children should not be concerned with family income and how it is spent.
8. Unhappy parents should stay together to protect the children rather than get divorced.
9. A close tie with family relatives creates family unity.
10. A one-parent family can't work out successfully for the children.

A person's life cycle is fairly predictable. Each family experiences many of the same joys and problems in life. Decisions have to be faced: to form a relationship with someone, to become a parent, to fit in with a partner's family, to establish a home, to fit into the community, to develop a variety of interests, to develop a career, and to develop skills to cope with all the changes that occur in each stage of life.

WORD POWER

adolescent stage
anthropologist
family
family customs
family functions
family life cycle
family traditions
family tree
launching stage
life-style
parenting

TAKE ACTION

Obtain some examples of marriage contracts. Discuss their purpose in class. What would you like to see in your marriage contract?

1. Some people marry these days and make a conscious decision *not* to have children. What will the stages of their life cycle be like?
2. (a) What are some alternative lifestyles to that of the traditional family?
   (b) Collect information on one of these alternatives.
   (c) Report your findings to the class.
3. Form buzz groups. Design a marriage contract acceptable to your group. Read the finished contract to the class.
4. Complete the following statements:
   (a) The family I most admire . . .
   (b) The family I least admire . . .
   (c) The family I would like to form would . . .
5. Give examples to prove Margaret Mead's statement, quoted earlier, that the family is the "toughest institution."
6. (a) Are the functions of the present-day family different from those of American pioneer families? Explain.
   (b) List community and government organizations that have taken over some of the traditional family functions.
   (c) Do you feel that some of the traditional family functions now lost should be reinstated? Should some of the present functions be delegated to specific organizations, such as schools, religious organizations, or state health departments?

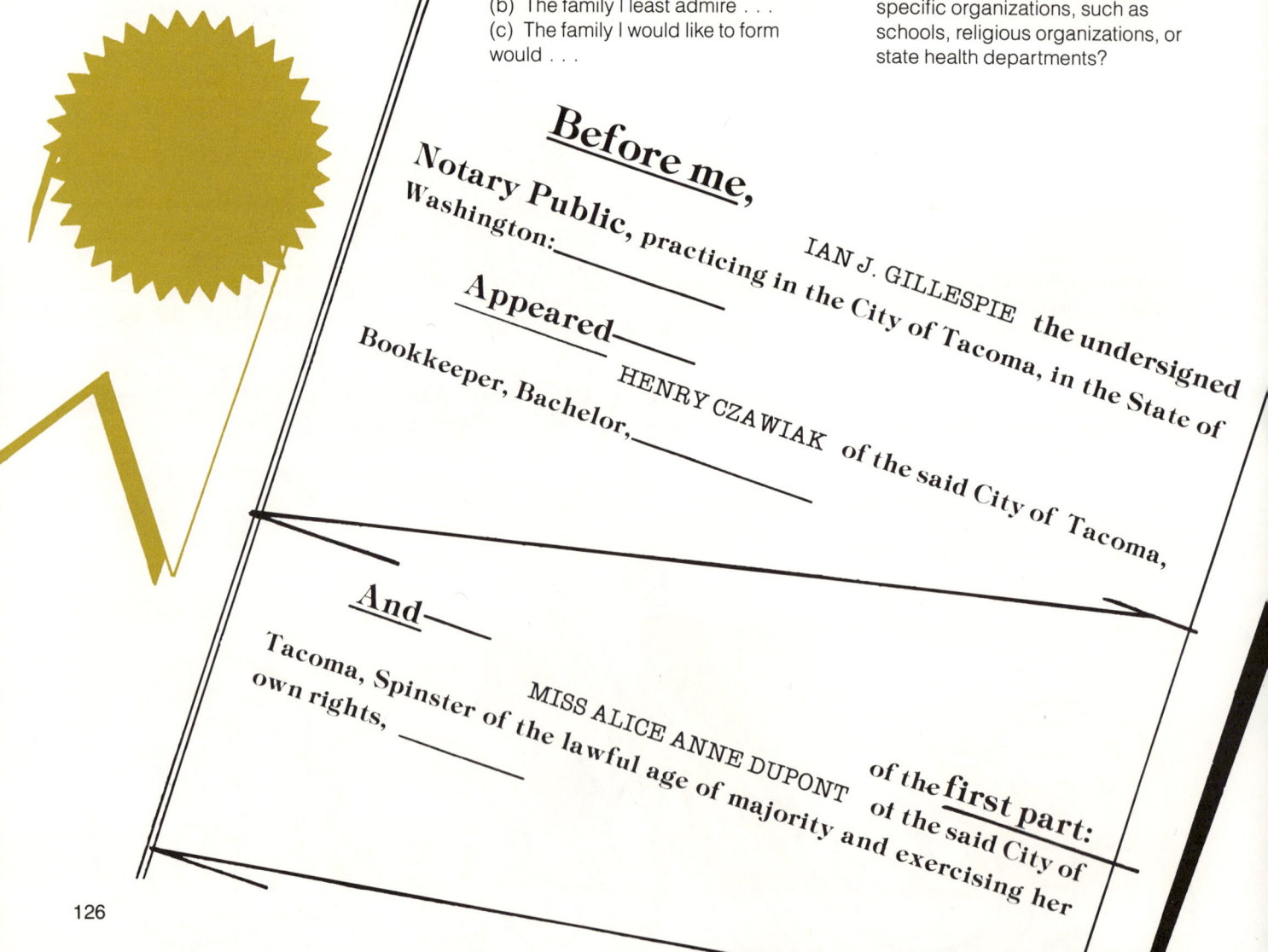

Before me, IAN J. GILLESPIE the undersigned Notary Public, practicing in the City of Tacoma, in the State of Washington: _____

Appeared _____ HENRY CZAWIAK of the said City of Tacoma, Bookkeeper, Bachelor, _____

And _____ MISS ALICE ANNE DUPONT of the said City of Tacoma, Spinster of the lawful age of majority and exercising her own rights, _____ of the **first part:**

7. I Think I Can Game
   (a) As a group, clip pictures from a magazine of activities you can do: they may include skiing, tennis, styling hair, preparing breakfast, delivering papers, caring for a pet, applying makeup, doing the laundry, choosing suitable clothing, etc.
   (b) Have one person sort out the duplicate activities.
   (c) Place the pictures on a large sheet of cardboard in the shape of a snake and square off each picture. (This game may be played by two teams or by individuals.)
   (d) Players will roll the dice and move ahead the indicated number of spaces.
   (e) When you land on a square, decide if you can carry out that activity in at least an average manner. If you can't, score 0. (If playing in teams, score 5 if at least half of the team members can do the activity.)
   (f) The person or team with the highest score wins.
   (g) Now determine who in your family has helped you achieve the ability to perform each activity.
8. You are a family counselor. It is the evening before the marriage of a couple you have been counseling. You would like to pass on congratulations and a wish for future happiness. You decide to send a night letter and you are allowed fifty words. Give the couple some advice that you feel would be important for a young couple beginning a life together.

127

12 Influences on You

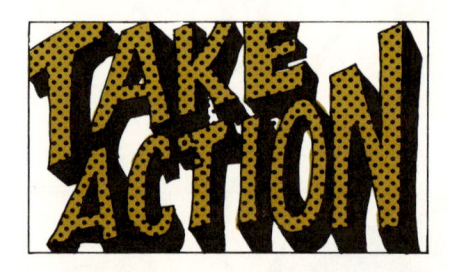

TAKE ACTION

Look at the following diagram.
1. Would you say that each of the things named in the circle has an influence on you?
2. Which things do you influence?
3. Could each area be a source of conflict?
4. Can you see how all of these influences work together to shape the person you are and the world around you?
5. List some positive influences each area has on an individual. Now, add some negative influences to your list.

Family Influences

Your family is the first and the most steadfast group to which you belong. It is the group that cares the most about you. Even though it knows your shortcomings and hang-ups, it won't make you turn in your membership. Even though you may argue with, disagree with, and misunderstand each other, your family members will stand by you when you need them.

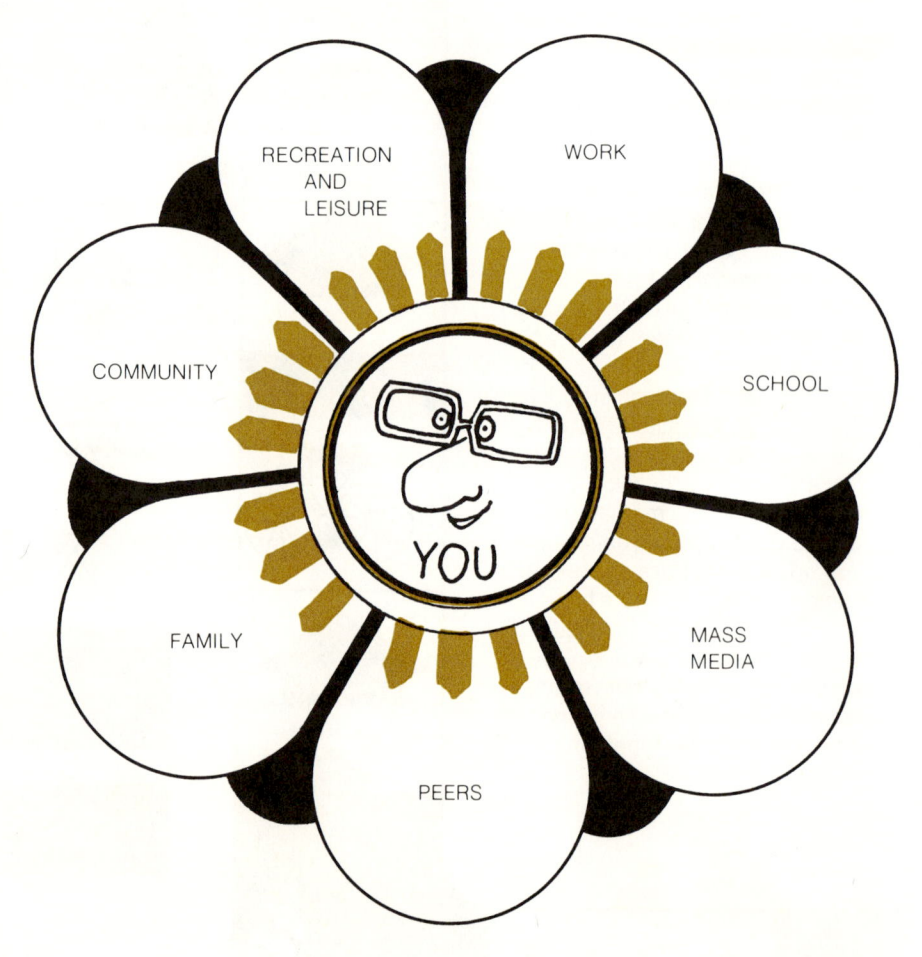

A group of students were talking about themselves and their families . . .

Susan: "I'm one of four children. I have an older brother and two younger sisters. I'm on the school track and gymnastic teams. I love children and spend all my spare time assisting with elementary school programs."

Anna: "I have an older brother and a sister who left home at 18. I help in the school library and spend a lot of time on school work and family events."

Brian: "I'm the youngest in the family. I'm really not unconventional, but my mom worries about my wild clothes and guitar playing. I don't always go by what my parents say because I want to find things out for myself."

Linda: "I have two sisters and a little brother. Right now, I am a ward of the court because I was a victim of child abuse. I am working with young children to help them get through some of the family problems I've experienced."

Tim: "I am in the middle of six children. I am actively involved in sports and love all outdoor activities. I find it hard to keep up with all my school assignments."

Anna: "My mother and older brother are my influences. My mother's terrific sense of humor and her understanding have really helped me to get along with people and understand them."

Brian: "My parents influence me, but I don't always go by what they say. I usually want to find out things for myself. I can't learn by their telling me what's right and wrong; however, I am influenced by the way they act."

Tim: "Parents have to be understanding, but I feel they should be courageous too – courageous enough to stand up for what they feel is important. I feel that if they are understanding and progressive, they can influence you in finding something to excel in."

Write a statement about the ways your family influences you.

The relationship of the parent and child changes during adolescence from the protective-dependent situation of childhood to one that involves more equality. It can be a time of turmoil. Both parents and children learn to play new roles and experience new feelings as the children move towards a more independent identity.

Adolescence is a time of change, a time in which there are many decisions to be made and in which new problems surface. Parents cannot provide their adolescent children with a detailed blueprint for coping with all of these changes, but they can provide models of flexible, problem-solving behavior so that adolescents may observe ways of successfully dealing with problems. A loving and secure family environment also helps adolescents cope with changing demands.

There are numerous patterns of parent-child interaction that have been found to influence the child's behavior and adjustment. No two parents will behave in exactly the same manner towards their child, so every adolescent is influenced in a unique way during the transition into adulthood.

Although parents have a great influence on you, it should be remembered that you are developing more control over your behavior and attitudes and can rise above negative influences. You can grow beyond the models your parents provide, but parents are still influential in determining the type of person you will become in the future. Let's look at some of the specific ways you are influenced by your family.

Home Environment	Responses to Environment
loving with age – appropriate freedoms	active; out-going; independent; friendly; creative; lacking in hostility towards others or self
loving and strict	dependent; conforming; dominant outside the home; competitive with peers; less friendly, creative, aggressive and more hostile in fantasies than the above
restrictive child-rearing with concealed hostility	angry feelings are internalized (often results in nervousness); introverted adolescent
hostile atmosphere with few limits	resentment is acted out; often leads to delinquency in adolescence

130

Community Influences

Do you think any community groups or facilities have an effect on you?

Community Quiz (Use a separate sheet of paper.)
1. Determine what facilities are available in your community.
2. Decide how each community group or facility may influence you and your family.
3. Identify how you could influence any of these areas or community resources.
4. Which community resources are missing? Could these missing resources be beneficial to you?

Community resources	Influences of community on you	Influences of community on family	Your participation in and influence on community	Needed resources	Benefits to you of these resources
Schools					
Religious institutions					
Community clubs					
Rinks					
Swimming pools					
Scouts					
Well-baby clinic					
Child-care centers					
Public library					
Law enforcement					
Athletic fields					
Arena					
"Help" (phone in or drop in)					
Recycling depot					
Others:					

The ability to take responsibility and to offer your services to the community does provide personal satisfaction. We all have something to offer to aid friends and others less fortunate than ourselves. Often this involvement can help you decide what career you will choose in the future. Do you help others in your community? Make a list of ways in which you could.

Leisure-Time Influences

Right from early childhood, the way we play or spend our leisure time is influential in shaping our personalities. The very small child's life is composed almost entirely of play. Some people don't see the value of play for little children. They forget that through play a child creates, experiments with alternative roles, and develops physical and mental skills. Play also helps children learn about themselves and their world.

Leisure may be described as a way of being at peace with oneself and with what one is doing.

We forget that everyone needs time to think and relax without the company of anyone else. On the other hand, when Johnny's mother asks him "Why aren't you doing something?," it is because she realizes that he needs to be exposed to leisure experiences that will help him develop appreciations and skills for personal satisfaction and future leisure time.

Do you ever feel bored or say, "I have nothing to do" during school vacations? The feeling of uselessness and worthlessness can disappear through planning activities or getting involved in existing groups and programs.

List some activities you or others you know have taken part in and write about the benefits of each activity. Did you think of some of the activities listed on the next page? Which others did you think of?

Type of activities	Benefits
lying on a beach	good tan, relaxation, reflection, conversations, communing with nature
sports team	physical development, sports skills, social relationships, acceptance of winning and losing
debating team	public speaking, becoming a good listener, controlling emotions
family camping	communication, shared responsibilities, fun, survival skills
swimming, horseback riding, reading, cycling, jogging, etc.	individual enjoyment, meets your personal pace and skills, personal vs. team competitiveness
volunteering	sharing with others, learning about handling problems and people
hobbies – photography, collections, mechanics, cooking, crafts, painting, etc.	personal development and knowledge, possible source of income or gifts
music – chorus, festivals, concerts, musical instrument	personal pleasure and shared enjoyment of expressing emotions
entertainment – movies, plays, museums, circus, TV	relaxation, education, source of conversation and amusement
parties, dancing	togetherness in conversations, social relationships – fun

Leisure activities can help you relieve your frustrations and tensions. They answer the need for personal relaxation. Leisure gives you the opportunity to consider other and often freer methods of handling situations. It provides you with the time to pursue more interests and, as a result, develops your personality.

Leisure activities can improve your knowledge, skills, and understanding so that you have more to exchange with others. These activities provide you with abilities to compensate for other not-so-successful areas in your life. You can learn to make decisions about your free time. You can plan activities that provide personal satisfaction, fulfillment and opportunities for interpersonal relationships.

How Work Influences Us

Work begins at an early age. Play is child's work. School becomes a job even though it is not exactly like the adult work world. Good work experiences give you a sense of worth. They help you understand the adults you work with, as well as your family's work responsibilities. Through any type of work experience you learn what is expected in society and also what you may choose as a future vocation. Like Ray on the opposite page, you will have some ideas about what you would like to work at in the future. The only difference is that you will now have to be more realistic about your choices. You will have to work hard on courses that will give you background for a future vocation. For example, if Ray wants to be a scientist he will need to do well in science-related courses. Eventually he will have to choose courses that will provide him with the knowledge he will need for the specific area he has chosen.

WHO AM I?

I am 9 years old.
I wants to be a scinctist
I wants to be a fireman
I wants to be a bird.
I want to be a cartoonist.
I sometimes sell my drawings for 5¢ each
I made $2.50 with my drawings.
I wrote to a T.V. staition and they wrote back about cartoon

What Do You Think?

The type of work one or both parents do affects the whole family. Discuss how their work may affect the following:

- amount of time the family spends together
- meal hours
- quiet hours
- vacation periods
- absence of parent(s)
- participation in your activities
- adolescents making meals
- personal attitudes towards work
- required baby-sitting
- amount of household chores
- tired parents
- parents' contribution to school and community projects
- opportunities to live in different communities due to job transfers
- influence on your future career choice

Work experiences influence the adolescent's sense of responsibility and self-development. Studies have shown that males tend to be most concerned with "getting the job done well" and females stress the social aspects of the job and the importance of good relationships with fellow workers.

Everyone has in-home jobs. Sometimes the job done by a child is essential to the running of the home. A child in a rural family, for example, may do the same work as an adult, plucking chickens or canning vegetables and fruit. Because this child gets to eat the "fruits of labor" and share them with the family members, the child feels productive.

Although there may not be the same satisfaction to be gained from cleaning your room or taking out the garbage, you should realize that all in-home work is necessary for the well-being and comfort of all family members. Further, any job teaches responsibility and how to build happy relationships by an equal division of labor.

How many real jobs are available to you now? Think about things you could do in your neighborhood. List some of the jobs you might do.

Did you consider these?
- minding pets or the house while people are away
- gardening, lawn-mowing, or flower-watering
- delivering flyers
- shopping for elderly people
- reading to elderly people
- working as a cook's helper, dishwasher, or waiter at a dinner party or club social
- preparing and selling baked goods to neighbors or teachers short of time
- selling art works or crafts to a specialty store
- helping out in a florist shop during the busy season
- sewing clothes for little children or their dolls
- cleaning windows

Do you belong to any organization where you raise money? This is definitely important work which gives you the benefits of being a real producer. Such organizations include Boy Scouts, Girl Scouts, 4H, church and school groups, Y.M.C.A., Y.W.C.A., choirs, orchestras, athletic teams, and community clubs. When your performance is judged "good" by peers and leaders, and when you get signs of recognition (badges, pins, awards, and so on), you feel you have done a good job and you develop a sense of industry.

School Influences

Today's adolescents are able to spend more years in school before becoming full-time workers than their parents or grandparents did. What is it like in school if you are twelve, thirteen, or fourteen? What does school mean?

Early adolescents are testing or exploring various vocational identities. They have the opportunity to explore various interests, talents, and achievements. In senior high school, the demands of school increase as students must choose courses that will lead to suitable work roles.

The greatest influence of the school for some of you may be the social opportunities and extracurricular activities it provides. It may influence others academically; it may provide a sense of achievement. Some students may be influenced in all these areas.

Response to questionnaires indicates that adolescents expect the school to offer other kinds of education besides the three R's. They feel a real need to have opportunities to make a place for themselves among those of their own age.

"I used to hate school in third grade because my teacher treated us like dirt. She did not treat us as people."

"My seventh grade teacher was one of the most understanding, kind, and considerate persons I have ever met, so I try to be the same."

"I really enjoyed the courses in which we discussed dating, group pressures, sex, and marriage."

"My mother is happy that girls have the same option choices as boys. In her school days, they didn't believe in equal opportunities for girls because they figured they'd just get married anyway."

"I always wanted to make the school basketball team, but they said I was too short. There should be enough teams so everyone can play."

"I think it's great that our school takes us on so many trips. Our extracurricular program plans camping and canoeing trips, field trips, student exchanges throughout the country, and trips to other countries. It was the first time I had been away from my parents and had an overnight train trip."

"We have a journalism class and I love it because it really lets us develop our own ideas and creative abilities."

"My older brother learned about photography in a special activity class and now he has an interesting career in aerial photography."

"Everyone used to ask in fun, 'What are you going to be when you grow up?,' but I didn't think it was so funny because I was so confused. I'm glad we have weekly sessions with the guidance counselor to discuss careers and hear talks from people in various careers. Do you know how many thousands of jobs there are?"

"We had a big food sale to raise money for the school play. I'd never seen half of the foods before, let alone tasted them. It's interesting to be involved with so many people of different ethnic backgrounds. We're making a foreign food cookbook in family studies class now."

"I used to think everyone thought the same way I did, but that was because we stayed together in a small group. It's neat to exchange ideas and values and gain the experiences of teachers and others in the class."

Sometimes students think schools don't teach anything that is worthwhile for the future, or that schools don't consider individuality. But most twelve-year-olds think of school as the place "where it's at." When people ask if you like school, you may say "no." But do you really mean it? School is a comfortable place where you are wanted. Although adolescents don't always like to admit it, most of them feel that school is important as well as being fun.

Mass Media Influences

Messages, programs, or ideas are communicated to a large number of people through the mass media. The mass media include radio, television, newspapers, and any other form of communication that is available to large groups of people.

You pick up information from what you hear others say, from what you see, and from what you read. Many ideas come from TV, because young people tend to believe TV before the printed word. Communications on TV have a greater immediacy and credibility than those in books and conversations.

We are subject to the influences of the mass media during much of our free time. Mass media are related to other forms of recreation: they may provide music to dance to or as inspiration for creativity; they can inform us about travel and sports; and so on.

Can you think of a situation from your preschool years in which you were influenced by a TV advertisement? Maybe someone in your family can help you recall a situation.

Susie kept asking her mother for a whosit. It was a special toy she saw on TV that could do magic tricks. Susie babbled so much about wanting this toy that her mother bought it for her birthday. Susie was really happy until it was time for the whosit to demonstrate the tricks she had seen on TV. Somehow it just didn't do them very well – in fact it really didn't do anything except look kind of cute. Susie didn't pay much attention to it after her birthday.

1. Why did Susie want the whosit?
2. Why did Susie stop playing with it soon after she got it?
3. (a) Should Susie's mother have bought it for her?
   (b) What would you have done?

Parents, broadcasters, and governments have been concerned about misleading advertising and its influence on children. The National Association for Better Broadcasting, P.O. Box 43640, Los Angeles, CA 90043; the National Citizens Committee for Broadcasting, 1028 Connecticut Ave., N.W., Washington, DC 20036; and local Parent, Teacher Associations are among the groups working to improve the standards of programs offered.

TV and radio invade the privacy of your home. Some cultural groups ban both completely because the values and environments depicted are contrary to the beliefs of their communities. Programmers are aware of the sensitive nature of some viewers and so they air controversial programs later in the evening to eliminate the possibility of young people viewing them.

Some people feel that TV is a method of bringing families together. Family members may have conflicts about what program to switch on, or some activities (such as meals) may have to be planned around programs, but generally TV provides an opportunity to share some entertainment and occasional conversation.

- Do you enjoy watching an exciting football game with Dad?
- Does TV provide topics of conversation to discuss with your friends?
- Do you feel the violence shown on TV influences young children?
- Have you learned a new dance step by watching it first on TV?
- Is a current song more appealing after seeing the artist perform it on TV?

Very few reports of typical family life situations appear in the newspapers and other media of mass communication. We are mostly bombarded by sensational, bizarre, attention-getting situations. Unfortunately, some adults are so influenced by the mass media that they form a negative attitude towards adolescents. Their attention has been drawn to the maladjustment and negative behavior of a very few adolescents.

We still know little about the influence of mass media on young people, but most parents and educators feel the positive effects outweigh the negative ones.

1. Sound of clock

2. Voice: "Hey Jimmy, what they need is a little touch of happiness...

3. ... what they need is WOW!"

4. Music

5. Music

6. Voice: "let WOW bring you together."

141

Peer Influences

Peers, or people your own age, influence your search for identity. Never again in your life will peer groups have such a strong influence on you.

There is a tendency to conform to the opinions of parents or peers. Decisions that have immediate consequences, such as choosing a new outfit or solving school problems, are influenced more by peers than by parental pressures. More lasting decisions are still made with parents.

The friendships of pre-adolescents are usually between the same sex; girls select girls as friends, boys choose boys. Friends and enemies play a large part in your life. You go to school happily to see friends, but also fearfully because there are enemies there too.

Adolescence is a time of intense friendships and groupings. The peer group is second only to parents in socializing the individual. If the individual is isolated from peer groups, it is very painful, because it is important to belong and to be like everyone else. This is a time when changes in physical, intellectual, and emotional development are so great that many individuals are ahead or behind their group of peers in development. Adolescents can be very cruel and take delight in pointing out people's differences.

This is a time of total commitment. You and your peers may be interested in only one thing: the school team, new clothes, or the latest model bikes. You will find that at one moment you have a great passion and enthusiasm for ideas, activities, or events, but the passion can vanish as quickly as it appeared.

The influence of peers is so great that you are willing to conform totally to the styles, values, and behavior of your group. Your affiliation with peers results in a questioning of adult and parental values. This questioning is the beginning of your shift from the family of origin to the eventual family you will begin as an adult.

Conclusion

The values, standards, attitudes, and expectations of all the people and forces in your life influence your development. The school will influence your learning capacity and attitude to future learning. Your peer group will influence behavior and the activities and friends that you prefer. Mass media will influence the way you dress and the things you buy. Available recreation facilities will influence your development of skills and use of leisure time.

The type of community you live in will influence your sense of belonging and the contributions you make. Work will influence your work habits, sense of achievement, and concepts regarding the value of money. The family, as you know, can have an influence in all of these aspects as well as providing you with the environment to develop your potential. Each of these forces has its influence and they all have an effect on the person you become. Each also has its negative sides. Evaluate each force and choose the influences that are the most beneficial to you.

community resources
influences
job availability
leisure time
mass media
negative influence
positive influence

TAKE ACTION

1. (a) Have you acted or do you act as an influence on others?
   (b) Describe how you may have been an influence:
   (i) on a preschooler while baby-sitting or being a group leader;
   (ii) on a friend selecting a record or article of clothing;
   (iii) on the community by collecting for UNICEF on Halloween or for the Red Cross;
   (iv) on a group by selling articles to raise money;
   (v) on a parent about a new car, choice of food, birthday gift, a movie, or a book.
2. List people who are in "influencing" positions. Why do you think they choose these positions? Are they influencing in a strictly positive way? Explain.
3. *Influence Questionnaire*
   On a separate sheet of paper, complete this questionnaire by writing down the first letter of the name of the person or thing influencing you. Choose from parents, friends, teachers, mass media, community, recreation leaders, work, or yourself (use "I").

(a) Who most often suggests that you sign up for a variety of school activities? ☐
(b) Who most often suggests that you have a group of friends? ☐
(c) Who tells you most about upcoming TV shows you would be interested in watching? ☐
(d) Who keeps you most up-to-date on fashions and fads? ☐
(e) Who gives you most suggestions on good books to read? ☐
(f) Who gives you most help in making decisions about your future? ☐
(g) Who gives you the most help in deciding what to do with your leisure time? ☐
(h) Who helps you most in learning about your development as an adolescent? ☐
(i) Who helps you most in learning to take care of yourself in the areas of grooming, rest, food, and fitness? ☐
(j) Who listens to you most when you have problems to solve? ☐

13 Siblings

Sibling Rivalry

Can you remember the biblical stories about Cain and Abel, Jacob and Esau, or Joseph and his brothers? Do you recall fairy stories such as Cinderella? In all of these stories the brothers and sisters were jealous of each other. We call such jealousy *sibling rivalry*.

Sibling rivalry is still a common cause of family conflict. It usually develops because the older sibling is jealous of the younger one. The older child enjoyed the individual, undivided attention of both parents until the new baby arrived. This jealousy is common only when the older child is still young. Once both children reach elementary school age, they become less dependent on parental attention.

Rivalry is seen in various ways. If the children are close in age, they will want the same kind of attention from parents and the same play equipment. Although siblings close in age are good playmates, their competitiveness presents the largest conflict in the family.

Sometimes in large families the siblings form cliques for attention and protection. The younger ones gang up on the older ones, the strong harass the weak, and the boys torment the girls. Each sibling looks to another one for support or for companionship. These bonds between siblings sometimes shift as a child takes sides first with one sibling and then with another. As brothers and sisters grow older, their annoyance with a particular sibling will disappear and they will become closer.

Everyone was watching the new mother open the gifts at the baby shower. Everyone "oohed" and "aahed" at the cute clothes and toys. It was a night for the mothers to recall their memories of bringing their babies home.

"I'll never forget what happened to Susan, my oldest, when she was three months old. She was sleeping in her carriage outside on the porch when I heard her howl. I ran out and saw little three-year-old Dougie from next door running down the steps. Well, he had thrown stones at Susan and they had left a couple of really big bumps and bruises on her head. Dougie had a new baby at his home, too, and I guess this was his way of acting out his hostility. His mother had to keep very close watch over him and his baby brother."

"Isn't it amazing how the older child will do anything for attention? Mine wanted to have a bottle again when the baby arrived, and wanted to wear all her baby sister's clothes."

"Well, Darren was four when his sister arrived, and he began wetting his pants. I thought he'd be remembered as the only kid in kindergarten leaving class with wet pants!"

1. List the different incidents of sibling rivalry given here.
2. Try to explain each incident.
3. Have you ever had such experiences? Discuss your own experiences in class.

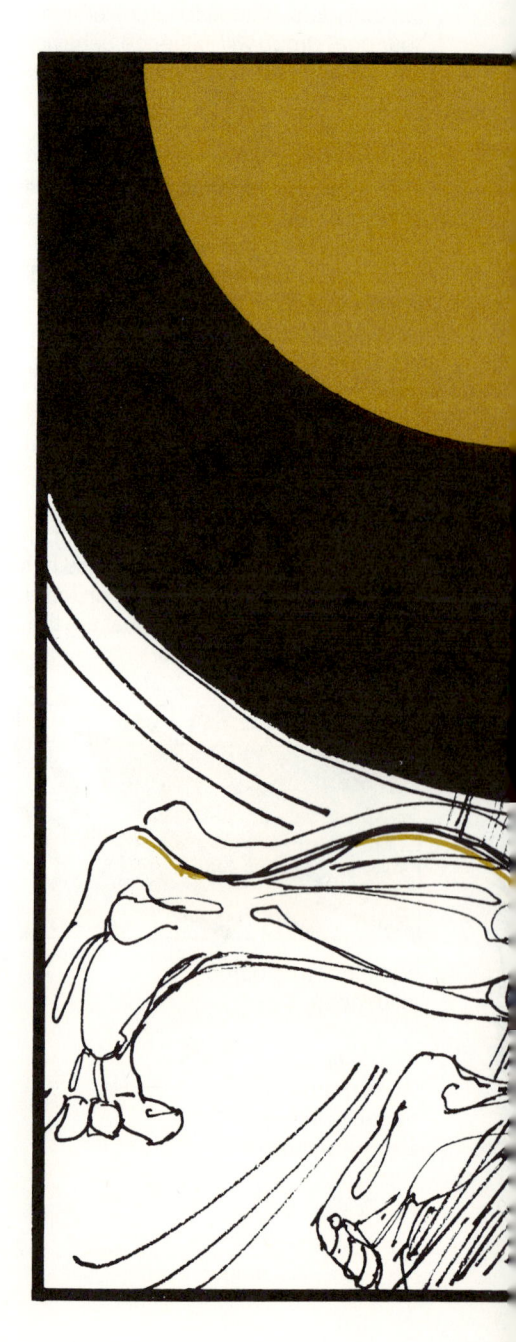

CAIN & ABEL

What causes sibling jealousy and rivalry? Jealousy and rivalry are two different emotions brought on by a feeling of frustration. Jealousy occurs when you are frustrated in your competition for attention and love. Rivalry occurs when families consciously or unconsciously compare siblings and expect them to be alike. One sibling will feel rivalry towards another when frustrated because he or she cannot win or do as well as the other sibling.

The tradition of *primogeniture* is another cause of sibling rivalry and jealousy. This used to be a common system by which all the family inheritance, power, and possessions went to the first-born son. Many fairy tales and other stories tell of a power struggle in which the "underdog" or last-born is usually the winner.

The "Can't Live with You or without You" Relationship

In one's own family, it is difficult to be objective about sibling rights and attention. However, visualize another family situation – perhaps at a friend's home or at some outing. What might you see?

- An older brother pushing a younger sister, then offering to fix her bike.
- A little brother running off with his older sister's doll, then coming back to play house and have a friendly cup of tea.
- An older sister yelling at her younger brother for not doing his homework, but promising not to tell on him.
- A sister who crosses the days off on her calendar until her older sister goes to camp, and then misses her so much that she writes almost every day.

There are times when you wouldn't care if your brother or sister disappeared from the face of the earth. But there is also a lot of affection in these relationships that can never be replaced. This is a time when there is a tremendous pull of opposite feelings.

Possessiveness towards Parents

Small children, as you know, think that love cannot be equal for everyone, and so they can't bear to see a sibling, or even the opposite-sexed parent, getting attention. Every child wants to be loved "the best" not merely "as much as" a sibling. Children overcome sibling jealousy as they learn to share their parents' love with the others in the family.

Competition

Competition plays a major role in our society. Most games involve competition. You may compete for a parent's, teacher's, or friend's attention. You may compete for grades at school. Perhaps the degree to which you compete begins when you have to share your parents with a sibling. Some people may only compete in skills and activities they know they can succeed in. Others may compete in everything – whether it's to be the first one to the bathroom in the morning, or the one to get the last piece of cake, or the only one with some ice cream left after everyone else has gulped theirs down.

Give and Take

Children have to learn to give and share. Small children can be heard saying, "That's my bulldozer!" or, "That's my fire engine!" as they pass a construction site or a fire station. They think anything they see could be theirs. They can triumphantly offer a candy to a little friend and then burst into tears when the friend eats it. Only emotionally mature people can give freely.

Giving must start on a small scale and be practiced often. Gift exchanging is a practice that helps children understand the giving and receiving procedure. Giving starts early, as this story indicates.

Because of the possessiveness they feel towards parents and because they are forced to share, siblings are often striving for what they think other siblings have. Parents must be loving and aware of these struggles. Rather than forbidding arguments and forcing siblings to suppress feelings, parents could help siblings work the problems out by listening to them and by helping them to develop suitable communication patterns.

Melanie helped her father wrap the Mother's Day presents. She examined each gift thoroughly and listened intently as her father explained about Mother's Day and told her that these were gifts from Melanie and Daddy especially for Mommy. Melanie burst in to wake up her mother, shouting in her two-year-old voice, "Happy Muber's Day, Mommy!" Then she quickly began unwrapping everything.

Your Place in the Family

Family Climate

The climate or environment in a family is determined by the individual personalities of each member. Each partner in a marriage contributes his or her own energy, feelings, attitudes, values, and abilities.

What other factors affect the family climate? The parents' expectations of each other, of family life, and of their children set a mood. The way parents relate to each other, their happiness or discontent, their adjustment to marriage, and their ability to cope with conflict all have an effect on the climate in the home and the well-being of the children.

The differences in appearance and talents between siblings can affect their self-concepts and development. The personality of each sibling is affected by the sex of all other siblings in the family. This fact, along with the age gap between siblings, has a great effect on individual personality development. Siblings do influence each other.

Birth Order

The order in which you are born into the family (first-born, second-born, etc.) is your birth order. Birth order research is interesting, but produces conflicting results.

Quiz (Use a separate sheet of paper.)
1. Complete the following statements:
   If I had the choice, I would like to be:
   (a) the _____ (which position) child in the family.
   (b) the _____ (same or opposite) sex.
   (c) a member of a family with _____ (more or fewer) children.
   (d) a member of a family that consists of:
   _____ M F M F (male, female, male, female)
   _____ M M
   _____ F F
   _____ F M M
   _____ M F
   _____ (you choose a combination).
   Write a paragraph in which you give reasons for the choices you make.
2. Ellen is the oldest in a family of four children. Her code is FFFM – she is the first child followed by two sisters and a brother. (F-female, M-male.) Heather's code is FMF. She has an older sister and brother and she is the third-born. What is your special code?

TAKE ACTION

Discuss sibling interaction either in groups or with the class as a whole. The following questions can be used to get started.
1. How do you "stake out a claim" to a certain area, or where do you put the things that you designate as personal?
2. Has a system been worked out to share responsibilities? Is it effective, or does it need some modifications?
3. (a) How can you get a brother or sister to do something you want him or her to do?
   (b) How has he or she gotten you to do something he or she wanted?
4. Recall an incident in which your brother or sister really upset you.
5. What do you do when a sibling is mad at you?
6. Does your sister or brother tease and harass you? What is your reaction?
7. Who bosses you the most? Does it irk you, or do you ignore it, or do you tell a parent?

Some individuals develop certain capabilities in one position within the family constellation; others thrive in another position. It is important to realize that no one birth order is preferable. The value of knowing about birth order and its effect on personality development is to create sensitivity to each person's position in the family. A person aware of the influences of each position can change or modify behavior in a positive way.

Here are some conclusions about birth order from students:

- If the age gap between the last child and the preceding child is great, the last child is treated like an only child.
- Only children are more likely to go to college.
- Last-born children are as likely to go to college as the first-born.
- Middle children are most likely to go to college.
- First-born children tend to identify more with parents' values and parental discipline.
- Second-born children are more likely to be resentful, appeal to parents for help, cry, pout, and sulk.
- First-born children often blaze the trail.
- Second-born children take on the characteristics of the older sibling.

Sibling Relationships Quiz (Use a separate sheet of paper.)

		Yes	No	Sometimes
1.	Most of the time we get along well together.			
2.	Too often my fun is spoiled.			
3.	Siblings are a nuisance.			
4.	Siblings can be fun.			
5.	Someone is always complaining.			
6.	Siblings make me feel sad.			
7.	Siblings stand up for me.			
8.	Siblings will listen to my problems.			
9.	Siblings tease me.			
10.	Siblings can make me happy.			
11.	Siblings are kindhearted.			
12.	We like to do some things together.			
13.	Siblings take things that belong to me.			

Draw some class conclusions about this checklist. By a show of hands, tally the number of people who noted "yes" and "no" for each of the thirteen questions. Determine the area of greatest difficulty and of least difficulty. Those who were able to answer positively in the areas that are difficult for others in the class could give some ways to solve these problems. Have your siblings do this checklist so you can identify problem areas in order to develop a better relationship.

Positive Side of Siblings

Siblings form strong bonds. Younger ones identify with older ones. Older siblings are a model for appropriate sexual behavior and provide sex education for the younger siblings. Siblings can also meet each other's needs for attention and affection. They can be advisers, leaders, protectors, and holders of secret information.

We all know the problems in sibling relationships. Let's try to strengthen the positive side so the problems become less important. What can you learn from these case studies?

Holly and Allison were planning their first mixed party in great detail. It was to be held at Holly's home and they wanted to enhance the atmosphere of the rec room. Holly asked her older brother, Larry, if they could use some of his far-out posters, and his purple light bulbs. The girls were thrilled when Larry agreed, and they got busy fixing up the room. Larry even helped them.

Later they asked Larry if they could use some of his tapes. He said, "No, there is nothing there that would interest you." The girls knew this wasn't true and that a lot of them were favorites, but they decided not to push the matter.

1. Why do you think Holly was thrilled at Larry's interest?
2. Larry usually referred to Holly as "shrimp" and didn't show any awareness of the daily events of her life. Do you think this attitude might be changing?

The Browns spend their vacation at the lake and all the family are excellent swimmers. Bill, Bob, Kim, and Sara really want a sailboat. Together they decide on a strategy for approaching their parents, and what points to bring out in the actual discussion and the follow-up. As a united group, they speak to their parents.

1. What do you think is the result?
2. Is "ganging up" a good idea?
3. What types of "ganging up" can cause problems within the family?
   Give an example from your experience or that you know about from your observations.

It is the middle of August and the Jones family has just moved to Dallas. Susan will be entering ninth grade; John, seventh grade; and Kendra, third grade. The move has meant that dad will have a more challenging job – everyone in the family could find some advantages in moving.

The first few days after their arrival everyone is busy unpacking, arranging rooms, and discovering where schools, stores, community centers, and various points of interest are situated. The family works together to decide where various pieces of furniture will be placed, and a general feeling of excitement prevails. Soon, however, they are settled and they have time for other activities.

During the first month of their move to Dallas, Susan and John spend more time doing things together than they ever have previously. Kendra frequently joins them in their activities.

1. Discuss reasons for the togetherness that the Jones family shows.
2. Describe a situation you are familiar with that illustrates sibling closeness.

Joanne is the eldest child in the family. As soon as her college classes were finished, she left to work at a summer job. She really enjoys receiving letters from home and wants everyone to write her each week. Margo writes to her regularly. Joanne's letters are also eagerly read. She writes in one that Margo, her "little sister" (eighth grade), is really growing up.

1. Do you think Joanne has mixed feelings about Margo's growing up? Suggest some of her feelings.
2. (a) Does Margo's communication by letters make Joanne more aware of her growth? Why?
   (b) Do you sometimes "listen" more to a written letter than you do to a conversation? Explain.
3. Joanne's seventeen-year-old brother has refused to write to her and says he is "much too busy." What is your reaction to this?

Siblings can help you with homework or with chores; they can loan you money or clothes; and they can help you solve a problem. They can make you feel good about yourself by the way they admire you. Siblings can bring you pride and prestige through their accomplishments. Absence seems to make the heart grow fonder as you separate and go your own ways. Sometimes there are bonds with a particular sibling who will always be close and on whom you can call for help throughout your life. Siblings can learn to handle competition, set a balance between work and play, and share family ups and downs. They are really going through a training course for their future life and successful relationships with others. The ability to handle feelings of hostility, jealousy, and rivalry will result in your being able to grow into a cooperative person capable of giving and receiving. All of these capabilities will eventually help you to become a positive influence on your future family, friends, and community.

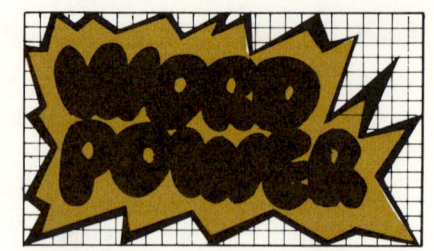

Word Power

birth order
family climate
family constellation
primogeniture
sibling jealousy
sibling relationship
sibling rivalry

Take Action

1. Collect cartoons illustrating sibling relationships. Interpret the meaning of each.
2. Write a description of your feelings on sibling love.
3. Relate experiences of a happy situation concerning one or all of your siblings.
4. Discuss what the term "sibling substitute" would mean to an only child.
5. Write some statements like the following about siblings in the form of similes, metaphors, or analogies:
   (a) Having a sixteen-year-old brother with a car is like living with a grease monkey (simile).
   (b) When my sister meets a new boy, she escalates herself into another true romance (metaphor).
   (c) Sisters are like a swarm of bees: some are drones, some are workers, and some are queens (analogy).

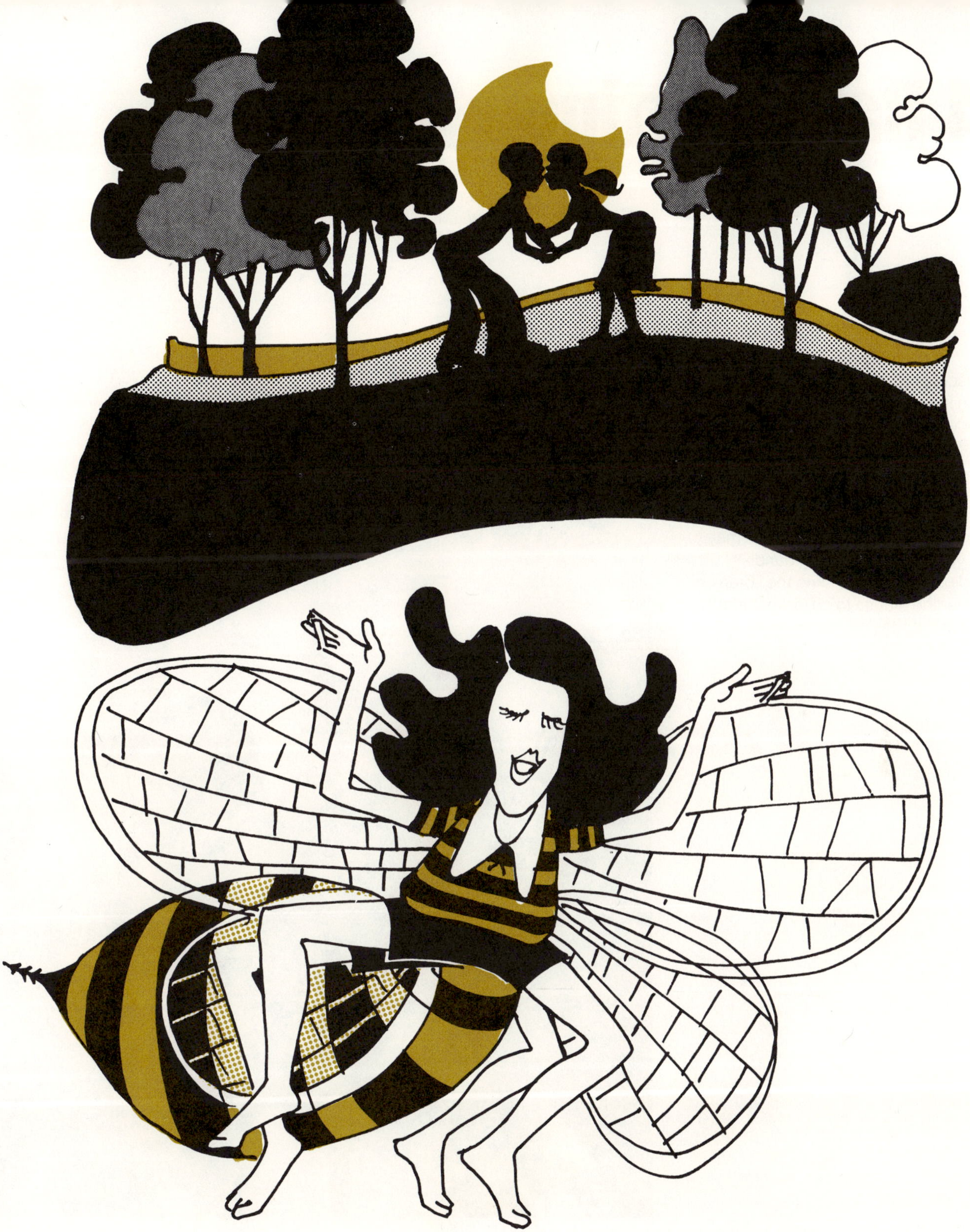

14 Baby-Sitting

Adolescents form relationships with children in a variety of situations. Almost everyone has a younger sister, brother, or cousin to care for or has had a baby-sitting experience. Perhaps you interact with children by teaching them games on the playground or by helping out in a community club group. You may have a volunteer job helping handicapped children or assisting the librarian by reading stories to children during story hour.

Roger and Jason were walking through the shopping center and suddenly Roger started waving and smiling at someone. When Jason asked who he was waving at, Roger felt a little embarrassed. He was returning the greeting of a small boy in a nearby shopping cart. When Jason looked at the jolly little boy, he waved and smiled too.

1. What is it about small children that makes us respond so spontaneously to them?
2. Do you find it easy to communicate with small children? Is it easy or nerve-wracking to care for them?
3. Could you list some of the reasons it would be helpful to learn about children? Consider the following questions:

   (a) Are children's needs the same all over the world? Will knowledge of these needs help you understand how children develop, as well as increase your awareness of how you developed?

   (b) Will the ability to get along with children make baby-sitting more fun and help you develop positive attitudes towards children?

   (c) Could experiences and a rapport with children help you decide whether or not to choose a career working with them?

By observing and working with children, you will probably be able to clarify the theories you've discussed about behavior, emotions, and self-concept. Will these experiences with children improve your communication skills and help you develop caring relationships?

Let's learn about children through the baby-sitting experiences of Diane Nagy.

July 3rd – 7 p.m.

Dear Diary:

You are probably wondering what I am doing in bed so early when it is still light and my friends are still out on their bikes. Well, I'm exhausted.

It all started last week when our neighbor, Mrs. Parker, asked my mother if I could baby-sit for little Benjy. (He may be little, but so are sticks of dynamite.) We only moved here last fall so I really haven't gotten to know Benjy. Mrs. Parker was taking a three-week nursing retraining course so she could go back to nursing in the fall. I only had to sit from 9 a.m. until 2 p.m. It sounded really easy and like a lot of fun playing with a two-and-a-half-year-old and getting paid, too.

Well, let me tell you about my first day. I arrived early. Mrs. Parker explained everything about the house and what I was to do. Benjy was smiling happily and playing with a truck. When his mother said "good-bye," he went wild. She tried to soothe him, but finally had to push him into my arms and run, as she was late. I could show you my bruises from the kicks I got. I thought someone would think I was murdering him – he was screaming so loudly.

I finally convinced him to sit on the floor and look at a picture book. All seemed well. We went outside to play. Benjy was really good playing with his bulldozer in the sand. He even made me some delicious sand cakes in a tart tin. "You like my cake?" he said. He can be really cute. He loves to talk and ask questions. He says "why" to everything.

We went for a walk to my house, and he was really good. He talked to my mom and horsed around with Jeff. I let him hold my stuffed animals and then I gave him some milk and cookies. He wouldn't leave my animals, so we took them to his home.

Dear Diary:
I only had to sit from 9 AM to 2 P.M. It sounded really easy and like a lot of fun playing with a two-and-a-half-year-old and getting paid too.

Benjy was supposed to eat at noon and go to bed about 12:45. Well, he wouldn't eat the lunch his mother had prepared. He took the sandwich all apart and left it, ignored the fruit, and yelled for the cookies his mother had promised. He got them, too. Finally I thought if we fooled around, he'd get tired. So we played piggyback and he walked on his hands while I held his feet, did somersaults, and hopped around. At about 12:55, I put him to bed. (I could have gone to bed too!)

Benjy wouldn't stop talking and he kept getting out of bed and running in with another request. "I want water." "I want my blanket." "I want my mommy." "I don't like you." I kept putting him back to bed and then he said, "I go toidies."

Sure enough – there it was right in the bed. All his clothes and the bed were soaked. I took off the sheet and his clothes. I didn't know what to put on the bed or him. What a mess. It soaked everything, even my favorite teddy bear. By this time his mother walked in and I really felt dumb as it looked like a tornado had hit the house.

I thought I would write some rules for baby-sitters. Who knows, someday these may come in handy for someone.

Rules for Preparing to Baby-Sit

1. Nobody's born a baby-sitter. Take a baby-sitting course *before* you are ever face to face with any child. Read some books or interview mothers about baby-sitting.
2. Make sure you like children.
3. Don't baby-sit if you can't make decisions. You have to be one step ahead of the child with lots of suggestions.
4. Watch children at a playground, on the street, or at a nursery school *before* you baby-sit. That way you'll learn some things about them.
5. Get to know the family, the child, his or her routine, and your duties.

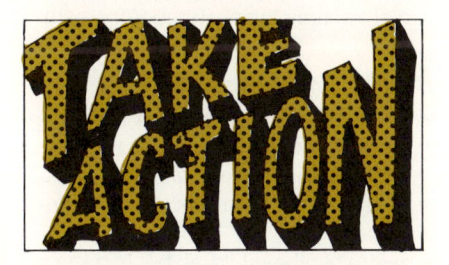

TAKE ACTION

Discuss Diane's rules in class. Follow her suggestions as much as you can to learn more about baby-sitting. Find out about:

1. Children of different ages (the charts on the following pages will help you);
2. hours of work;
3. rate of pay;
4. skills required of a baby-sitter, e.g., first-aid, lunch-preparation, and so on;
5. what emergency telephone numbers are required;
6. the schedule to be followed during the baby-sitting period.

Child Development

Infants to Toddlers

Physical
- a period of rapid growth
- move from complete dependence to ability to raise the head, lift chest up, roll over, reach, sit, pull body up, stand, creep, walk, climb up
- at no other period in life is there such rapid development and growth as from birth to one year of age
- eye-hand coordination is gradually developing
- recognize specific people and things
- develop from sucking to swallowing first liquid, then solids, and finally to chewing and feeding themselves
- by one year, infants may have two to eight of their twenty temporary teeth

Behavior and Needs
- from smiling, cooing, babbling, playing "pat-a-cake" to speaking words and having outbursts of anger, sadness, and joy, to speaking short sentences
- aware of other children but engage in parallel play (side-by-side) rather than playing with each other
- indicate wants by pointing or vocalizing
- begin to explore – ask numerous questions
- like to "show off"
- emotions are self-centered
- tend to dawdle over food; time means little to them so they don't hurry decisions
- need to be watched continuously: due to tireless curiosity, infants can easily harm themselves

Interests
- in the first year, interested in themselves and their families, gradually become curious about their environment
- exploring – may pull up a plant to see what it is like
- play-talking

Preschool

Physical
- large muscle development and coordination quality increases, e.g., jumping
- small muscles and eye-hand coordination only partly developed, e.g., prefer large pieces of paper to print on
- need a rest period but regular naps gradually given up
- toilet training completed during this period
- increased skills in dressing and undressing
- rapid language development
- increased sensory awareness

Behavior and Needs
- change from "NO" to gradual acceptance of limits
- need guidance
- learn to understand many things about their environment
- imitative; like to help and copy manner, language, and method of doing things
- short attention span; need patience
- very curious; ask many questions and eager to know "why?"; need new and varied experiences
- very active; tend also to tire easily
- easily frustrated; need help with the task or a change of activity
- like to be with family
- gradually develop skills for cooperative play; enjoy other children

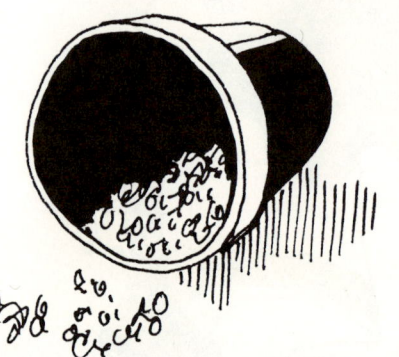

Interests
- string beads, load a truck, use blunt scissors
- want to do things themselves
- like to run, lift, build with blocks, and have active play activities
- like to help put things away
- picture books and short stories delight a two-year-old
- "finger plays" are fun
- playground activities – swings, sandbox
- painting, writing – large paper, large crayons
- stories; looking at pictures, nature, water play
- role-playing – house-keeping, dressing up, store, cleaning up
- interested in TV, puzzles, blocks, blackboards, excursions (such as to the zoo), walking in the park
- exploring

Elementary Schoolers (five to twelve years)

Physical
- continuous slow growth
- development of large-muscle skills
- development of fine-motor skills, e.g., writing
- permanent teeth
- eyes maturing to full size and ready to take on close work
- development of competence in athletics, music, art, etc., varies with children

Behavior and Needs
- highly active
- attention spans gradually increase
- exuberant enthusiasm, but easily lose interest; need adult suggestions
- planned group activities
- interest in opposite sex develops but need friends of same sex
- learning acceptable forms of behavior – at the end of this period they understand responsible behavior, and develop values and a sense of right and wrong
- like to discover and experiment

Interests
- people
- reading – real-life stories
- active learning
- crafts, collections
- regular activities, such as swimming, music lessons
- being a member of a team or a club, such as Brownies, Cub Scouts
- TV and continuous radio programs
- having an allowance or having money
- making own activities
- interest "fads" are prevalent

Baby-Sitting Workshop

When you baby-sit, you will be faced with many problems. It is much better to try to foresee them and have solutions ready than to be surprised. The following are some common problems. Work on them individually, in groups, or in the class as a whole. Discuss your solutions together and spend enough time on each problem to find the best solution.

1. What do you do when the child acts up after the parent leaves?
2. What do you do when the child bites you or kicks you?
3. What do you do when the child cries or acts up?
4. What should you feed the child? What do you do if the child won't eat?
5. What should you do when you put the child to bed? What should the child wear?
6. How can you prevent a child's bed-wetting?
7. What special provisions will you need to make for a baby?
8. What do you do when the child's friend from down the street drops in?
9. What should you do when someone comes to the door? Let them in? Not answer it?
10. What do you do if the child chokes on some food?

Here are some checklists that you might like to copy out for your baby-sitting notebook:

Don't:

- ☑ Leave a baby or young child alone.
- ☑ Let the child have sharp objects or small articles that could be swallowed.
- ☑ Give foods such as raw carrots, hard candy, and gum that could cause choking.
- ☑ Bring a friend unless you have permission from the child's parents. Remember, it is your job and most parents expect you to come alone.
- ☑ Fall asleep even if the parents give you permission. You are not used to "listening" for a child's cry, and it is best you stay awake and aware.
- ☑ Baby-sit if you have a cold or do not feel well, without phoning and telling the parents and asking if you should get a replacement.
- ☑ Open the outside door unless you are *sure* about the person who is there.
- ☑ Eat food unless you are given permission.
- ☑ Use appliances without permission (stereo, stove, etc.).
- ☑ Let children misuse furniture. Take special care of all articles in the house.
- ☑ Neglect to make regular checks when children are sleeping.
- ☑ Have long telephone conversations.
- ☑ Forget to write down all telephone messages and mention any phone call where messages were not left.
- ☑ Have the TV, radio, or records on too loudly.

Do:

- ☑ Be adaptable.
- ☑ Be dependable.
- ☑ Be honest.
- ☑ Be responsible.
- ☑ Be alert and aware.
- ☑ Show your empathy for children.
- ☑ Understand the needs and behavior of children.
- ☑ Accept each child as an individual.
- ☑ Be polite and set a good example for the children.
- ☑ Provide interesting experiences for children.
- ☑ Make sure parents have left emergency numbers.

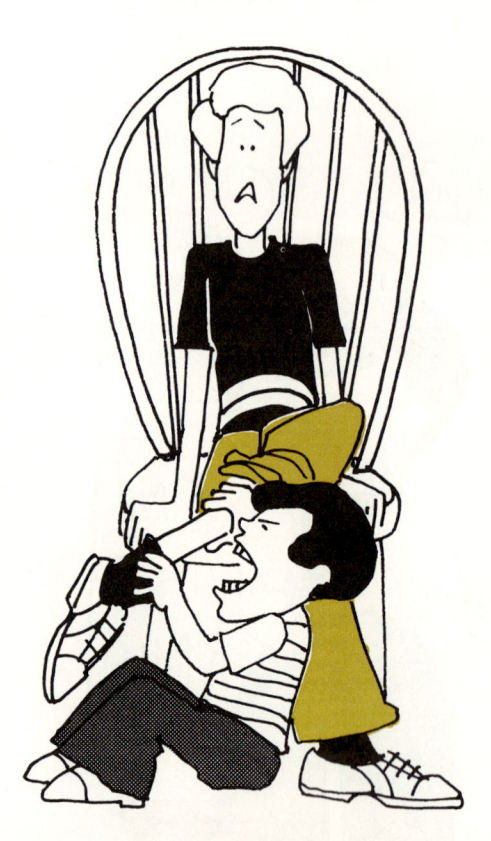

General Hints for Discipline

- ☑ Physical punishment should never be given by a babysitter.
- ☑ Give either/or choices where possible. For example, "We can go for a walk or we can read a book."
- ☑ Give warnings or advance notice of what you expect. Tell the child that in 10 minutes you will have lunch ready, for example.
- ☑ Avoid commands. Instead, use a statement, such as, "It's time for bed," in a positive, pleasant voice.
- ☑ You can sympathize with a child about some rules. Always explain the reason for the rule.
- ☑ Be consistent. Don't let the child get away with things one day and then be very strict the next. The child will become confused if you do.
- ☑ Praise and approval of good behavior help prevent discipline problems.
- ☑ Remind the child of the consequences of his or her actions.
- ☑ Try a variety of positive methods until you learn what gets the most satisfactory response.
- ☑ Rewards can be effective if used wisely. Choose a reward that consists of doing a special project or favorite activity, rather than a treat that costs money.
- ☑ Accept the child's feelings. Perhaps you can find an outlet for his or her anger, such as "punching the cushion."
- ☑ Try to anticipate problems of rising frustration. A change of activities may avert a problem.

CHILD SAFETY in the HOME

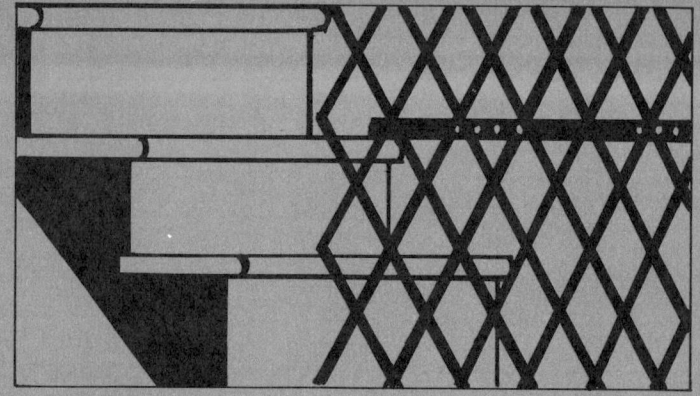

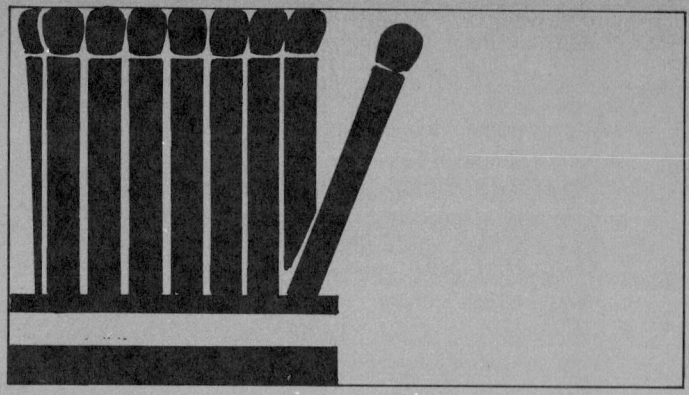

Make a list of as many household safety tips for baby-sitters as you can.

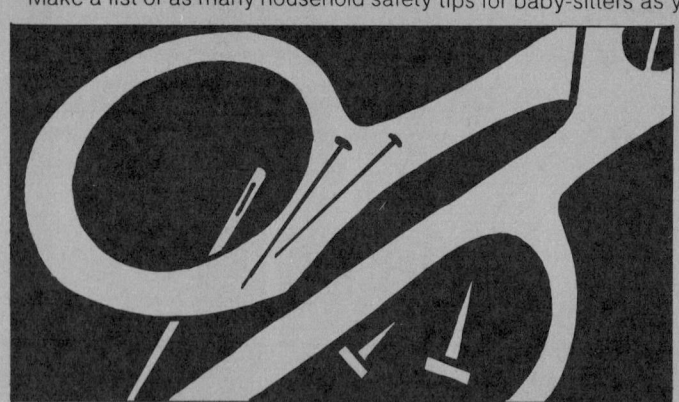

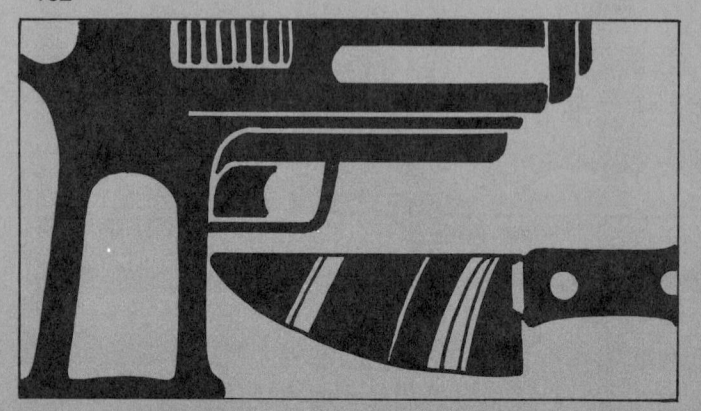

163

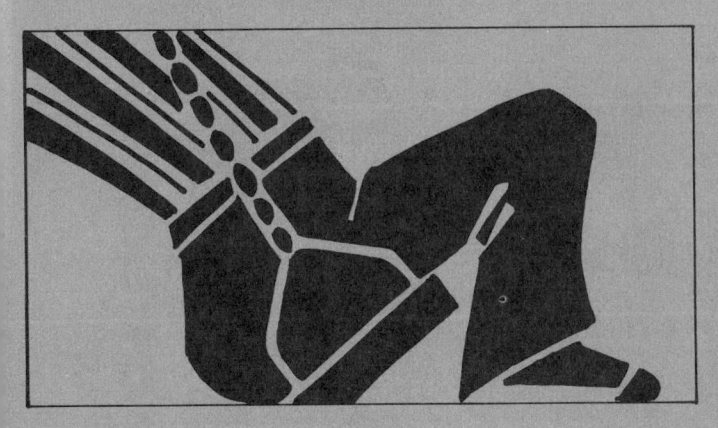

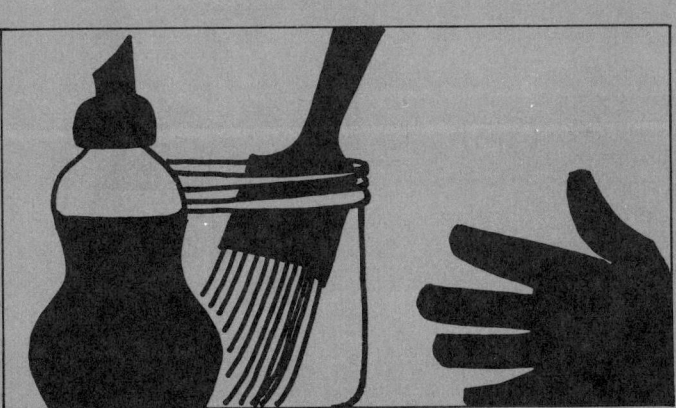

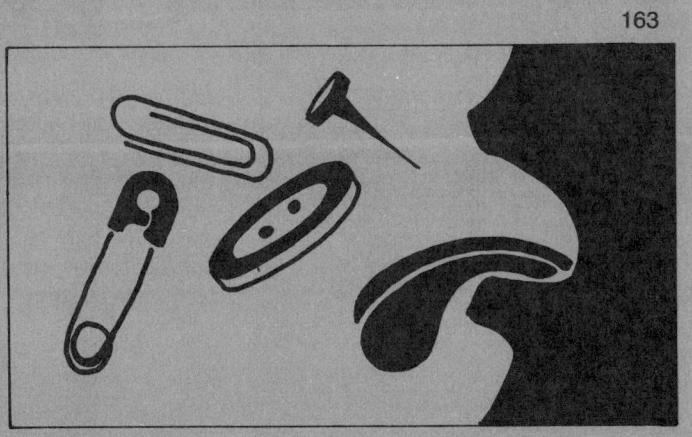

Baby-Sitter's Idea Book

Here are some things to do with children when you baby-sit. Can you think of any more?

Use Your Imagination

Bring a couple of empty cardboard cartons for daytime baby-sitting.

Make a car.
1. Cut open one side so it can be opened and the child can sit inside and close the car door.
2. The child can then make noises to pretend he or she is in various things – a car, train, boat, fire engine.
3. You could cut out a cardboard steering wheel, or use the top to a plastic ice cream carton and draw spokes on the wheel.

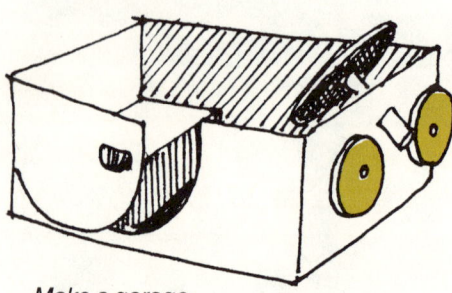

Make a garage.
1. Cut out a flap, which will open up and allow trucks, cars, etc., to drive in and be parked.

Make a house.
1. Cut the lid off and put pieces of cardboard in for floor- and room-dividers.
2. Make furniture out of empty spools, soap boxes, etc.

Make a boat.
1. Another box with the lid off could be a boat. The child could sit inside and pretend to row.
2. You could have the child make an anchor out of sticks.
3. A buoy could be a plastic bottle.
4. An empty nylon net onion bag could be the fishing net.
5. Perhaps you could improvise a pole with a line and a clothespin on it.

A special big box can be a tent, a house, a store, a fort, a barn, a hospital. You could find various things to play with inside the box: empty packages to play store with or you could put stuffed animals in the barn. Such toys provide hours of fun and usually the child will contribute all sorts of ideas.

Art Play

Most children enjoy playing with paints, crayons, or clay. Be sure to use lots of newspaper to keep things clean and make sure the child understands where to paint, print, or work with clay. Be careful the child doesn't knock paint over or get it in his or her mouth. If possible, cover the child's clothes.

Finger painting

250 mL [1 cup] sugar
250 mL [1 cup] flour
 60 mL [¼ cup] pure soap flakes
 30 mL [2 Tbsp.] powdered alum
a few drops of mint extract
vegetable coloring

Mix sugar, flour, and soap. Add water and cook until thick. Add alum. Beat until creamy. Add mint extract. Add color to suit. Store in a covered jar.

Creative clay
250 mL [1 cup] cornstarch
250 mL [1 cup] baking soda
250-300 mL [1-1¼ cup] cold water
Mix cornstarch and baking soda together in a saucepan. Add water and stir. Heat mixture, stirring, until it resembles mashed potatoes. Remove from pan and form into a ball. Cover and let cool. Dye different colors by kneading in dye. Use as clay for jewelry, etc. Varnish when dry. The more coats of varnish, the shinier it will be. String beads, etc., and they're ready to wear.

Potato printing
Cut a potato in half. Dip it in paint in a shallow container. Use to make a design on a large sheet of paper. For variety you could cut a shape in half and then print with it.

Toilet paper roll dolls
Draw a face on the roll. Glue on hair if you wish. Glue on fabric.

Modeling clay

Paper bag puppets

Or tie up for ears.

Finger Plays for Preschool Children

1. *A Little Ball*
   A little ball,
   A bigger ball,
   A great big ball I see.

   Now let us count
   The balls we've made,
   One, two, three.

2. *Here's a Bunny*
   Here's a bunny
   With ears so funny, [*Raise two fingers*]
   And here's his hole in the ground. [*Make hole with fingers of other hand*]
   At the first sound he hears
   He pricks up his ears, [*Straighten fingers*]
   And pops right into the ground. [*Put into hole*]

3. *Mother's Knives and Forks*
   Here's mother's knives and forks [*fingers interlocked showing fingers*]
   Here's father's table [*showing flat side of interlocked hand*]
   Here's sister's looking glass [*first fingers forming triangle*]
   And here's the baby's cradle. [*little fingers forming triangle and rock back and forth*]

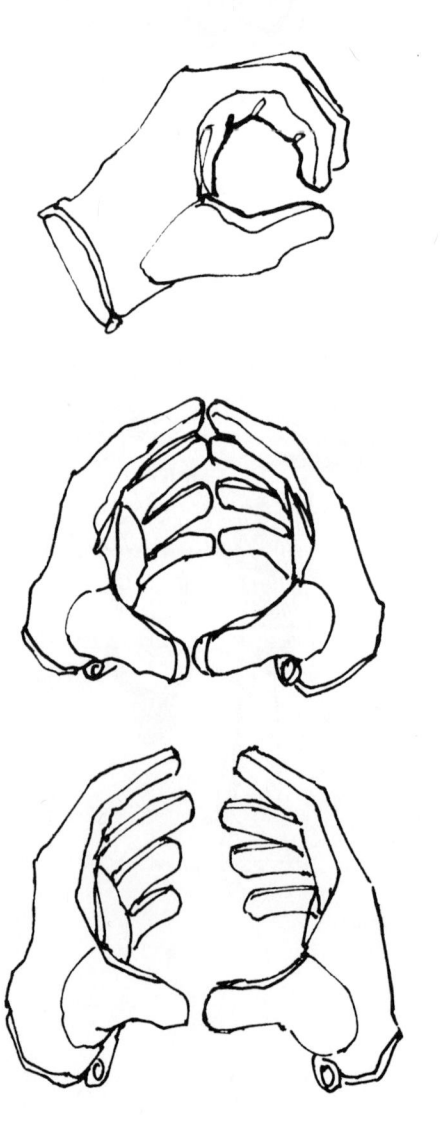

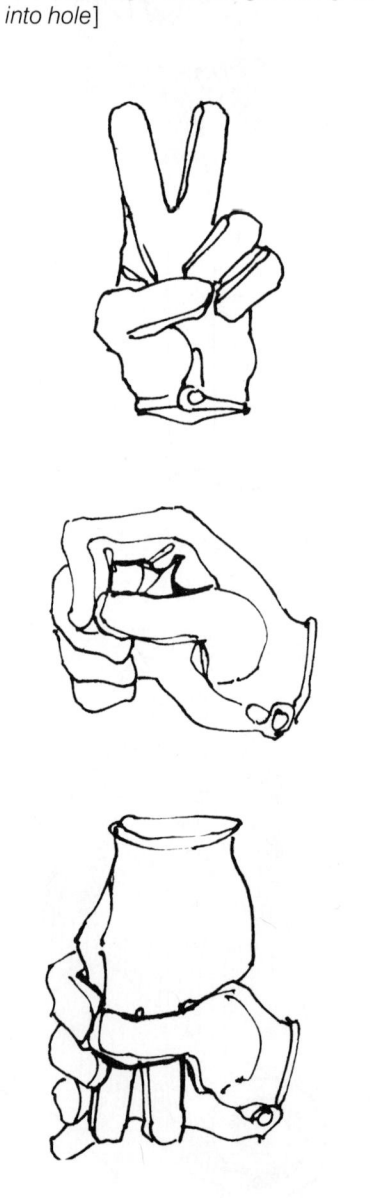

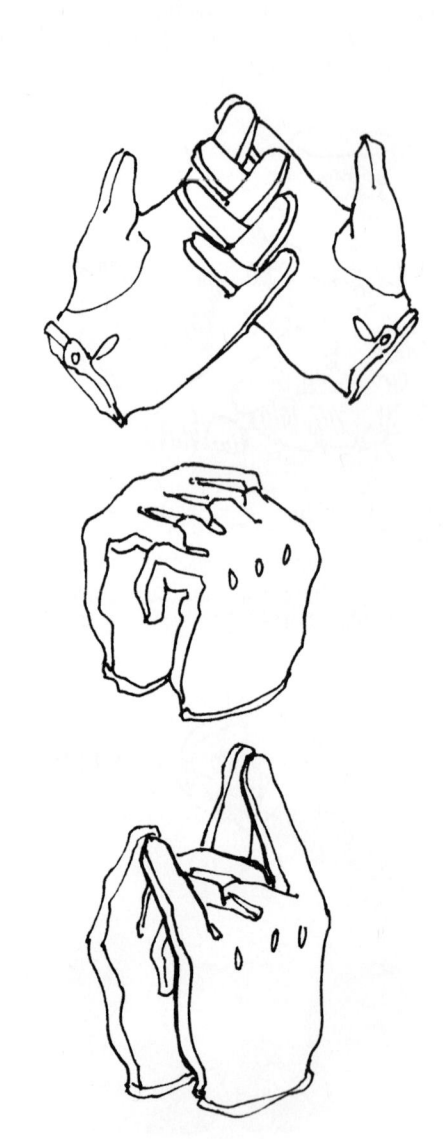

4. *The Mice*
   Five little mice on the pantry floor,
   [*hands out, fingers outstretched*]
   Seeking for bread crumbs or something more,
   Five little mice on the shelf up high,
   [*right hand fingers together pointing on the back of left hand*]
   Feasting so daintily on a pie. [*two hands form a circle with thumbs and first fingers together*]
   But the big round eyes of the wise old cat [*with each hand separately hold thumb and first fingers*]
   See what the five little mice are at.
   Quickly she jumps, but the mice run away, [*left hand lowered suddenly – right hand brought behind back*]
   And hide in their snug little holes all day.
   "Feasting in pantries may be very nice
   But home is the best," say the five little mice.
   [*hands folded*]

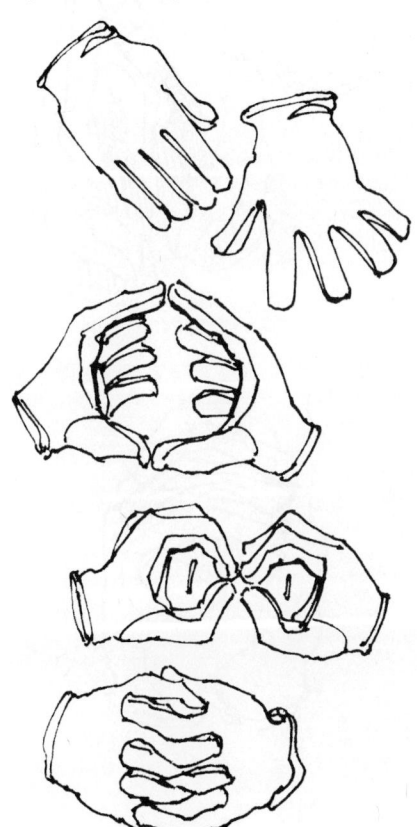

5. *The Five Little Pigs*
   This little pig eats grass [*touch little finger*]
   This little pig eats hay [*touch ring finger*]
   This little pig drinks water [*touch long finger*]
   This little pig runs all day [*touch pointer*]
   This little pig does nothing
   But lies in the shade all day. [*lay thumb over in palm*]

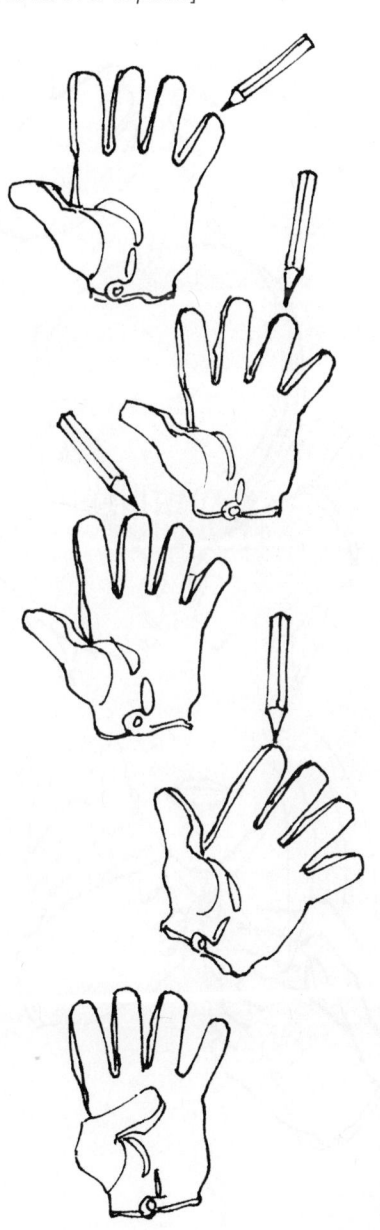

6. *Ten Little Soldiers*
   Ten little soldiers [*ten fingers stand, line them all up in a row*]
   Standing in a row
   The captain says salute [*each salute*]
   And they do so.
   They march to the left [*show by hand*]
   And they march to the right [*show by hand*]
   When the gong goes bang [*clap the hands*]
   They run with all their might. [*put hands in the back and imitate running*]

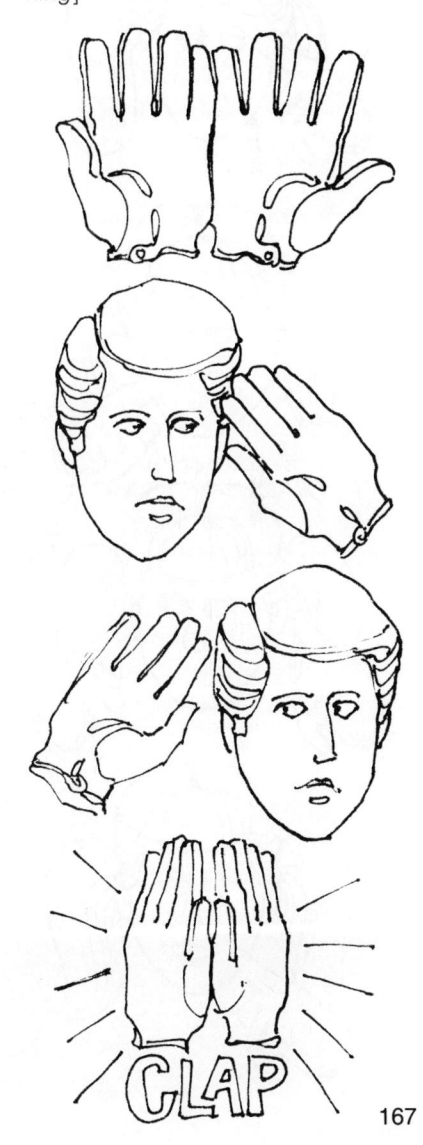

7. *The Senses*
   Little eyes see pretty things [*point to eyes*]
   Little nose smells what is sweet [*point to nose*]
   Little ears hear pleasant sounds [*point to ears*]
   Mouth likes good things to eat [*point to mouth*]

8. *Birds on a Fence*
   Two little birds sitting on a fence [*thumbs up*]
   One named Jack [*one thumb lifted*]
   One named Jill [*other thumb lifted higher*]
   Fly away Jack [*put Jack behind head*]
   Fly away Jill [*put Jill behind head*]
   Come back Jack [*back in former position*]
   Come back Jill [*back in former position*]

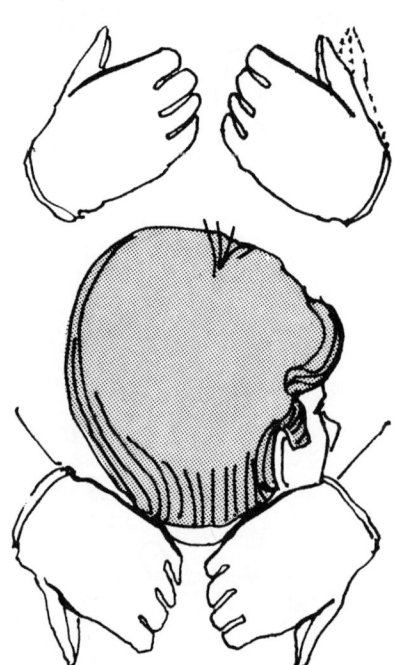

9. *Church and Steeple*
   (a) This is a church [*hands folded*]
   This is a steeple [*two initial fingers out*]
   Open the door [*open the thumbs*]
   There is no one in
   They are all gone home.
   (b) This is a church [*interlocked fingers folded the opposite way*]
   This is a steeple [*same as above*]
   Open the door [*same as above*]
   And see all the people. [*wiggle interlocked fingers*]

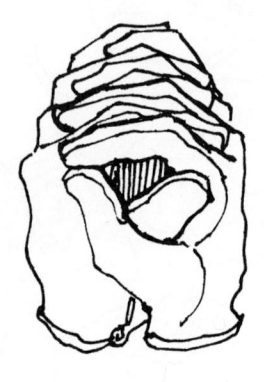

Water Bubbles
1. Mix a strong solution of soap. Melted small pieces of soap are excellent or just have them soaking in water.
2. Add a few drops of cooking oil or glycerin.
3. Blow bubbles through a straw or use a piece of plastic.
4. Dip the plastic in the solution. Then blow through the film which has formed.

Conclusion

This chapter was not designed to emphasize the principles of child development, or to prepare you for parenthood or a lifetime career. It was designed to help you as a baby-sitter in caring for young children, and to give you a little insight into children's needs and intellectual and physical capabilities. You should now know what to expect in the way of behavior and interests at various ages and stages. It is hoped that you have learned to make a distinction between discipline and guidance so you can guide and direct children's activities safely.

WORD POWER

art play
child development
discipline
eye-hand coordination
finger plays
guidance
large-muscle skills

TAKE ACTION

1. From a magazine or catalog cut out pictures that illustrate the orderly stages of motor development (lying on back, rolling over with chin up, sitting up . . . walking).
2. Examine children's books. List the characteristics that make certain books popular with certain age groups. Mary has been asked to help in selecting books for her niece and nephews. What would you suggest for Judy, age three; Jimmy, age six; and Ricky, age ten?
3. Observe pre-verbal children and describe how they communicate.
4. Prepare a baby-sitting kit for one of the following:
   (a) a toddler before an afternoon nap,
   (b) a four-year-old sick in bed with a cold,
   (c) a three-year-old playing outside in the summer.
   Explain how each item would be of enjoyment for the child and would aid in his or her development.
5. Select toys out of a catalog or magazine and decide on the following:
   (a) the age of child the toy is suitable for,
   (b) the purpose of the toy,
   (c) the type of development the toy encourages (hand or body, intelligence, imagination).
6. Recall some games and activities you most enjoyed as a child. Decide how you could pass on these games and activities to other children.
7. Behavior problems: plan a sociodrama based on the following situations – a child's refusal to go to bed, fear of the dark, temper tantrum, refusal to share with others, boredom with play activities, etc.
8. Write a page from a baby-sitter's diary including your baby-sitting experiences.
9. Prepare a checklist to determine "How I Rate as a Baby-Sitter." Score yourself and have a person you sit for score you, too.
10. Form groups and have each group brainstorm to make up "A Baby-Sitter's Code."
11. Have a round-table discussion on the topic: "Children are just miniature adults."
12. Make a list of as many things you can do with the children you baby-sit as you can think of. Share your list with your classmates. Keep your list handy for when you are baby-sitting.

171

4 YOU AND YOUR FRIENDS

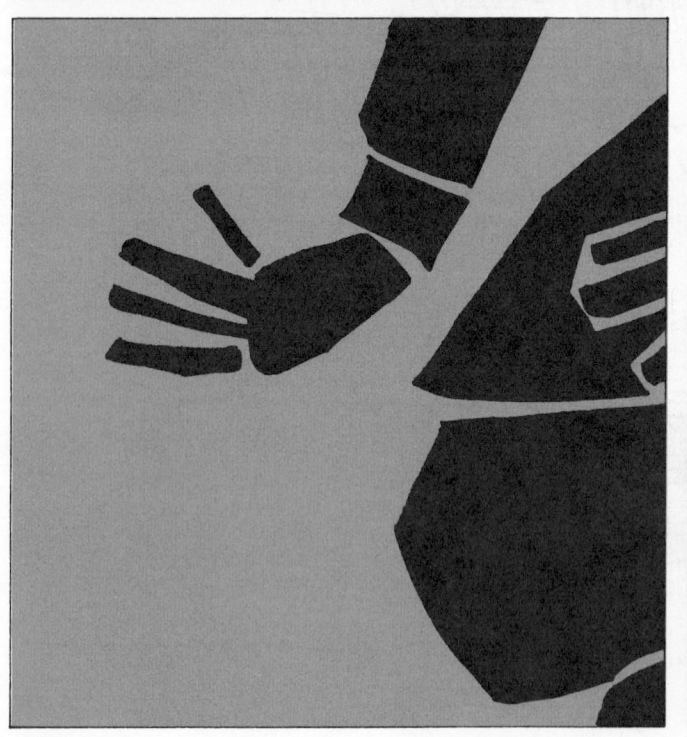

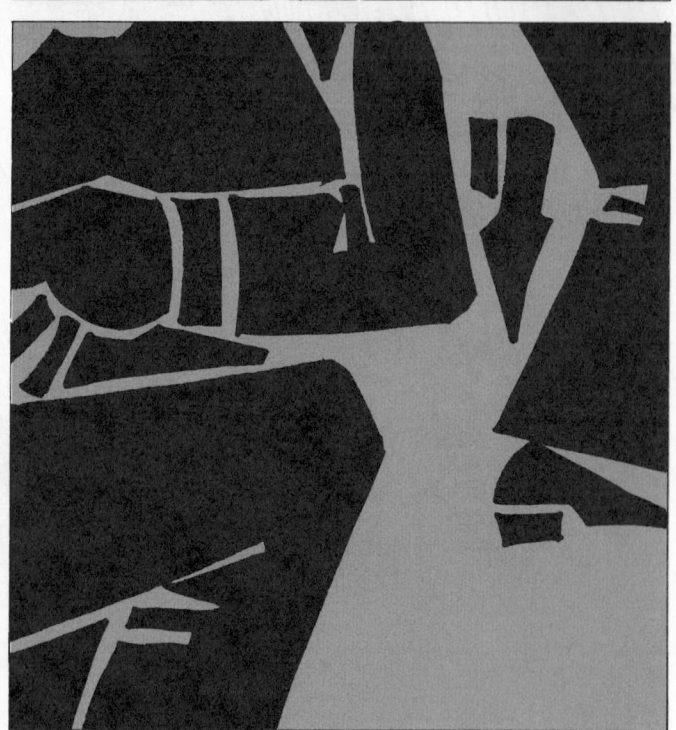

173

15 A Place in the Crowd

The way you feel about yourself is partly a result of how others react towards you. Do you see yourself as a reflection of the approval or disapproval you get from adults?

Often the reference group, or people who give you important feedback about yourself, are your peers. Because we all seek approval, there is a tendency to conform to the values and expectations of the crowd.

Dual Membership

As an adolescent you have two social roles: child to your parents and friend to your peers. You have memberships in both the family group and in the peer group. In order to gain personal and social growth, you need to develop the ability to get along with peers as well as maintain close ties with family members. At about eleven or twelve years of age, children begin to spend less time in family activities and more time with their peers. The affection and approval of peers becomes more important than that of the family. This is a time when you seek more independence, and when parental influence and authority diminishes in importance.

Parental values can come into direct competition with peer values. Thus, this dual membership can cause conflicts, because the interests and characteristics of parents and peers are sometimes very different. You may experience difficulties reacting to the change in the situations and expectations of each group. When the ties of family affection are weak, and the parents lack concern for, or even reject, the children, there is a tendency for a young person to become exclusively peer-oriented. The peer group will provide the approval and acceptance the child is seeking.

Affiliation with the family and peer group is not an either/or situation. Commitment to both groups is important for developing social awareness, independence, and a positive self-concept.

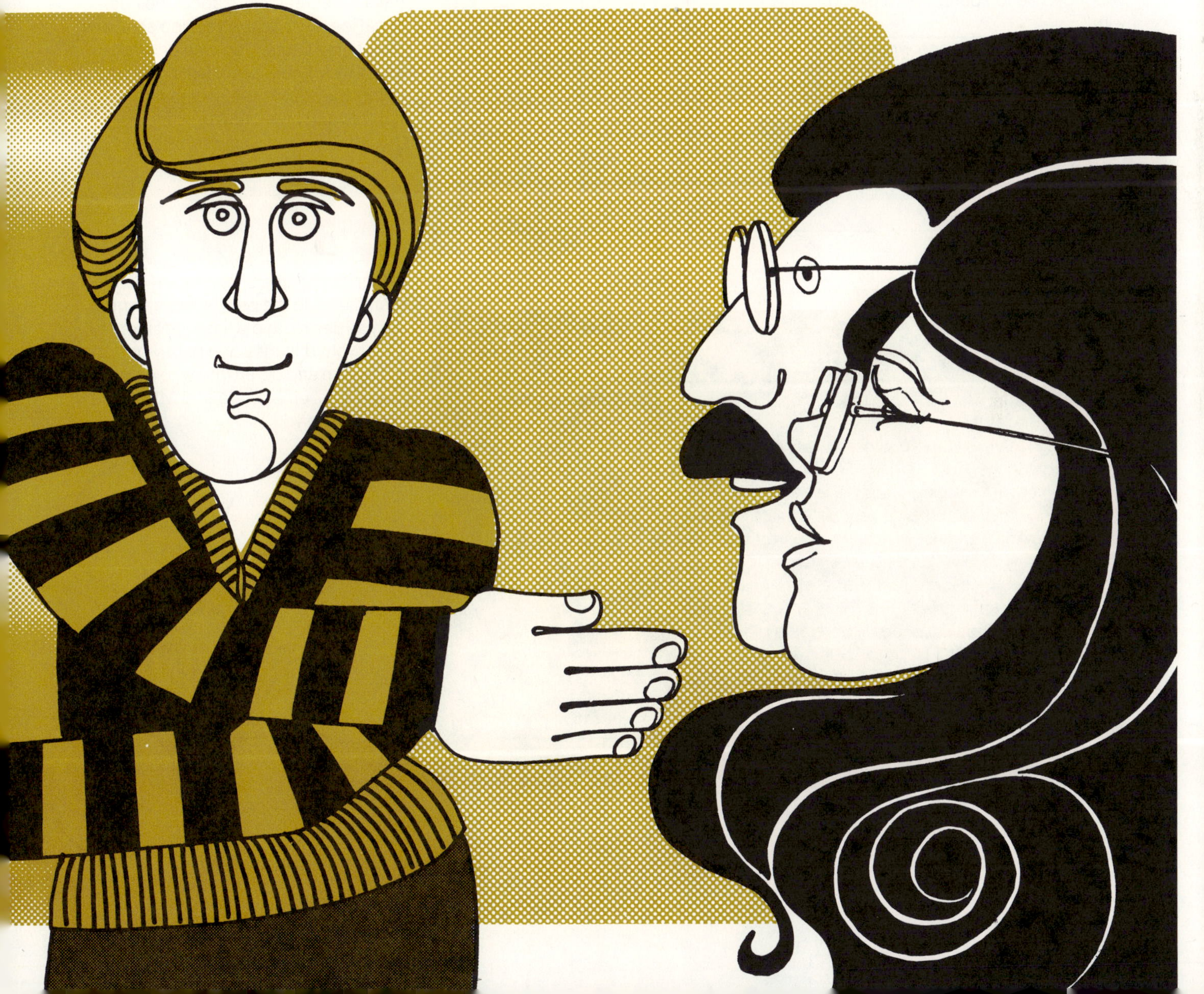

Try this quiz. (Write your answers on a separate sheet of paper.)

Quiz

	Family	Friends	Equal or Uncertain
Which group understands you best?			
When you grow up, who would you rather be like?			
Which group do you most enjoy doing things with?			
Which group would you most like to spend the evening with? Which would you most like to spend the weekend with?			
Whose ideas of right and wrong are most like yours?			
Whose ideas of fun activities are closer to yours?			
Whose ideas of the importance of school are yours the same as?			
Are your manners most like your parents' or your friends'?			

Dilemma Test

Frequently you will find yourself in conflicting situations. Test yourself with these dilemmas.
1. One day, one of your friends, whom everybody admires, comes to class with his T-shirt on backwards. Soon all your friends, boys and girls, are wearing T-shirts the same way. They want you to do it too. However, you realize your parents do not approve, even though they have not specifically said you cannot do it. What would you do?
2. The girls in your class are all having their ears pierced, and you think it's a terrific idea. Your mother dislikes the fad, but has not forbidden you to have yours done. What is your decision?
3. Your friends have recommended a movie, but your parents disapprove. Would you go to see it?
4. Your parents feel school attendance is very important. It is a beautiful afternoon and the group decides to skip out and go to the park. Where would you spend the afternoon?

In a study, these questions were answered by children in grade 4 to grade 10. Nine-tenths of the fourth grade children were more influenced by family than by friends. By the eighth grade, the influence of peers and family became equal. By the tenth grade, the orientation was shifting to the family again.

Peer opinions about school, clothes, and friends are very important. Opinions about situations that have long-term consequences are usually gained from adults. By the tenth grade, students have a clearer picture about their personal identity and are seeking solutions about their future. Because decisions about their future are of lasting importance, they tend to seek ideas from parents and other adults.

"Significant others" is a widely used term meaning the people whose approval you desire, and whose judgments affect your attitudes and behavior. Make a diagram and determine who your "significant others" are and why they are important to you.

Characteristics of the Group

There are a variety of peer groups. The high status group is the most visually or verbally active group in the school. They may be the high scorers on a team, they may be on the student council, or they may be the trend-setters.

The accepted groups of lesser status are those groups that are not in the spotlight, but it's still desirable to belong to such a group.

The non-accepted, low status groups consist of those who reject most of the values of the school and those who support school-oriented programs, but are not active participants.

There are the "faceless" people in the peer culture who do not belong to any group, usually through no fault of their own. They may be new members in the school or they may not express any distinguishable characteristics to make others aware of them. They may choose to remain "faceless," or perhaps they do not know what is expected of them in order to become a part of a peer group.

Many individuals in a peer culture choose not to belong to any one group. They may move in and out of different groups but never feel the need to be a full member in any one group.

A group of peers can be made up of both boys and girls, people of the same sex, small groups, or pairs of friends. Often you belong to several groups with conflicting interests and values, so you must determine ways to get along well in each group.

Give examples to illustrate how a group can achieve each of the following:
- a "we" feeling
- acceptance of abilities
- a place for self-evaluation about the individual's sexuality
- standards of dress, behavior, and language
- communication
- security of people experiencing similar problems
- strength to assert individuality and become independent
- a place to try on different roles
- an atmosphere of fun and comfort
- an opportunity for "idiot" behavior
- a broadening of ideas and values

Although the group seems a comfortable place to be, it can also be a very competitive place where you are expected to demonstrate your abilities. You have to develop a thick skin because of the group tendency to exchange friendly insults and put down your achievements. Sometimes you have to be careful about what you do, or the feelings you express, because you may be laughed at.

Everyone's group experience is not always the same. Individuals differ in the ways they need friends and interrelate with them.

Why Is Everyone So Stupid?

by Francine Himelfarb

Why is everyone so stupid?
Is all they care about themselves,
And pleasing the opposite sex?
Do they have no feelings?
Why don't people accept other people
Less privileged than themselves,
Who can't wear the latest styles,
Who can't express their emotions in large crowds,
Who can't seem to grasp friends?
Oh why? . . .

Grant Park High School
Winnipeg, Manitoba, Canada

Friends

What makes a friend a friend?

I guess I'd say that my friends and I spend most of our time hanging around together just talking. We spend our time at a couple of club activities and we have similar hobbies. I never like to do anything alone 'cause I feel self-conscious, so it's great to have a best friend to go out with.

Let's see. I guess my friends and I spend most of our time playing organized team sports. I really don't have one close friend, but I'm friendly with a lot of good guys in the crowd and do different things with them. I really like movies and I feel weird if I go alone, so I usually go with the crowd.

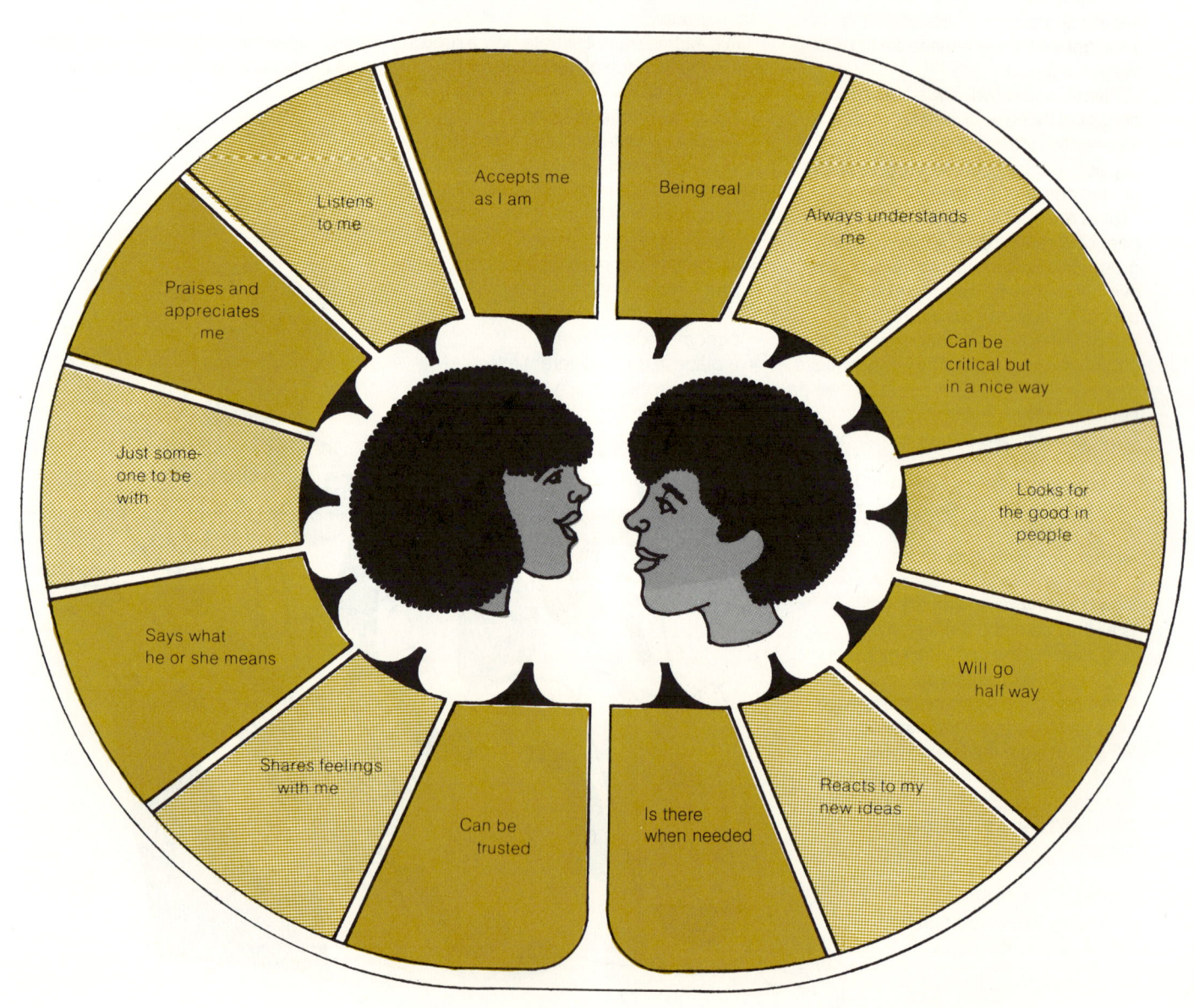

- Listens to me
- Accepts me as I am
- Being real
- Always understands me
- Praises and appreciates me
- Can be critical but in a nice way
- Just someone to be with
- Looks for the good in people
- Says what he or she means
- Will go half way
- Shares feelings with me
- Reacts to my new ideas
- Can be trusted
- Is there when needed

One of my best friends is a boy. He and I can be so open and honest with each other. If I have a problem, I can talk it over with him. He listens, and then tells me his point of view.

There are girls I can talk to easier than I can with the guys. I like getting their point of view and enjoy having someone of the opposite sex who is just a friend. Sometimes the girl may be having the same problem as I am, only the other way around. So, she can answer my question, and maybe I can answer hers.

I can really trust Sue. I know that some of my other girlfriends will repeat to others what I say, so I never tell them about anything that's important to me.

My sister is behind me in school and I can relate to her situation. It's really great to sit and listen to her, and I feel good that I can give her some advice. At other times, I try out one of my problems on her, and she quickly comes up with a suggestion.

I don't like it when my friends try to push their standards on me. I like to play baseball, and if there are a group of guys I know playing it in the park, I want to join in. My girlfriends think I look awful – the only girl playing with a bunch of guys.

I have another friendship problem. I feel smothered at times because my friends are too dependent on me. They want me to do everything with them and this makes me angry.

1. Have you had any of these problems or experiences?
2. What solutions have you found to the problems?
3. What different friendship experiences have you had? Discuss your experiences in class.

"You have to be a good friend to have a friend." What does this slogan mean to you? Do you think of a best friend as someone of the same sex? Does a friend help you understand yourself? Do you find that you can test out different roles and identities on a friend? Do you feel more secure knowing there are two of you with the same ideas? Does your best friend like the same things you do? Do you have the same hopes and dreams and problems? Do you depend on friends for understanding and advice?

Did you answer "yes" to most of these questions? In most cases, a best friend helps you to find your identity and to meet some basic needs.

A sense of intimacy is first developed with a close friend, and the development of this sense helps you to form permanent relationships in the future. All young people are trying to find their identity or figure out who they are. The sooner you discover this, the more easily you are able to put yourself in the background and be truly concerned about another person's thoughts and feelings. Oh yes, there are problems with friends at times – such as when they disappoint you or are a little too critical or compete with you.

Have you ever had a close friend move away? At the time, did you think you wouldn't be able to exist without that person? One of the facts of life is that friendships and relationships can change. This is part of the meaning of growth and maturity. Interests may change, or intimacy may shift to a special friend of the opposite sex. Relationships might start up again, but be on a different level of appreciation. As you mature and become your own person, the need to share all your feelings diminishes. What should be remembered is that it is inevitable that relationships change and that different people or different levels of friendship will satisfy your needs at different times.

How Do You Rate Your Friends?

Keep one friend in mind and choose an answer to each question. Write your answers on a separate sheet of paper. When you finish the quiz, you will have an idea of what you are getting out of this relationship. Would your friend rate you the same way?

1. You and your friend enjoy conversing best
    (a) over the phone.
    (b) in your bedroom.
    (c) at your friend's house.
2. If you have a disagreement,
    (a) you always apologize first.
    (b) your friend makes the first effort.
    (c) you work it out together.
3. You have to play softball. Your friend did not make the team. You feel
    (a) that your friend should come and cheer the team.
    (b) happy for your friend to spend his or her time with other friends.
    (c) that your friend should stay at home and enjoy himself or herself there and you'll come over when the game is finished.
4. If something your friend does is upsetting you,
    (a) you would find it easy to tell the friend the problem.
    (b) you would put off telling until the time was appropriate.
    (c) you would keep it to yourself.
5. If your friend heard some gossip about you, the friend would
    (a) tell you what was being said.
    (b) pass it on.
    (c) try to squash the rumor.
6. If your friend has an embarrassing habit,
    (a) you would inform your friend through indirect statements.
    (b) you would correct your friend.
    (c) you would criticize constructively, since you find it easy to praise your friend's good points.
7. You feel friends should
    (a) be frank and honest always – even if it hurts.
    (b) avoid embarrassing you.
    (c) always ask what is bothering you and try to work it out with you.
8. If your friend is mad at you, you
    (a) fight back.
    (b) first decide if you are the real target of his or her anger.
    (c) help your friend express anger so the friend will probably soon forget it.
9. If you overheard your friend describing you,
    (a) the description would be similar to the way you would describe yourself.
    (b) the description would be unflattering.
    (c) the description would not be at all as you see yourself.
10. Your friend
    (a) accepts you as you are.
    (b) tries to make you change.
    (c) looks down on your family.

WORD POWER

dual membership
family groups
peer culture
peer groups
reference group
relationship
significant others

TAKE ACTION

1. Re-read the poem "Why Is Everyone So Stupid?" in this chapter. Write a poem or list the things that bother you about the groups in your peer culture.
2. Make a collage entitled "Friendship."
3. React to the following form of discipline. "Go to your room and think this situation out." What effect does isolating a person from a group have on the individual's behavior and feelings?
4. Banishment has been an effective method of social control. Research the history of solitary confinement. Describe your feelings about solitary confinement.
5. The United Nations Declaration of the Rights of the Child reads: "No discrimination based on race, sex, religion, language or national, political and social origins."
   (a) Discuss what is meant by discrimination and how it may or may not relate to classroom situations.
   (b) How can a family with friendships among people of different races or religions make children more tolerant of peers in school or other social settings?
6. (a) Interview some first grade students and ask them to describe what "best friend" means to them.
   (b) Ask the same question of an adult, having them explain if what they expect from a friend today is similar to what they expected in the past.

16 Dating

Personality and Social Acceptability

What makes some young people accepted, others neglected, and still others rejected in a social situation? A study and understanding of personality characteristics could help those who are not accepted in some social situations to improve their acceptability. A questionnaire completed by students produced this list of characteristics for peers who were socially accepted and for those who were not:

High social acceptability	Low social acceptability
cheerful	restless
enthusiastic	talkative
friendly	fighting, aggressive
good sense of humor	shy, withdrawing
attractive	noisy
active in games	boastful
lots of friends	few friends

What attracts you to other people? List some characteristics that determine your preferences for certain people.

Would you say that having athletic ability makes a person appealing? What other involvement could you undertake in the school to improve your acceptability? Did you consider inter-school quiz shows, science fairs, social or fund-raising committees, the drama group, or the school newspaper?

Would you say you have to conform totally to the ways of the crowd to be popular? Actually, individual attributes are more appealing and contribute more interest to the group – so keep your individuality. Research has shown that adolescents who are not accepted by their peers are more peer-conforming than the out-going, individualistic students who are accepted.

Social acceptability can be achieved by becoming self-aware. You require some knowledge of personality development, and of your strengths and weaknesses, and you should have plans for self-improvement.

Personality is the sum total of behavior, character, abilities, temperament, habits and motivation.

Your personality is formed and influenced by many factors, such as

- heredity – physical appearance, race, instincts
- environment – home, peers, community, religion, social situations
- learning patterns – attitudes, habits, decision-making
- health and fitness – physical and mental disabilities, reaction to stress and pressures, illness, diet
- emotional expression – joy, anger, fear, deprivation, satisfaction, love, hate

Think of a person you enjoy being with. Consider his or her appearance, home privileges, habits, reaction to problems, and general emotional reactions. Describe how each of these factors has influenced his or her personality.

Personality Development

As an adolescent you are searching for an identity. This is a time for trying on a variety of personalities to determine the one that fits you most comfortably. You integrate the roles you like to form a personality or state of being. Roles may be adopted from parents, friends, or media. Development of your personality helps you to find your sense of identity. There are six stages in the development of personality.*

*This is fully explained in *Childhood and Society* by Erik Erikson (New York: W.W. Norton, 1963).

Stages	Explanation
I. Trust versus mistrust Infants develop a sense of trust in mothers and in their environment.	Consistent love and care versus neglect and separation. The skill of a mother in handling material needs is not nearly as important as providing love and security.
II. Autonomy versus shame and doubt Infants discover they have a behavior of their own. They realize their own will. However, they should have to encounter manageable frustrations so they are aware of limits.	Development of muscles and control of choices versus inability to control body, emotions, and environment.
III. Initiative versus guilt Environment challenges children and they attempt to master specific tasks.	Increased mobility and communication versus feelings of guilt and anxiety.
IV. Industry versus inferiority Children develop a realization of competence and they gradually fend off a sense of inferiority.	Working, producing, and knowing the rules of the game versus inadequacy and inferiority in ability to meet standards of work.
V. Identity versus role confusion Adolescents acquire a sense of identity while overcoming a sense of instability due to conflicting demands.	Integration of childhood identification with social roles.
VI. Intimacy versus isolation Young people take their place as members of society.	Ability to understand self and others and be understood. Lack of this causes feelings of isolation and aloneness.

There is a positive and negative side to each stage, and no one achieves all positive characteristics. However, a healthy personality can balance these various feelings and achieve positive growth.

Dating

Relating to the opposite sex through dating is a stage in personality development that occurs in adolescence. It is a time of fun, when you can learn what various individuals are like. It is a time when your need for affection transfers from family members to those outside the family and of the opposite sex. Many aspects of dating widen your educational and personality development.

- ☑ Having fun in groups helps you become comfortable with the opposite sex.
- ☑ You learn acceptable social behavior with both sexes.
- ☑ You can learn of others' interests, attitudes, and ways of thinking.
- ☑ You recognize the different ways in which people express emotions and learn how to handle your own.
- ☑ You may become more aware of, and try to improve, your personal grooming.
- ☑ Dating promotes personality development by helping you identify the characteristics that are most favorably accepted by others.
- ☑ Dating helps you to develop and exercise good manners.
- ☑ Dating increases your talents, skills, and activity involvement.
- ☑ Dating helps you develop communication skills.
- ☑ You will realize that you are responsible for your own conduct.
- ☑ You will develop an interest in other people and things besides yourself.
- ☑ You will learn to respect other people's choices, decisions, and life-styles and learn to settle differences maturely.

Parental Conflict

If you developed all these terrific talents, skills, and attitudes, parents wouldn't be too concerned about your dates. In reality, dating can become a cause of friction between teenagers and parents. If parents and teenagers work out an agreed-upon set of guidelines, dating doesn't have to be a problem.

Why do parents make rules? What would happen if they didn't? Why is it difficult to talk about sex?

What Do You Think?

1. Parents should know who you are with and where you go.
2. Teenagers of any age do not require supervision at dances and parties.
3. Teenagers should decide their own time limits.
4. Boys and girls should be able to have opposite-sex friends over even when no one else is at home.

Sexual Identity

As an adolescent you have several adjustments to make while developing a positive sexual identity. There is a need to adjust to your body and all its changes in order to see yourself sexually as a male or female.

If you understand the physiological and psychological differences between males and females, it will help you develop better relationships with the opposite sex. Your understanding of possible differences in perception, emotions, and sensitivity in your partner can lead to a stronger dating or personal relationship.

Sexual Stereotyping

Here are some characteristics that describe stereotypes of the sexes.

adventurous
aggressive
ambitious
artistic
aware of others' feelings
crude
direct
dominant
excitable
gentle
gracious
impulsive
independent
logical
needs security
practical
quiet
reserved
romantic
self-confident
tactful
talkative
unemotional

Which of these characteristics would you apply to a male student? Which would you apply to a female student? Which could apply to both? Discuss your reasons for your choices in class.

It is important not to stereotype or class people according to their sex. Discuss in class why the characteristics you thought were masculine could also be feminine and vice versa.

Put yourself in these shoes....

Derek and Pam were expecting a baby. They were very excited about this happy event. They were concerned about raising a child in a non-sexist manner. They wanted to raise their child so as to develop the child's human potential. They wanted to promote equality of the sexes – legally and socially, as well as in schools, work, and politics. They decided to join a group of other parents interested in a caring but non-sexist approach to child rearing. Pam and Derek were asked to try to change the stereotyped thoughts they had about "masculinity" and "femininity." For example: Pam had to stop thinking of a little girl in frilly pink clothes and of a very dependent, reserved nature. The group tried to list all the situations in society that were not acceptable for one sex or the other, e.g., specific athletic teams, political positions, handicraft courses, service clubs, etc. Finally the group decided to list all the characteristics they wished their children could possess regardless of their sex. They listed characteristics that would describe a healthy human being.

1. How might parents raise a child in a sexist way?
2. (a) Have you been raised in a sexist way?
   (b) If so, give some examples of sexual stereotypes that have been applied to you and try to explain why.
3. What is the importance of raising a child in a non-sexist manner?

TAKE ACTION

1. Some characteristics of a healthy human being might be independence, honesty, initiative, sensitivity, compassion, courage, and tenderness. What characteristics do *you* feel are important for a healthy, well-balanced person?
2. List situations or statements you have experienced or made that indicate you have developed sex-role stereotypes.
3. Discuss how the ability to look at equality for males and females can help you to combat other prejudices towards people and things.
4. List all the activities – of a work, religious, or social nature (like clubs) – that exclude one sex or the other. Find out why this kind of policy exists and suggest some solutions. Do you want changes or not?
5. Listen to a recording of *Free to Be . . . You and Me* (Bell Records, 1974) or read "X: A Fabulous Child's Story" by Lois Gould (in the appendix at the end of this book). What is this record and/or the story trying to say? Do you agree? Why or why not?

Dating Problems

For the past week, the class had put questions in the question box outlining their concerns about sexuality, dating, and sexual codes. On Friday afternoon the teacher and the class discussed solutions to these problems. Have you been involved in similar situations? What answers would you give?

Question: When you move to a new school, or go away for a summer vacation where you don't know anyone, how do you meet people? I miss being "somebody." I still look and act the same as I did before, and I just want to be liked.

Answer: Your basic physical appearance and your ability to present your most attractive appearance will have an effect on the attraction process. Sometimes your body "language" or your actions are misinterpreted. Certain body motions or habits, such as never sitting still or constantly pushing your hair back, may make a person think you are nervous and jittery. How can you present an attractive image? You may emphasize your actions to project a social image that is desirable to another person or group. If they appreciate athletes, you might wear your letter sweater and join a variety of sports activities or spectator events. Remember, though, that what is considered attractive to one observer may be undesirable to another. It is best to present a natural image rather than playing a phony role. Be patient – you will soon make new friends and feel you are somebody.

Question: I have a friend who is really shy and I end up passing messages to this other person for him. He has never ever talked to her. I really don't mind since I'm not involved, but how do you break the ice and actually get to meet someone?

Answer: The logical, but not necessarily the easiest, thing would be to set up an introduction. Meeting is a difficult situation: apparently, and sometimes unfortunately, the first five minutes of contact after and including the ice-breaking statement can make or break a relationship because everyone forms such definite first impressions. Have you ever changed your opinion of someone after you finally got to know him or her?

If you feel a fairly high sense of worth and have some self-confidence, you might initiate a meeting and introduce yourself. Of course, you also take the chance of being rejected or ignored, and that's rough. It might be worth making a note not to put down someone who tries to get to know you in this manner. If the person is rude or being a snob you could just ignore them.

You can overcome your shyness by thinking through how to meet the person. Work out what you will say to that person and practice it in front of the mirror or with a close friend. Try to list all the interests you know the person has, and ask questions that will get this person talking about these interests. They may not be the same as yours, but if you like the person, you will probably learn something and develop similar interests. It also gets you off the hook for making conversation – and everyone appreciates a good listener. If a third person is doing the arranging, it would be helpful if that person arranged for the least shy of the twosome to do the approaching.

Question: My friend Monica has asked me to give her some pointers on how to meet and get a boyfriend. Monica is kind of cute, has a good personality; she's smart but not a snob. Have you any suggestions?

Answer: Tell her to stop worrying. With the assets you have described – she will soon be discovered. There are several ways of meeting boys. Why not plan a party? You'll have fun putting it together and it gives everyone a chance to discover things about each other. If you decide against having a party at home, suggest that the social committee at school plan a dance soon, or maybe a youth group you belong to can plan a dance. Other ways people get together are through computer match-making, blind dates, or horoscope pairings. These might be fun activities to plan for a party.

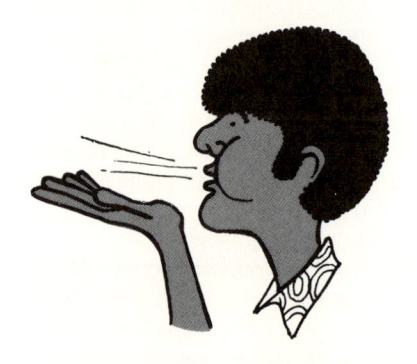

Question: I am going out with an older boy whom I really like. He's a big flirt with all the girls, and that worries me. Do you think he is just using me? Do you think he will stop flirting when I'm with him? I'm scared he won't quit when I'm not around.

Answer: Flirting is usually harmless. It is a way people use to get to know each other. Don't worry about being used. If he is sincere to you, and you have fun together, that is the most important thing. If you get too possessive about him, he will find more pleasure flirting with others. I'm sure you do a little friendly flirting yourself.

Question: My older sister had such a hassle about dating. My parents always asked a thousand questions and made her come in really early. My older brother says it won't be the same hassle for me as our parents are used to it all now. Can I be sure?

Answer: As the youngest, you are less likely to have to work out these problems because your parents have already set ground rules. Parents and the young person beginning to date usually have to work out acceptable guidelines for both of them. Because you have an older brother and sister, your parents will be more relaxed about the socializing process and you will follow along with the rules that have been set. Besides parents and your birth order, there are other factors that affect dating behavior. The behavior of siblings, family changes resulting from a move, death, or divorce all have an effect. Also your place in the peer group, the amount of money your family has, where you live, transportation facilities, living conditions, and religion all have an effect on your social behavior.

Question: My friend and I go around with two boys who are friends and most of the time it is great. However, they never leave us alone and we never have a day just to ourselves. How can we make them realize that there are times we don't want them over?

Answer: Lots of girls would like to have your problem. The best way is to explain to the boys you really want a day to yourselves and suggest something for them to do. There is room for both girlfriends and boyfriends in your lives, so be honest with them and arrange it that way.

Question: I have a BIG problem. My girlfriend is really attractive, and all the guys are envious, but I find time with her is frequently boring.

Answer: It is hard to carry on a one-way conversation – or is this a case where she never stops talking long enough for you to get in a word edgewise? Such situations can happen on the first few dates, and you can either stop dating, or remedy the situation through developing better communication skills. Often people fear they will say the wrong thing or fumble their words. It may be worthwhile planning some time at a movie or concert or sports activity where you are not forced to carry on a conversation all the time. Boredom is a confusing emotion. It is important for you to look at the situation and see why you are really bored. Don't worry, you'll meet someone to hold your interest after the novelty of the first few dates wears off.

Question: I am involved in a lopsided relationship. I like this person but not nearly as much as he likes me. I don't want to get serious because I want to go out with other people too. He is so possessive and gets jealous if I even look at anyone else. I can't go on much longer, but he is too nice to hurt. Help me.

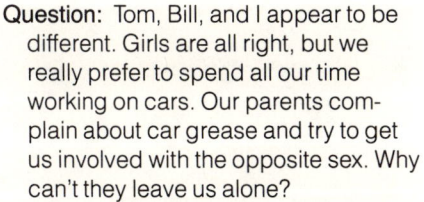

Answer: It might be helpful to determine at the beginning the type of relationship you feel you want. Do you want to be friends, date often, or go steady? If you know how deep you want the relationship to go, you would be doing your friend a favor by letting him know. The longer you continue, the harder it is to break off and the more pain the other will suffer. If you don't level with him, you are just setting him up for more pain. He'll soon discover something is wrong and feel like a dummy. He'll also think you don't respect him enough to think he has the ability to accept the breakup. You really are not helping his sense of dignity by trying to spare his feelings. Leave him with enough self-respect to heal his wounds. There are nice ways to say you don't want to go steady. Never say, "I don't like you anymore," but say the relationship is too demanding, argumentative, or restricting for both of you.

Question: Tom, Bill, and I appear to be different. Girls are all right, but we really prefer to spend all our time working on cars. Our parents complain about car grease and try to get us involved with the opposite sex. Why can't they leave us alone?

Answer: Peers and adults tend to apply pressure towards dating. They are just trying to get you to develop other skills. Why not take time off occasionally and give the girls a break?

- List some activities that would be enjoyable for a first date and that would make conversation comfortable.
- List the characteristics you like and dislike in a dating partner.
- Give examples of how you or someone else gracefully broke up a relationship so there was little conflict or upset.

189

Personality Quiz (Use a separate sheet of paper.)

		Yes	No	Sometimes
1.	Do you make your friends feel you are superior to them?			
2.	Do you like to make the final decision?			
3.	Can you always be depended upon to keep your word?			
4.	Do you make fun of others behind their backs?			
5.	Are you ever sarcastic?			
6.	Do you go out of your way to help others cheerfully?			
7.	Do you smile easily and often?			
8.	Do you try not to laugh at the mistakes of others?			
9.	Do you have a tendency to find fault with everyday things?			
10.	Do you avoid jokes that will embarrass others?			
11.	Are you a good listener?			
12.	Do you let others have their own way?			
13.	Do you avoid flattering others to gain something for yourself?			
14.	Do you give praise or genuine compliments?			
15.	Do you avoid asking snoopy questions?			
16.	Can you laugh at yourself when something ridiculous happens?			
17.	Do you and your friends make fun of other people?			
18.	Do you gossip about others?			
19.	Are you enthusiastic?			
20.	Do you try to be natural in your manner?			

Meeting and Talking Tips

- ☑ Be interested in a variety of things.
- ☑ Avoid interrupting.
- ☑ Show a real liking for people.
- ☑ Avoid embarrassing topics.
- ☑ Be an alert listener.
- ☑ Don't be too opinionated.
- ☑ Listen to the opinion of others with respect.
- ☑ Don't talk excessively about yourself.
- ☑ Avoid sarcasm.
- ☑ Give the other person a chance to talk. Be a good listener.
- ☑ End the conversation with a pleasant feeling.

Sexuality begins at birth. Adolescence is a time when the need for both sexual identity and love from those other than family are very strong. Dating is an exciting time that can provide personal growth, but it can also be confusing, competitive, and tense. There are no easy steps to follow to become popular. In fact, too much emphasis is placed on "when you date," "who you date," or "if you date." All of the advantages of opposite sex relationships and personality development can be achieved by mixed group activities and do not require one-to-one dating.

MIND POWER

dating problems
peer conforming
personality
sexual identity
sexual stereotypes
social acceptability

TAKE ACTION

1. What's Your Advice?
   Set up a Dear John and Dear Joan column. Answer these concerns and collect replies to others submitted to this column.

   Dear John and Joan:
   He says he doesn't like me, but sometimes he acts as though he does. How can I find out for sure?
   Confused

   Dear John and Joan:
   I'm 17 and my girlfriend is 14. Her father says we can't see each other or talk anymore because I'm too old for her. We don't want to sneak around. What can we do?
   Concerned

   Dear John and Joan:
   I baby-sit regularly Saturday nights. When the baby is asleep, my boyfriend comes over. My mother doesn't approve.
   C.F.

2. Discuss:
   (a) Would you be most attracted to someone with similiar interests and past experience or someone from a completely different neighborhood and life-style?
   (b) Would you say you are attracted to those who make you feel good about yourself? Would you say you seek someone who fulfills a need?
   (c) All boys and girls should have group dating experiences before having one-to-one dates.
   (d) An older date is more interesting than one your own age.
   (e) Playing "hard to get" is better than showing too much interest in someone you like.

3. Form groups of three with the people sitting beside you (not necessarily people you know well). Have Person A talk to Person B for one minute about the things that Person B is interested in. Person A is to avoid the use of "I," "my," and "mine." After one minute, Person C comments on how well Person A picked up Person B's interests. Change roles.

4. Do a school questionnaire and survey the students on "the characteristics of a good date."

5. Have a debate on one of the following topics:
   (a) Resolved: Males pay for all dates. If he has no money, then no one gets to go out.
   (b) Resolved: When going to a dance on a date, it's O.K. to mix as long as you dance with your date at the beginning and go home together at the end.

6. Set up a panel with parents and teenagers to discuss what parents expect of teenagers and what teenagers expect of parents.

5 YOU AND COMMUNICATION

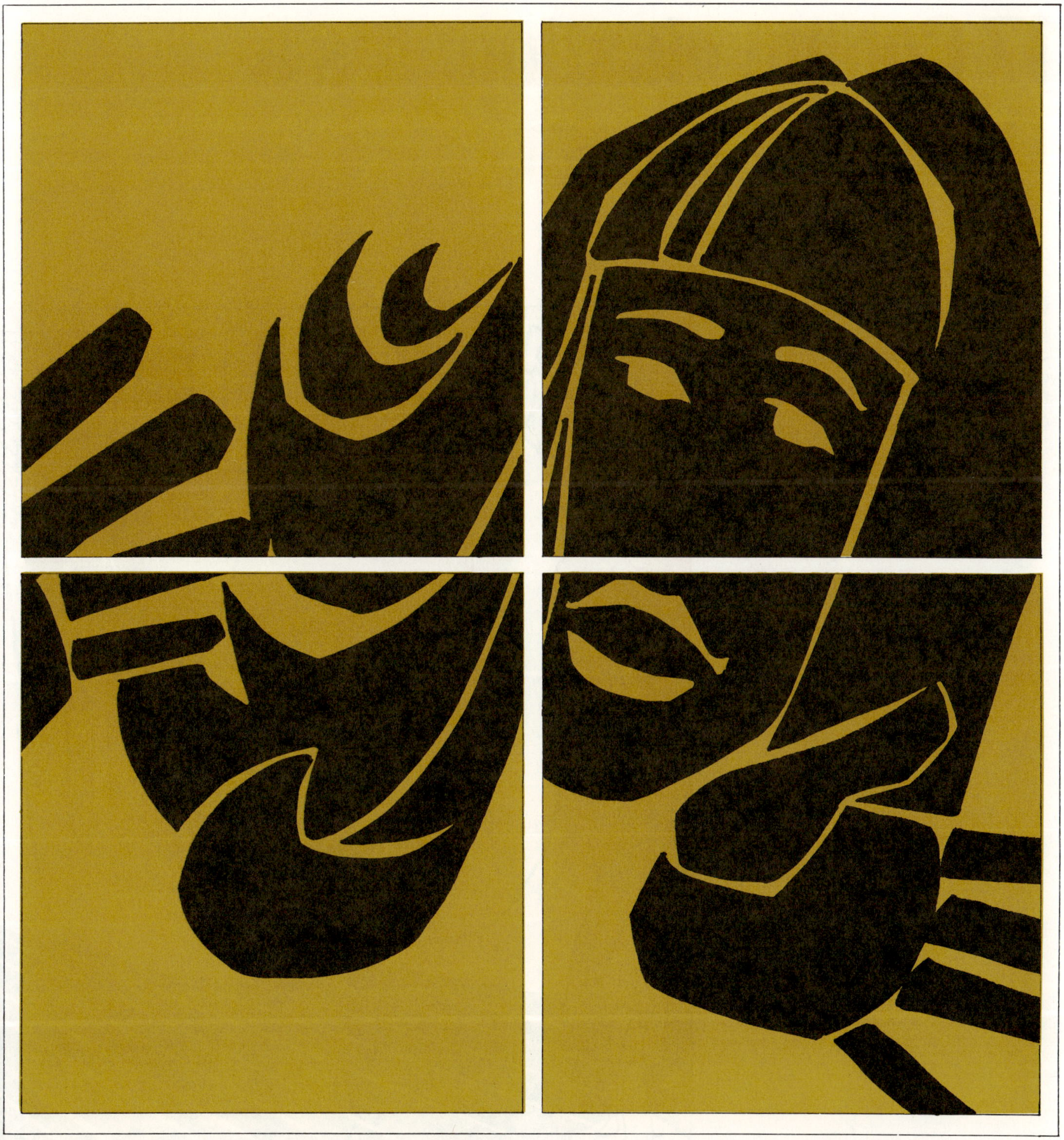

17 Communication: It's a Two-Way Street

What is good communication? Why is it necessary? How can good communication improve your relationships? Have you ever been a victim of misunderstanding due to a lack of communication?

Elaine and Ruth were discussing a mutual friend. Elaine said she noticed that Sandy had put on a few pounds. The next Saturday Ruth and Sandy were shopping and trying on some new pants. Sandy said, "I'm not in the mood because nothing seems to fit. I guess that snacking after school isn't agreeing with my old body."

Ruth replied, "I know what you mean. Elaine even said the other day that you looked fat."

"Well, that's really catty of her. Tell her I think she's fat, too!" cried Sandy as she stomped out.

Ruth later told Elaine that Sandy was mad at her and why. "You sure aren't using your head. Thanks a lot for nothing. I'm never going to say anything if you plan to repeat it. Anyway, if you do repeat it, the least you could do is not twist it so it sounds worse. Putting on a few pounds is hardly the same as being fat!" yelled Elaine as she went to call Sandy to explain.

1. Why is this an example of poor communication?
2. How could this situation have been avoided?
3. Who is at fault here?
4. Discuss in class any similar experiences you have had.

What ways do people use to communicate? We mostly think of verbal communications, but messages are passed by many methods. Babies, for example, know that they are loved by the cuddling they get, even though they don't understand the words their parents use. We know many things about prehistoric people by being able to interpret the symbols and art forms found on cave walls. Let's explore the many ways that people send and receive messages without speaking.

Non-Verbal Communication

Symbolic Communication
Here are some symbols that are used and understood all around the world.

Non-verbal messages of this kind are transmitted through a shape or symbol. People of all languages can travel anywhere and understand how to get around and also how to find food and places to rest.

Did you, or anyone you know, belong to a group where you learned semaphore? Semaphore is a sign language in which the positions of your arms represent specific letters. There is one position for each letter of the alphabet. It is a language that is fun to know, as you can use it to communicate with a friend from a distance or when you don't want to share your message with others who may be around. Deaf-mutes also use a type of sign language. Their fingers and hands shape symbols that have specific meaning. Deaf-mutes can enjoy plays and TV shows as they watch a person translate the words into symbols in their language.

A group of high school students were interested in learning more about forms of communication among deaf people. They arranged a field trip to the School for the Deaf. While there, they attended an assembly program which presented the candidates for Valentine King and Queen to the student body. Each candidate appeared twice. The first time, each candidate modeled an outfit, and the second time, the candidate made a speech or acted out a pantomime. The program on stage was conducted in complete silence. Body language played an important part, with students clapping, waving both arms, and standing to show enthusiastic approval.

The school president was master of ceremonies and had excellent support from his audience. The visiting students and their teacher had to rely completely on body language and they showed their approval like everyone else.

Some of the teachers at the school were deaf-mutes. Others had taken immersion courses that had taught them how to speak with sign language. Here is the alphabet. Perhaps you are interested in learning some of it.

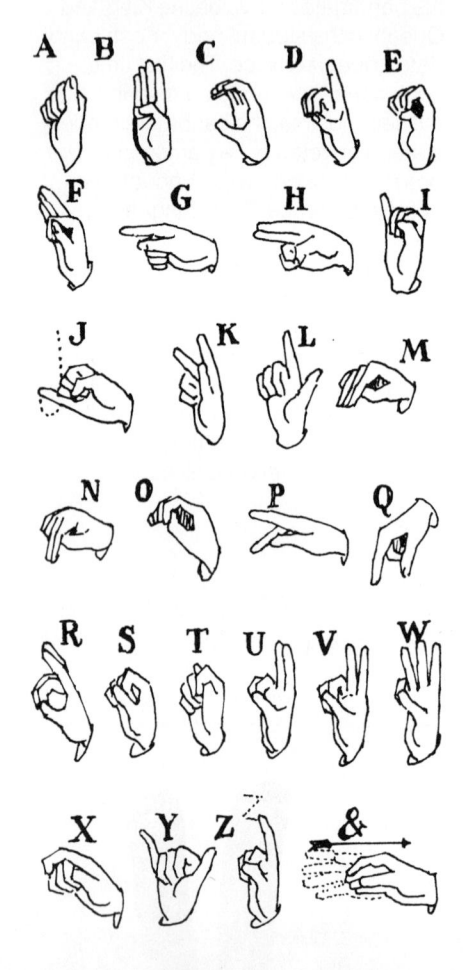

Investigate and report to the class on the use of symbols (with examples) from any of these areas:
1. astronomical language
2. surveyors' markings
3. blueprints
4. Indian signs
5. editing symbols
6. shorthand
7. sports

Body Language

Body language is the name given to the messages that we transmit through our body. These actions help explain our emotional state. Body language gives you clues to people's real feelings while they are carrying on a conversation. Body messages may give a truer picture of what a person is feeling then what that person says. The message may even be the exact opposite of what the person is saying.

Have you ever been with a friend at school who was really mad at someone and didn't want to make a scene, so he or she just kept silent and pretended not to be angry? How did you recognize that your friend was angry? Did your friend act or use his or her body in a certain way that showed anger? Some people get unusually quiet or red in the face. They may cross their arms and legs in a self-protecting manner that is a shut-out sign to everyone. How do you try to conceal your anger?

What other messages do people send by their actions? Write down a feeling or emotion on a piece of paper. Act out your emotion without using words and see if the class can guess what you are feeling. You could be showing sadness, embarrassment, anger, boredom, loneliness, fright, joy, confusion, satisfaction after a good meal, surprise, or empathy.

Have you ever observed people on a bus or at a shopping center? Can you guess what they are feeling from their body movements or behavior?

Touching can be a loving gesture. It can indicate a need to be close to someone, or it can show empathy. A raised eyebrow often expresses surprise or disbelief. Crossing of arms on the chest often indicates personal satisfaction. A shoulder shrug can show indifference, or imply, "I don't know." A wink is a way of sharing a thought or of expressing intimacy. Tapping fingers or shuffling feet may indicate impatience. A slap to the forehead says, "I sure was dumb."

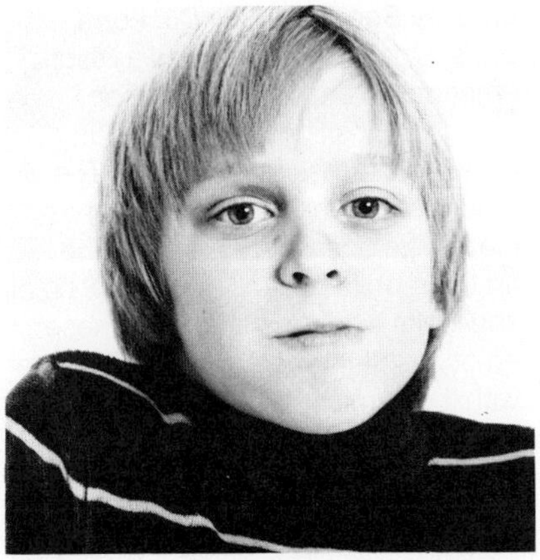
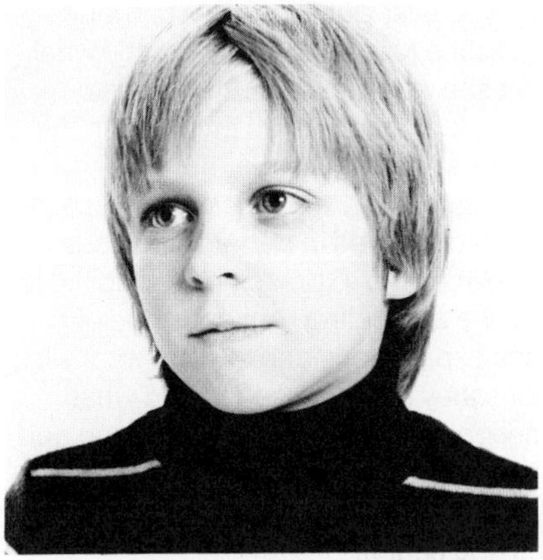
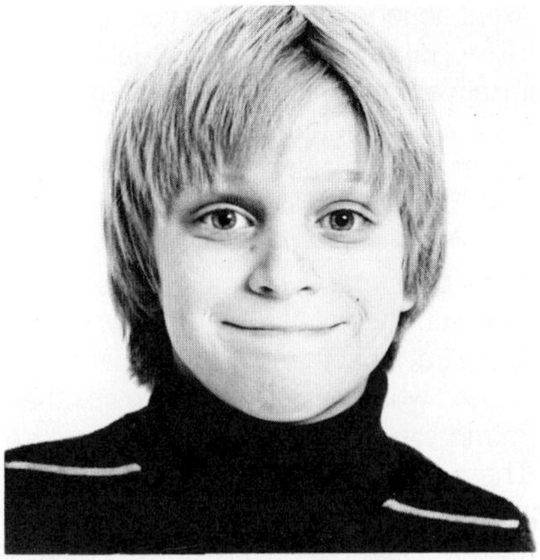
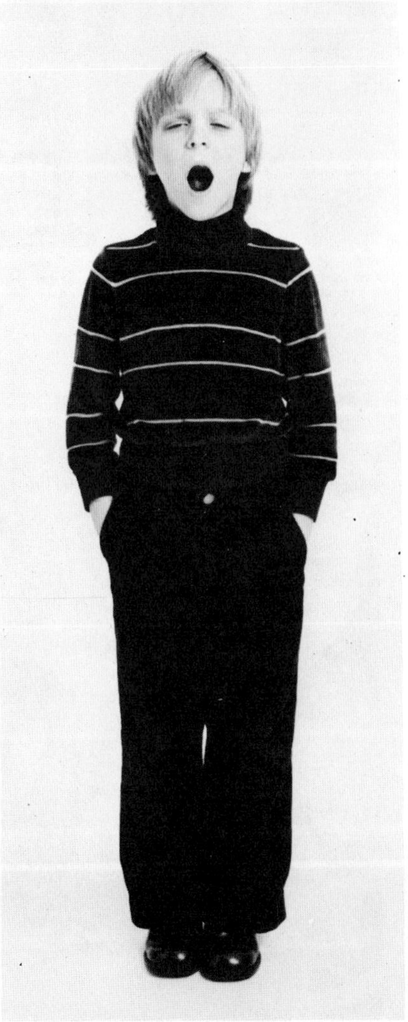
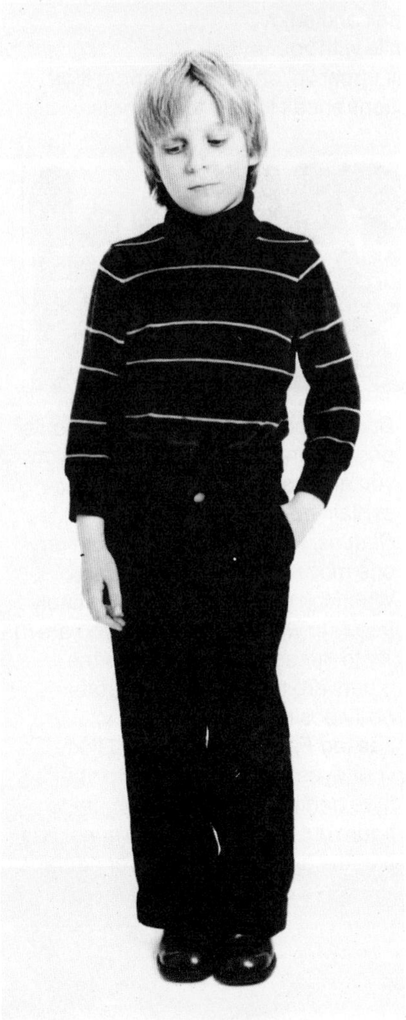
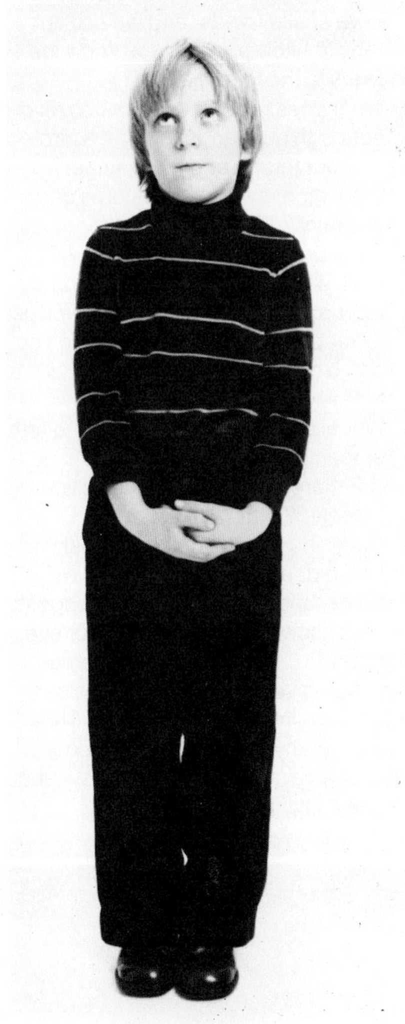

What actions or habits do you have that are triggered only when you feel a certain emotion? With your friends and family analyze each other's body language. Do you pull at your hair, rub your nose, clap your hands, chew your fingernails, crack your knuckles, rub your hands over your eyes, pick at your face, chew your pencil or turn your back? Figure out what these actions mean to you and what messages they give others around you.

There are many signs that are universally understood. Think of the signs we make with our hands that convey different messages. We wave hello or goodbye, we shake hands, and we use our thumbs to hitch-hike. Do you know the answers to these questions?

1. What does it mean when we cover our ears with our hands, or form a circle with our thumb and index finger? What other symbolic gestures can you think of?
2. What does a handshake tell you? And, what message do you send by the way you shake hands? Do you like to keep at an arm's length, or do you come close and put the feeling "it's a pleasure" into your handshake?
3. When do you embrace someone rather than giving a handshake?
4. Are there certain handshakes you object to? Why?
5. Have you ever used a handshake to seal a deal or a bet?

How can the eyes pass on messages? Studies show that the pupils of our eyes increase in size when we view something that gives us pleasure. Eyes can laugh, be sympathetic, or angry. They express many emotions. What about wide open eyes or squinted eyes? What are they saying?

Did you ever get a look from a friend across the room and know exactly what he or she was thinking? It's a terrific feeling to know that you are both on the same wavelength.

There are many expressions we use to control ourselves in certain situations. Sometimes the expression is opposite to what we are feeling. Act out some of these expressions and explain what situations they may be used in and what emotion is to be overcome. Can you add others?

Grin and bear it.
Bite the bullet.
Relax and enjoy.
Smile with your eyes.
Stiff upper lip, chin up and shrug it off.
Actions speak louder than words.

TAKE ACTION

1. *Body Feedback:* Take on a particular posture and have others guess how you are feeling. Each person is to explain how he or she thinks you feel.
2. *Statues:* Play music and have everyone move freely about the room. When the music stops, immediately freeze in whatever position you are in. Try to guess what messages the others are transmitting from their body positions.
3. *Feeling Faces:* Form pairs. Close your eyes and explore each other's face gently with your hands. Try to figure out the other person's feelings and the expression on his or her face.
4. *Monkey See – Monkey Do:* Form pairs. One person receives a list of emotions to act out. This person moves or positions his or her body in a way to express that emotion. The other person mimics the partner as closely as possible. This gives the first person feedback about how he or she looks when experiencing these emotions. If the person doesn't agree with the mimic, then the whole group can try to mimic the action.

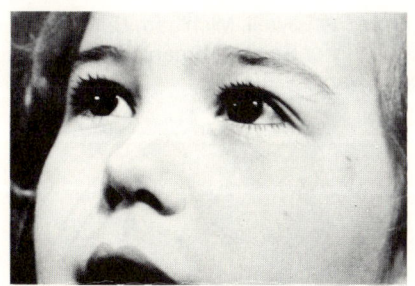

Verbal Communication

These components are necessary to establish good communications:
1. a message
2. a sender
3. a method of sending the message
4. a receiver
5. a clear message
6. interpreting skills
7. response or feedback

Hi John. Want to go downtown with me now? We can get a ride with my mother.

Sure Gerry, but I can't go until I cut the grass. So, I better meet you about noon.

Okay. I'll meet you at Stonewall's Department Store under the clock at noon.

Great! See you there.

201

It is obvious that Gerry is the sender of the message. His method of communicating the message is over the phone. John was the receiver. Was it a clear message? Would John be certain about where to go and when? Gerry made it clear that he was going downtown, right then, and getting a ride with his mother. John understood the message, agreed to go downtown, but at a later time. Gerry concluded his conversation by stating exactly what store he would be in, at what time, and the specific meeting spot. There was little skill needed to interpret this message. The words and expressions were easily understood. There were several points that had to be clear though, or John might have gone to the wrong store or the wrong meeting place.

What about the response or feedback? Did John give Gerry positive feedback? Do you think Gerry got the message that John really wanted to meet him?

This is an example of a verbal communication. There are many other ways that a person can communicate, but all ways follow the same process. Remember that all face-to-face communications include body language as well as spoken language. Many also include symbolic language. We communicate for several reasons. It may be to pass on some information, facts, or a message. Advertisers communicate to try to convince us that their product is the best. We also use communication to convince people that we are concerned, care for them, or are annoyed with them. By communicating, we learn more about ourselves and about others. If you communicate well, it will help solve a lot of problems and people won't feel they need a fortune-teller's crystal ball to figure out what you mean.

Mixed Messages

Church note in *The New Forest Magazine,* England: "In future the preacher for next Sunday will be found hanging on the notice board."

From the Frederick, Oklahoma, *Press:* "Sam Haskins accidentally shot himself while hunting. One of the wounds is fatal, but his friends are glad to hear that the other is not serious."

From the Lowell, Michigan, *Buyer's Guide:* "For Sale – Woman's Coat, never been warm."

The chairperson and the guest speaker were chatting as everyone moved into the auditorium. The chairperson got up and introduced the speaker in very glowing terms. At the end of the introduction, the speaker very lightly and humorously said, "I would be honored to have done all those things, but you have just introduced Mrs. Jeffries who is speaking in the next conference room."

What is wrong in each of these situations?

Communication Behavior

When we talked about behavior, we learned that people develop their methods of behavior through imitating those around them, from their inherited characteristics, their culture, their environment, and their life experiences. Will the way a child communicates also be a result of all these factors?

Children observe how those around them communicate. Later in their development, their senses and experiences often tell them how they should communicate with certain people. You may communicate differently with a parent, teacher, sales clerk, friend of the opposite sex, and a close friend. But mostly you have a basic pattern of communicating. Here are four that have been identified.*

Pattern 1: *The super-agreeable or accommodating person.* This person always asks what *you* want to do and puts him- or herself in the back seat. Janie phoned Sue and asked, "Would you like to do something tonight?" Sue replied, "Sure, whatever you like." Janie said, "Would you like to go to the show or downtown shopping?" "Oh, I don't care, whatever you want to do." Sue sounds so agreeable, but she is depending on Janie to make all the decisions. She is not considering any of her own wishes. Janie won't know if what she decides to do is really what Sue would have most wanted to do.

Pattern 2: *Blamer, disagreeable, put-down person.* Bill arrived home on foot pushing his bicycle with the blown-out tire. His brother Jack came flying out of the house and said, "I told you that would happen. I said that the tire was getting bald. You never listen to what I say and it serves you right. Maybe you'll pay attention next time." Jack gets pleasure out of putting others down in order to make himself look superior. People like this always look for the negative side of any situation and fill their messages with "you always," "I told you so," "you never".... These comments always place the blame on the other person.

Pattern 3: *Irrelevant, off-the-track, or distracting person.* Don's father was trying to get to the bottom of the problem of who had left the stereo on all night. He wasn't particularly mad, but felt whoever it was should accept the responsibility. "Who used it last?" he said. Little Robbie said, "You know, Dad, we read this really neat story about Indians today at school." "That's nice. We'll talk about it later. Now, if no one can remember if he left the stereo on, I'm wondering how many days it's been on." "You see, Dad, they were out hunting antelope and they got trapped by a brush fire...." "Listen Robbie, this is serious. Would you quit changing the subject? I'm beginning to think it was you, the way you keep trying to get us off the track."

This kind of person seems to wander on and off the topic. Often these people get things out of perspective. Sometimes, if a situation is tense or uncomfortable, they'll crack a joke. They prefer to avoid the issue rather than state what is really on their minds. Their irrelevant behavior is unpredictable and makes it difficult for others to pass on a message. The feedback they give is also confusing, so the sender doesn't get a clear message about the receiver's reaction.

*From Virginia Satir, *Conjoint Family Therapy* (Palo Alto, Calif.: Science and Behavior Books, 1967).

Pattern 4: *"Congruent" or realistic person.* Sally called her friend Evelyn and asked if she wanted to come and sleep over on the weekend. Evelyn said, "I really would love to spend the time with you, but you know I am allergic to your cat. How about if you sleep here? What do you think about that?"

A "congruent" person is aware of self, others, and the real situation. Evelyn said how she felt, making it clear that she wanted to be with Sally. She didn't make up an excuse, but told why she felt the way she did. She also offered another suggestion and asked Sally to express her feelings.

1. What pattern do you follow in most of your communications?
2. Would your family and friends agree?
3. Can you see how the "congruent" person used the process for good communications?
4. Choose five people to role-play this situation. A mother, father, seventeen-year-old Grant, twelve-year-old Sheila, and eight-year-old Ray are sitting at the dinner table discussing Grant's vacation plans. Grant wants to spend his summer vacation hitchhiking across the country. Have each of the people role-play one member of the family. Each is to communicate in one of the four patterns just outlined. Act out the situation using the pattern you have chosen. Have the class determine whether you followed the pattern well or if you shifted into another pattern. Often, as you get involved, you automatically shift into your own communication pattern.

Conclusion

We all use three modes of communication – symbolic, body language, and verbal – when we are relating to other people. True communication occurs when the receiver interprets the meaning of the words in the same manner as the sender.

Communication is a two-way street with each person exchanging ideas and feelings. There must also be some feedback process through which each person shares what he or she heard from the other. Just as a carpenter or engineer uses his tools to erect a sturdy structure, we must explore words to determine if those we use are building a durable foundation for human communication.

WORD POWER

body language
communication patterns
communication process
"congruent" person
non-verbal feedback
semaphore
symbolic communication
verbal communication

TAKE ACTION

1. Research communication in the animal kingdom to see how animals communicate:
   (a) *Tactile signals:* the honey bee, scouting out a food source, will return to the hive and do a "waggle dance." This tail-wagging tells the bees the exact direction of and distance to the food source.
   (b) *Visual displays:* e.g., those of peacocks, stickleback fish, and chameleons.
   (c) *Acoustic signals:* alarm cries or mating signals, e.g., those of beavers, monkeys, and birds.
   (d) *Chemical signals:* e.g., those of skunks and dogs.
   (e) *Threat postures:* e.g., positions and movements of dogs and cats when threatened.

204

2. Think about communication between cats and dogs and humans. List at least five ways a cat or dog will announce that it wants to go out of doors.
3. Pantomime and discuss the following forms of non-verbal communication:
   (a) *Smiling and laughing*
   - the "say cheese" smile
   - the broad smile
   - the grin
   - open- and closed-mouth smile
   - wide-mouth laughter

   (b) *Eyebrow flash*
   - lowered
   - raised
   - bunched
   - one lowered and one raised

   Match these eyebrow movements with the following messages: flirting, greeting, arrogance, disapproval, worry, surprise, inquiry, attention-getting, "yes" response.

   (c) *Hiding the face during slight embarrassment*
   - hand over face
   - fingers over lips
   - lowering of head
4. When you hear these words, describe what they communicate to you. Determine why people's descriptions may be different.
   - fire engine
   - blue
   - beauty
   - night
   - dog
   - clock
5. One expert lists three hundred body movements used in body language. If you can recognize and understand these symbols, you will realize how important body language is in the communication process. List as many of the body symbols as you can and tell what they communicate to you.

Some examples are:
- squinting
- winking
- pouting
- clapping hands
- teetering on toes

6. Can you interpret some of these messages in nature?
   - dark clouds
   - stillness
   - crack of thunder
   - "sun dogs"
   - red sky at night
   - cloud shapes

205

18 Developing Your Communication Skills

When you are communicating with someone, many factors come into play: the actual content of the message, your feelings about the message, and the way you are feeling at the time of communicating. All of these factors affect how the other person interprets your message.

Dave kept checking the clock and hoping this last class would end. He felt kind of badly that he wasn't taking part in the discussion, because this was really the best class of the day. He kept thinking about the new job he was starting for Dr. Procter at the veterinary hospital. He hoped he would have lots of opportunity to help with the animals. The information was always interesting in this class, but Dave's feelings of excitement caused him to drift away from the class discussion.

What you actually hear or get out of a message is colored by many factors. These factors include: your self-concept; your needs at the time; your goals and expectations in life; your cultural background, prejudice, and standards; language; and your feelings about the sender. Are you beginning to see how all of these factors and differences in people can cause problems in communication? Remember also that you send both verbal and non-verbal messages. In addition to the intended message, there may be some unconscious or unintentional verbal and non-verbal messages.

Willie (laughing nervously): I guess I should have been more careful on my bike, but I thought I was in control before I slammed into that car.
Doctor: Does your arm hurt here at the elbow? At the shoulder? Is that gash causing a lot of pain?
Willie: Oh, no. I'm O.K. It's not too sore.
Doctor: I guess we'll have to give you a needle to prevent infection, then stitch it up. Would you come into the other room please, and we'll fix this up quickly?
Willie (pale and in a kind of daze, looking at his arm): Oh, sure.
Doctor (reentering the office): Do you need some help? I thought you were right behind me.

Willie very confidently explained his accident in a light or joking manner. He intended to laugh it off as if it wasn't upsetting him. The nervous laughter, and the way he went pale and didn't move when the doctor asked him to, were unintentional messages that he was nervous and worried about the needle and stitches. Many messages are mixed communications: people may say one thing, but their actions may say the opposite.

Obstacles to Communication

Have you ever been in an obstacle race? In an obstacle race, the path is blocked by a variety of obstacles. Some jogging paths contain obstacles. There may be hills to climb, a creek to cross by stepping on stones, a log to climb over or one to go under, or a zigzag route. These obstacles mean the joggers need more time to run the course and they must think of what they will do when they reach these obstacles. When faced with physical obstacles of this kind, one has to coordinate both mind and body to overcome the obstacles. In communication, there may be language obstacles, sound obstacles, and obstacles of body movement and feelings.

There are many obstacles that can confuse the messages sent and the way they are received. You might recall watching a TV program or talking on the phone and being interrupted by static. You miss a part of the program or the conversation because of the interruption. Barriers in communication are a kind of static that interfere with the message. Can you list some things that could block communication? Let's consider some obstacles and some ways to improve the road to good communication.

Are You Listening?

The sketch of the teacher and students illustrates how the teacher gave a message that was not received because the two students weren't listening. At times this probably happens to you too. Have you ever been talking to someone and from that person's responses, you knew that he or she wasn't really listening? Sometimes if people don't look at you, or cut in with a completely unrelated remark, you can tell they are not really listening to you.

Listening is an art. Listening is not just hearing what people say, but sensing what they feel and what their bodies are saying. You can also pick up people's attitudes and values from what they say.

TAKE ACTION

1. Let's see how well you listen. Choose a partner. You are each to talk about a topic for two minutes. The topic could be "my most embarrassing moment," "my happiest experience," or "my parents." One person speaks first and the other listens without comment or asking questions. After two minutes change places. The second talker gives his or her talk. At the end of this, each person is to repeat the partner's story. Try to report the facts you heard and describe the feelings and attitudes experienced by the person speaking. Try to point out the good things you got out of your partner's story and the upsetting things. Tell what body language you observed and what message you received from it. Was it difficult to talk for two minutes? Was it strange to talk and have zero feedback from your partner? Was it difficult to listen without reacting or adding your two cents' worth?
2. Act out the part of a person who is listening to someone else. Show by your body posture, eye contact, and actions that you are really interested. How might people pretend that they are listening?
3. Choose an old saying, such as, "A rolling stone gathers no moss," or "Every cloud has a silver lining," or "Along the way, stop and smell the flowers." Now, divide into groups of four or five, each group standing in a straight line. The person at the extreme right of each line whispers this saying (once only) into the next person's ear. Then this person passes it along to the next, and so on. Have the last person say it out loud. Was the message changed? Now try it with a short joke. Have each person explain his or her understanding of the saying or the joke he or she heard.

Being a good, understanding listener means that you have to feel empathy with the speaker. You have to try to see the situation through the speaker's eyes. It is difficult to do, but you have to try to be impartial like a judge. Forget about your own feelings and values, and try to understand the speaker's feelings and thoughts.

Active listening, that is, giving the speaker feedback about what you think you heard, can lead to real understanding. You will have developed this skill when you are able to get outside of yourself and really feel empathy for the other person.

The Magic Formula for Instant Success

The six most important words: "I admit I made a mistake."
The five most important words: "You did a good job."
The four most important words: "What is your opinion?"
The three most important words: "If you please!"
The two most important words: "Thank you."
The one most important word: "We."
The least important word: "I."

Mixed Interpretations

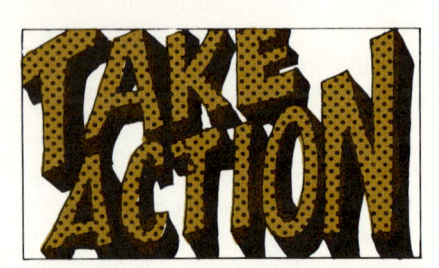

1. (a) Draw a circle about the size of a nickel.
   (b) Draw another circle with wavy edges around the first one.
   (c) At the right side of the larger circle, make a squiggly line going out to the right.
   (d) At the top of the larger circle, make a line up, curve it to the left, and zigzag it to a stop.
   (e) At the bottom of the large circle, make a line up, make a bump on a bump, then draw a line, then form a figure 8 to the left.
   (f) Put the small form of the ninth letter of the alphabet in the center of the small circle and put a dot over it. Turn the page and see if your figure looks like the one described.

   Is your figure the same as the others in the class? Can you see how words and directions are interpreted differently? Your learning experience, culture, and concentration may cause you to interpret instructions or a situation in a different way from others.

   Do words mean different things to different people? Is your idea of "squiggly" and "wavy" different from your friend's idea of them?

2. Get out a piece of paper. As soon as you read the following words, don't hesitate, but quickly write down the first thought that comes to your mind: a fruit, a piece of furniture, a flower, a color.

3. Read these words. Again, without hesitating, define them: baste, fold, bow, port.

4. Read these sentences and decide exactly what is meant:
   He has *several* sweaters. Exactly how many is several?
   She has *some* pennies. How many pennies?
   His grades are really *good*. What exactly is a good grade?
   She is wearing a *coffee-colored* skirt. Describe coffee-colored.
   That gives me a sense of *security*. What exactly makes you feel secure?

5. How well do you describe things? Pretend that someone arrived from outer space and you had to describe something to him or her. Write down a description of the object you chose (an apple, a shoe, a telephone, etc.). Do not tell what it is, but see if the others can guess from your description. A description should include color, shape, size, comparisons, and an example of usage.

6. Each part of this question has four lines. The first line – the one that is missing – is a noun (an object). The second line gives two descriptive words (adjectives) that describe the object. The third line gives two words derived from verbs associated with the object. The fourth line describes the kind of thing that each object is. You decide what each object (noun) is from the three given lines.
   (a) _____
   fuzzy, grizzly
   growling, prowling
   mammal
   (b) _____
   green, stringy
   crunchy, chewy
   vegetable
   (c) _____
   cuddly, talkative
   running, loving
   human being
   (d) _____
   soft, comfortable
   supporting, resting
   furniture

   Try making up some descriptions of your own and have others guess what you are describing.

7. Think of words that sound the same, but are different in spelling and meaning. Read these sentences and describe how they can cause communication static:
   "Shall I buy that (*pair, pear*)?"
   "That is quite a big (*waste, waist*)."
   "That (*buoy, boy*) just got knocked over."

   Make up some more examples for each of these seven exercises – for fun and to become more aware of possible misinterpretations.

Bias or Prejudice

A possible obstacle to communication is your feelings about the speaker or message sender. If you don't respect the individual, or find his or her ideas vastly different from your own, you will have a difficult time even listening to what is being said.

Mary attended a leadership-training course to prepare her for her volunteer job with preschool children at the local wading pool. The leader was rather pudgy, grubbily dressed, and not particularly appealing by Mary's standards. Although he really knew what he was talking about and had some terrific ideas, Mary was turned off. "How did it go?" asked her mother when Mary arrived home. "At first it was lousy. The speaker was a real grub," she replied. "But did you pick up any ideas to use with the children?" asked her mother. "Oh, yes. Finally I realized he had some really great ideas – like water play, sand toys . . ." She was off and running, expressing all the good ideas.

1. What made it difficult for Mary to hear what the leader was saying?
2. Did she gain from the course? Why?
3. Have you ever had this experience? Discuss with your classmates what happened in your case.

Mary's example naturally makes us think of the biases or prejudices that cause problems in communication.

The crowd unanimously decides to go to Leonard's house and listen to records. As they drive past a supermarket parking lot, they see a large display of vivid "paintings." Phyllis laughingly remarks, "Aren't those hideous? No wonder they have a special – 'Buy one and get one free!'" As soon as she has made the remark, she notices a horrified look on Leonard's face. She senses something is wrong and wonders what it can be. On arrival at Leonard's, she sees a pair of the pictures on the wall. She tries to figure out something positive to say to change the impression she previously gave.

1. Do Leonard and Phyllis have the same taste in art?
2. How could the situation have been avoided?
3. Discuss in class similar experiences you have had. How do you try to avoid such experiences?

What would happen if every suspect questioned by the police were judged by rash conclusions or hearsay rather than by the facts? What if a doctor drew rash conclusions about a serious illness instead of doing tests and getting other medical opinions? What would happen if people believed all the gossip they heard?

What is the difference between taking a person's word because you trust that person and being gullible?

Bias Quiz

On a separate sheet of paper, write down your first thought after you have read each question. Answer yes, no or uncertain to each.
1. Do you like cats?
2. Do you like raw oysters?
3. Do you like classical music?
4. Would you like to live in Europe?
5. Do you like to waltz?

Evaluate your answers to these five questions and determine if your answers are based on fact or experience, or if they are rash judgments.

Little Jeannie really idolized her older sister and was always talking about her and everything she did. Jeannie's sister realized this was a little out of proportion, and didn't like her business blabbed all over the neighborhood. She decided to fix Jeannie once and for all. Jeannie's sister had a very good singing voice and had had good parts in the high school operettas. She was going with a fellow who had a band at the university and they used to do a few group songs. She told Jeannie she was cutting a record and even sang her a song that sounded original to Jeannie. Well, Jeannie could hardly wait to tell everyone this great news. As the weeks passed, all Jeannie's friends kept asking when they'd hear the record and when it would be on the radio. Soon Jeannie and her friends realized they had been taken in. Jeannie's sister explained it to Jeannie and her friends, and suggested that they not be so gullible in the future. She also pointed out that repeating everything one hears is not such a great idea.

Can you list some of your rash judgments, biases, or prejudices? Are they illogical, or based on fact or experience? What are the dangers in these biases? How do you think you have developed each bias? Are you willing to check out your judgments and change your mind if you are shown to be wrong?

Checklist for Recognition of Communication Roadblocks

Section B below gives typical communication phrases. First, cover the answers with a piece of paper. Now read each phrase and choose the obstacle(s) from Section A which that phrase represents. Use a separate sheet of paper to write down your answers and then check them with the answers given below.

Section A
- (a) Bias
- (b) Avoidance
- (c) Sarcasm, teasing
- (d) Disbelieving
- (e) Commanding
- (f) Threatening
- (g) Giving solutions
- (h) Moralizing
- (i) Blaming
- (j) Excusing
- (k) Interpreting
- (l) Cross-examining
- (m) Persuading, lecturing
- (n) Negativism

Section B
1. That is not right.
2. I told you _____.
3. If you had listened to me, _____.
4. Are you sure you can _____?
5. You have to _____.
6. Don't tell me that.
7. It is your responsibility to _____.
8. If you don't, I shall have to _____.
9. Wait until _____.
10. Your problem is _____.
11. You should be the guidance counselor.
12. That's not true. You don't like it as well as _____.
13. The truth of the matter is _____.
14. Why don't you face up to reality?
15. You still haven't told me why.
16. Don't worry _____.
17. You never _____.
18. I insist _____.

Answers

1. (m), (n)	2. (h)	3. (i)	
4. (n)	5. (e)	6. (i)	
7. (f)	8. (f)	9. (b)	
10. (g)	11. (c)	12. (j)	
13. (k)	14. (c)	15. (l)	
16. (l)	17. (n)	18. (e)	

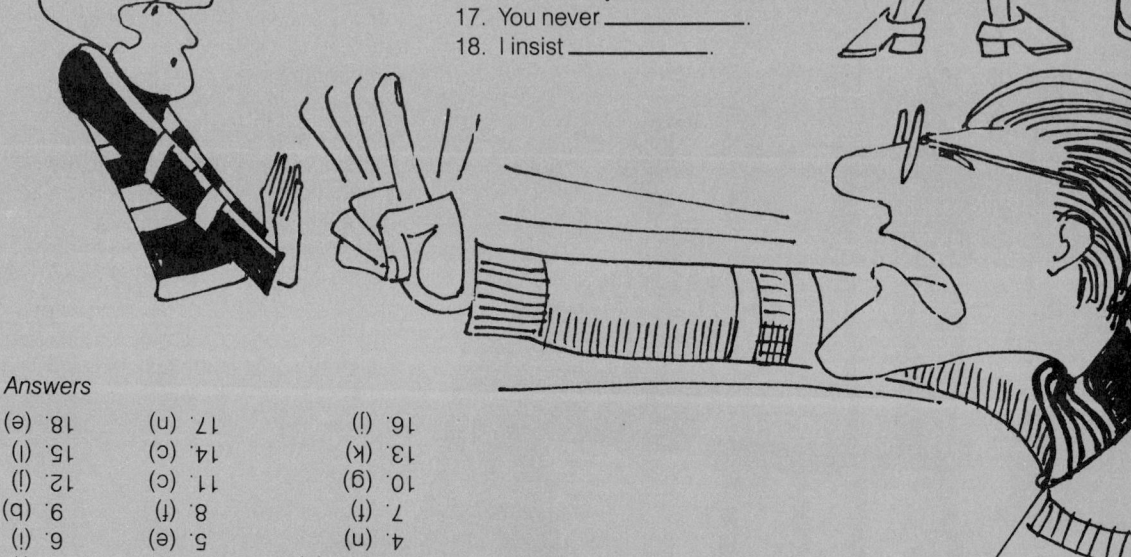

Space Relations

We all react to and use the space around us in different ways. The way a person uses space tells you something about that person.

Everyone was excited about attending the fifty-year reunion at the elementary school. Even though they had only left the school three years before, Dennis and Wes were anxious to see their old teachers and some of the people whose pictures hung on the walls. Everything in the school looked very attractive for the occasion. The assembly was fun, but a little sad, too. Refreshments were served in the gym after the ceremony and the old teachers were receiving people in the staff room. Dennis and Wes went to see them. They sat down to wait their turn to see their fourth grade teacher who had also been their softball coach. Soon a white-haired teacher approached Wes and said, "Excuse me, but you are sitting in my chair." She hadn't been there when Wes walked in, nor were there signs of any of her belongings. But nevertheless, Wes politely moved. When he finally talked to Mr. Petrie, he was told that the elderly teacher had taught in the school when it opened and that she had always sat in that chair at that exact spot at the table.

1. Do you have a favorite chair at home? Do your father and mother?
2. Do you like to sit in a particular spot on the bus?
3. Do you have a favorite spot in the cafeteria?

We all need to have our own space, a place to call our own, our personal territory. Have you ever watched a dog stake out its territory in its own yard? Other dogs will approach, shift about, and move out of that range because they know it belongs to another animal.

In *The Hidden Dimension* (New York: Doubleday, 1969), Dr. Edward T. Hall defines four different distances that we like to keep between ourselves and others: (1) intimate distance, (2) personal distance, (3) social distance, and (4) public distance.

Intimate distance is about 15 to 46 cm [6 to 18 in.], and is reserved for close relationships, like those with friends, family, and children. This is not so in all cultures: in some Mediterranean and European countries it is natural for friends of the same sex to kiss and walk with their arms about each other. If people are not on intimate terms and are physically close to each other, such as two strangers pushed face to face on a crowded bus, there is embarrassment.

A close *personal distance* would be 15 to 76 cm [6 to 30 in.]. You can hold hands, but still keep your own space. If you are not accepted in another person's personal space, this might indicate that the person finds you pushy and this makes him or her uncomfortable. If you are accepted, it probably means that you are appreciated. If you were having an argument with a friend, you would probably move 46 to 122 cm [18 to 48 in.] away. You are close enough to talk, but far enough away to retain some privacy.

Socially you relate to people at about 1.25 to 2.15 m [4 to 7 ft.]. This is the usual distance you maintain when you are talking to a sales clerk, a service person, or an employer. The farther away you are from someone, the less need you have to talk. If you were sitting right beside the doctor's nurse in the doctor's office, you might feel compelled to make a few pleasant remarks.

Public distance is about 3.7 to 7.65 m [12 to 25 ft.]. This is the distance at which you feel most comfortable when sitting and listening to someone speak in a classroom or at a public meeting.

214

NO SMOKING
HEH-HEH--- ER---EXCUSE ME MISS--- --ER--- HOW D-D-DO YOU DO?....
I WAS PUSHED! IT WASN'T MY FAULT. ---ER...UM---NOW THAT WE KNOW EACH OTHER WOULD YOU LIKE TO GO TO A MOVIE ¿?
15 TO 76 cm [6 TO 30 in.]
BOSS... MAY I HAVE A RAISE?
NO! BUT I DO ENJOY THESE LITTLE CHATS.
1.25 TO 2.15 m [4 TO 7 ft.]
EINSTEIN'S THEORY SAYS THAT E = A COUPLE OF SQUARE M.C.S
3.7 TO 7.65 m [12 TO 25 ft.]

A study of the number of seats used in a school study hall was really surprising. The principal couldn't figure out why students would go to the room, check it out, and then leave instead of going in to study. There were empty chairs, but the students wouldn't use them. Instead they would sit in the main resource room. It seemed that out of 50 chairs, on the average only 29 were filled when students would turn away.

What happened was that people had mapped out their privacy by putting books across from them on the table, and by putting their coats or bags on the chair beside them. They wanted this amount of personal and public space, and those who came in late wouldn't ask them to move their things. To study, a person needs this privacy of territory to feel secure and to be able to concentrate.

Have you ever been eating at a restaurant with a group of boys and girls or alone with someone of the opposite sex? Did you find it difficult sitting face to face? The most comfortable position in this kind of social situation is at right angles. You can easily turn your head to talk, but you can also look straight ahead without appearing to be avoiding eye contact.

Improving Communications

We have talked about many obstacles to communication and some solutions to problems. Let's summarize by listing some practices that help to improve communications. In order to be a truly "congruent" communicator, you should:

- Recognize that you have feelings and that they are a part of you, and so they will influence the way you communicate.
- Remember that each person is responsible for at least half of the communication; you should make an effort to be both a clear sender and a good listener.
- Try to be aware of the other person's feelings and learn to tolerate them even though they may be different from yours. Try to feel empathy.
- Try to give the other person positive feedback about what he or she says, and about your feelings.

Conversation is 50 percent talking and 50 percent listening. If we were certain to spend 50 percent of our conversation time listening to what is being said, we would probably be able to remove several of the barriers to good communication. Remember that listening involves decoding not only the meaning of the words, but also the intention of the sender and the tone of voice and body movements accompanying the message.

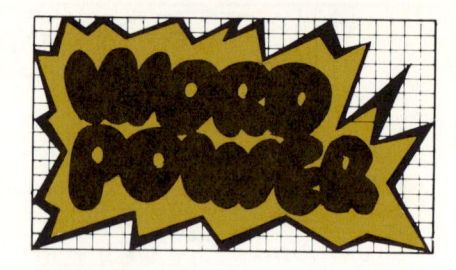

active listening
bias
feedback
mixed interpretations
obstacles
prejudice
space relations

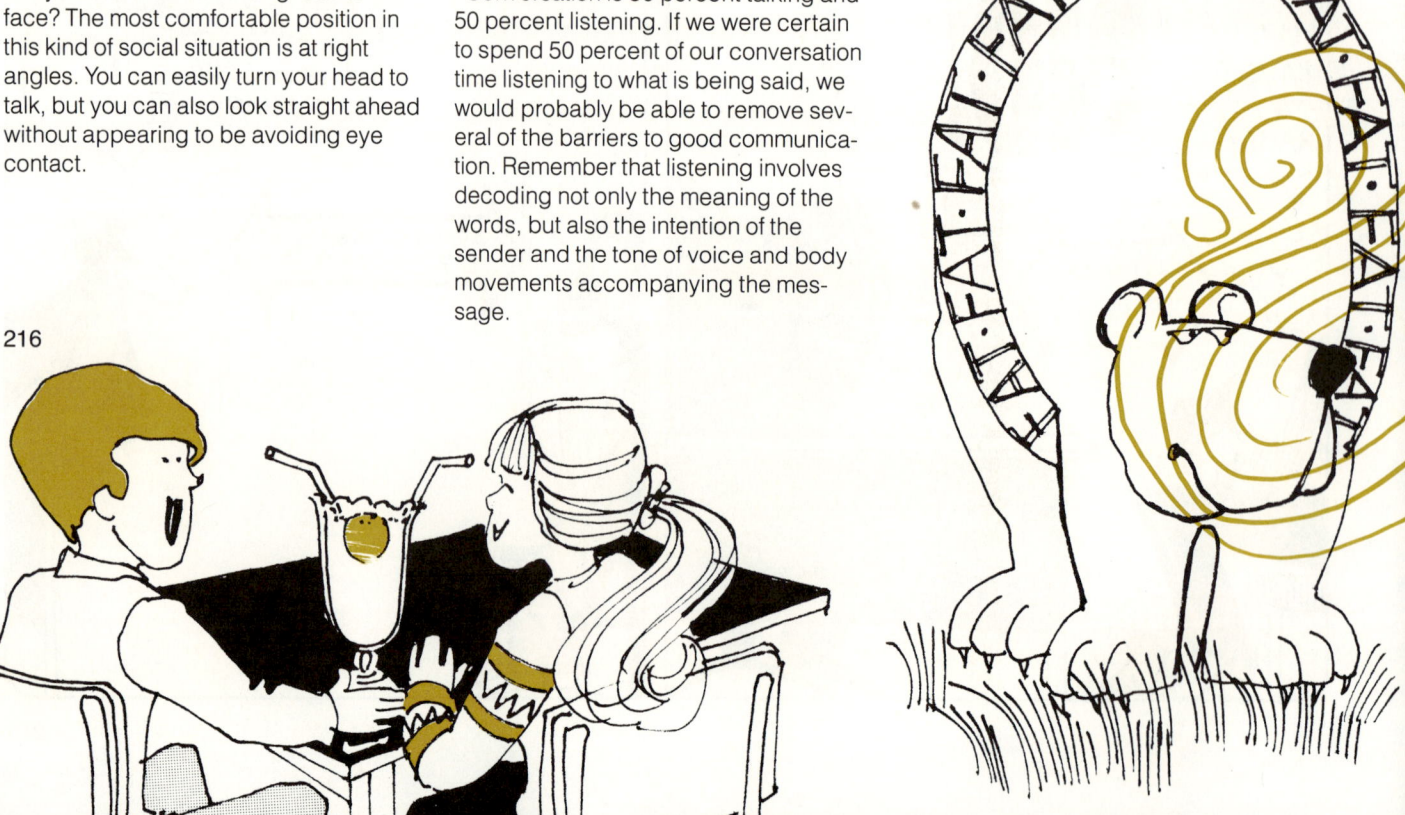

TAKE ACTION

1. If you were part of the animal kingdom, which animal or bird would you like to be? Explain why you chose this animal and what your choice may be communicating about you.
2. Read these examples and explain how one word can have so many meanings. Explain how this can be a barrier to communication.
   (a) Cook those hamburgers in that *fat*.
   (b) All mammals have a layer of *fat* for warmth.
   (c) What a *fat* little boy!
   (d) That guy's a real *fat* cat!
   (e) Will you get that summer job? *Fat* chance!
3. Imagine cave people before they developed a language. Act out how you would communicate this message: A woman, man, and six-year-old child live in a cave. The woman wakes early, feeds the child, and sweeps the cave. The man is still sleeping. The mother becomes ill and someone has to fetch the tribal witch doctor in the next village. Someone must wake the father and explain, and they must decide through sign language what to do, who will go, and who will stay with the sick mother.
4. Research the techniques of brainwashing to determine how a person's ideas, feelings, and behavior can be changed.
5. Parrot talk is an imitation of sound without meaning. People who use it just like to hear themselves talk. Give examples of people who are "parroting" the remarks of others.

19 A Series of Decisions

How many decisions have you already made today?
Were they forced decisions?

Were they automatic decisions based on habits?

Were they voluntary decisions? These are the decisions you make about what to do or what not to do. Often these voluntary decisions are made from a variety of choices.

Often when you have too many choices you suffer from "overchoice." It is easier to make a decision when you have just a few varieties or alternatives to choose from.

Susan was helping her mother by doing some grocery shopping. She had a list of only five items, so she rode to the store on her bike. Everything was pretty definite on the list except for the sugar. Susan wasn't sure whether her mother meant white, brown, or confectioner's sugar. She could get hung up on light brown, dark brown, or extra fine sugar, too. She recalled that "sugar" in a recipe book meant white sugar, so that's what she decided to buy. Now how much to buy? Which brand to buy? Luckily there were only two brands and one was cheaper, so she took that one. She remembered she only had enough room for a 2.27 kg [5 lb.] bag. Phew, thank heaven the list didn't include beans.

Life is really one decision after another. The ability to think through a situation before making a decision helps you to manage your life better. It helps you to avoid frustrations and so feel less hassled. Thinking through a situation is the way to solve problems; know what is involved, weigh all sides, and make the best choice for you.

The usual reaction when a problem arises is to talk it over with friends. Some people never get past this point. They expect the advice, plan of attack, and final decisions to be supplied by others. Often friends have just as much trouble making up their minds, so if you rely on them, you may find that a problem will eat away at you for days. This can be corrected and you can save yourself some worry if you learn to "personalize" your decisions. When it comes right down to the crunch, it's you who has to make the decision and accept the consequences of that decision. Do you think a checklist or step-by-step process would help you? These points can serve as your guide for making decisions and solving problems. They aren't foolproof, but they sure can help.

1. Analyze the situation or problem.
2. Determine what your values, goals, and standards are in relation to the problem.
3. What resources will help solve the problem?
4. Consider the alternatives for solving the problem.
5. What would be the consequence of each of these alternatives?
6. Choose one alternative. Make a plan of action.
7. Accept the responsibility for your decision.
8. Evaluate your decision and your plan. How was the situation or problem improved?

Now let's apply these points to a specific problem. When you arrived at school today, you were handed the following bulletin:

Student's Bulletin

Sign up for an activity immediately! Everyone has to be a participant in at least one activity. Indicate your first, second, and third choices. Some activities have limited enrollment. The places will be filled as applications are received.

Activity	Daily 7:00 – 7:45 a.m.	Daily 3:45 – 4:30 (or longer if you wish)	Special Activity Period (Fri. only) 1:00 – 2:15 p.m.
Archery (Friday only)			
Art Group			
Astronomy Group (Tues. & Wed. only, some evenings)			
Badminton			
Basketball			
Chess			
Choir			
Debating Group (Mon. & Wed. only)			
Drama Club			
Fitness Club			
French Conversation			
Gourmet Club (Friday only)			
Gymnastics			
International Relations (Friday only)			
Jogging			
Journalism			
Librarian's Aide			
Macramé (Mon. & Wed. only)			
Math Club (Mon. & Wed. only)			
Metal Art Sculpture (Mon. & Tues. only)			
Orchestra			
Photography (Mon. & Wed. only)			
Red Cross (Friday only)			
Referee clinic (Mon. & Tues. only)			
Remedial Math (Tues. & Thurs. only)			
Science Club (Tues. & Thurs. only)			
Sewing Skills			
Study Group			
Swimming			
This Is the Law (Friday only)			
Track Club			
Typing			

Let's work through the decision-making process to help you decide which extra-curricular activities to take at school. You also have a special activity period once a week that you want to sign up for. Let's set up a step-by-step approach to help you make your decisions.

The decision to be made is . . .

Which extra activities to take before and/or after school and in the special activity period?

1. Analyze the situation or problem.

What is actually available? Do you want a change in activities or do you want to do something you have done before? Will some activities require money and a great deal of time, effort, and energy? Is there a conflict of time? What do your friends want to do?

2. Determine values, goals, and standards.

Decisions are based on what you feel is important, what you hope to accomplish, and the standards you expect for yourself from the situation. What goal are you aiming for? What activities best suit what you feel is important? Is the activity fun? Will the activity or amount of instruction meet your standards? Will the activity help you relate with others or is it done alone? Will it help you develop a new skill or talent? Will it help you meet new people?

If one of your goals is to improve your singing voice, you might join the choir. You might take typing if you have high standards about the appearance of your schoolwork, or if you want to learn a new skill, or perhaps if you want to pick up some extra money by typing term papers for college students.

3. What resources will help solve the problem?

Resources are tools you use to make a decision or do a job. Everyone is really a resource person. We all have personal skills, talents, attitudes, interests, energy, and basic knowledge that can help us make decisions, solve problems, or tackle a job or activity. A sister might be skilled at sewing; a second sister might have a real knack for finding fabric bargains, or might be knowledgeable about colors and types of fabric. They could share their resources to make their wardrobes.

Non-human resources are time, money, equipment, and community facilities. The school is a resource center with equipment to teach new skills and teachers to share their ideas and knowledge with you.

What personal resources do you have? What equipment is available? Which resource teachers sponsor the activity? Are there books in the resource room or library that give information about the activity? Can someone at home help you if you need extra instruction? Are you really interested in the activity? Do you have a positive attitude about it? Do you have the ability to cooperate and share with others if you get onto a team or become involved in a group activity? Do you have time to fit in several activities? Will too much time on extra activities hurt your grades?

4. Consider all the alternatives.

How many activities are you really interested in? Which alternatives offer fun, skill development, group friendships, and realization of future goals? What time alternatives are there for the favorite activities?

5. What is the consequence of each alternative?

If you go to an activity at 7:00, what plans must you make to get up and get to school early? Will an after-school activity cause you to miss out on time with your friends? How will you feel if this happens?

6. Choose the best alternative and make a plan of action.

Make the final decision based on facts, your values, your goals, and the most manageable time slot. You should sign up immediately so you get your first choices. A decision must be made when there is a need to take action. Your plans might be to hand in your form, tell your family to make sure that no appointments or commitments fall on those days, and mark these activity sessions on your timetable and on the calendar at home. If you make a regular commitment of this kind, let friends know when you plan to be tied up. Start earning or saving money to pay for any needed supplies or equipment. Start reading or asking about the activity. Buy or collect and prepare the required supplies and equipment for the activity. Figure out how to make adjustments in routines in order to attend early morning sessions.

7. Accept responsibility for your decision.

Now that you have made up your mind you will feel relieved. Trust your judgment and don't fret about your decision. If your choice was based on your needs and wishes, then you will not regret it. If you are informed, interested, and positive about the choice, you will be able to carry through your plan and not wonder if you made the right choice. Another plus is that you will learn not to blame others for a choice that didn't work out. Most of your decisions will work out if they are planned to suit you. You will also learn to accept the consequences and learn to adjust the plan so everything will work out in the best possible way.

8. Evaluate your decision and your plan after a decision is made and the plan is put into action.

List your choices of activity. The following questions could help you check out your choices:

- Did your decisions work out the way you expected?
- Did you make your decision soon enough to get what you wanted?
- Did you anticipate all the consequences of your decision?
- Did you manage your time wisely?
- Did your plan of action include everything to prepare you for your choices?
- Would you use this approach next year when choosing school activities?
- Could you keep a record of this procedure to help you make a similar decision?

Eventually, arriving at a solution will be so automatic that the decisions will no longer require a great deal of concern, time, or worry. Decisions or problems that are never completely solved when they first occur will keep cropping up and be a continuous source of frustration. Remember too that we all fail at different times. We learn from these failures. In order to grow as individuals and develop skills, we have to take risks. Trial and error and some failures help us to know our limits. Don't avoid decisions because you are afraid of failure. By avoiding these risks, you will also limit your chance to succeed.

What have you learned about decisions? Could you list some rules or reminders about decisions?

Reminders when making decisions

- ☑ Decision-making skills can be learned.
- ☑ Decisions are obligatory, forced, or voluntary.
- ☑ The decision-making process aids in making lasting decisions and solving problems.
- ☑ Personal decisions are based on one's goals, values, and standards.
- ☑ The type of decision determines whether immediate action is required.
- ☑ One decision often triggers off other decisions.
- ☑ Available resources can influence the success of a decision.
- ☑ Resources like time, energy, and money must be organized to eliminate waste.
- ☑ The more knowledge and information one has about a situation or problem, the more successfully one can handle it.
- ☑ A well-organized plan of action will result in a decision being carried out.
- ☑ There is always more than one solution to any problem.
- ☑ Consequences of a decision can affect many people. The outcome of the decision should be positive and bring satisfaction to those involved.
- ☑ Decisions become difficult when wants, needs, values, standards, goals, or resources are in conflict. One may have to make a compromise.
- ☑ Some decisions are beyond your control.

Resources

Personal Resources

We briefly discussed resources and how they aid in making decisions. Remember resources are what you use to get what you want. Can you list your personal resources? Did you consider any of those listed on the Personal Resource Inventory?

Personal Resource Inventory

1. friendly
2. enjoy reading
3. good listener
4. like spectator sports
5. sincere
6. athletic
7. cooperative
8. neat worker
9. enjoy children
10. sympathetic
11. good conversationalist
12. enjoy outdoor activities
13. artistic
14. sense of humor
15. creative
16. punctual
17. responsible
18. a leader
19. musical
20. follow through and finish an activity
21. good at research
22. dependable
23. open-minded
24. willing to volunteer
25. will serve on committees
26. will head a committee
27. rational
28. happy most of the time
29. will share
30. truthful
31. conservative ideas
32. way-out ideas
33. enjoy traditions
34. aware of others' needs
35. aware of others' rights

Whether you are aiming for a goal, setting up a plan of action, or solving a problem, you always need to refer to your tools or resources. These resources provide you with the means to cope with situations.

What are some of the characteristics of resources?

Resources are limited. We can only expect some resources to last for so long. Time, money, or household equipment can run out or wear out. A skill such as sewing or typing, on the other hand, is a resource that can improve as we use it.

Resources are interchangeable. One resource may be substituted for another. Homemakers who are working, for example, will use their resources of money to save themselves time and energy. They may buy convenience foods rather than prepare homemade meals. They may have their children help them clean and run the house for an increased allowance.

Resources are often shared. In a home and family, the resources are shared. Each family member has some responsibility to keep the home in good repair so it can be enjoyed by all. If a resource such as a toaster is broken by one member, all members must alter their pattern and will be put out by the inconvenience. Money is shared in the home by all, but it may be shared unequally due to certain individual needs. A child suffering from an illness or taking a special course may require more money than others for a specific period of time. Schools, playgrounds, shopping centers, and recreation centers are examples of resources shared by the general public. If equipment is destroyed in the playground, everyone suffers. Those who use the playground no longer have the use of the equipment, and the whole community must pay for repairs through tax money.

Knowledge

Knowledge is an important resource and one you can increase through experiences, or by formal learning, or by learning from other people. Knowledge is a resource that grows. You can use your store of knowledge to help you make a decision.

Knowledge also consists of knowing where to get information on a subject. The more knowledge you have on a subject or item, the easier it will be to make a choice. Sources of knowledge include:

- People whose opinions you respect
- Library books
- Magazines and newspapers
- Sales clerks
- The Department of Agriculture Extension Service
- The Consumer Advisory Council of the Federal Trade Commission
- The U.S. Department of Health and Human Services
- The National Bureau of Standards
- The Chamber of Commerce
- The Better Business Bureau
- The *Buying Guide Issue – Consumer Reports* (the facts you need before you buy)
- Community, correspondence, or school courses

These are just a few ways to gain knowledge. Can you think of more? There are many sources that can be used to gain information on any topic. Have you considered all the people in your family? Make a list of all the types of information contributed by the community and family members.

Attitudes

Your attitudes are ideas you have that are colored by your emotions or feelings. Your attitudes, as you know, will dictate your behavior. They will determine whether you will act positively or negatively towards something. Your attitudes tell others the type of person you are.

A student's attitudes towards a second language will affect his or her success in that language. If you say you don't have a use for languages, you are approaching the subject with a negative rather than with a positive attitude.

If people have a positive attitude towards other people, they will most likely be accepted in a positive manner. If they are not positive about themselves but go about complaining and downgrading themselves, they will drive away those people who would normally be attracted to them. An open or positive attitude towards resources, people, ideas, the future, and decision making will lead to a more satisfactory and successful life.

Interests

Each person has specific interests. Some have many, while others have a select few. We do not share all the interests of our family members or friends.

A father who was athletic in his youth may pass this interest in sports on to his children. Interests are often learned from family members because we see how satisfying they have found these activities.

Being interested in the world about you, in others, and in learning will provide you with the knowledge and the positive attitude necessary to make life a success.

Skills and Abilities

Right from the day you are born you have certain abilities. Skills are learned through the use of your physical and mental abilities. Skills are abilities perfected to the point where they are carried out with a minimum of effort. The result is a satisfactory performance. Skills require muscular coordination, good management of resources, understanding of self and others, and emotional control.

☑ A skill requires study, demonstration, and observation.
☑ A skill requires practice.

We often learn a skill by exploring or figuring it out ourselves. At first, we may be clumsy; we may become frustrated; and we may waste time, materials, and energy.

A skill can
☑ contribute to an individual's feeling of personal satisfaction and worth.
☑ enable a person to meet some of the demands placed upon him- or herself at home.
☑ make it easier for an individual to find a job.
☑ save time, money, and energy.
☑ increase opportunities for creativity and personal recognition.

Think about your attitude and interest in working in the kitchen to prepare food. Some people look on this as a dreaded job. Be positive and develop your resources of knowledge and skills and organize a way to manage in the kitchen.

When you first start to prepare your own lunches or dinners, use good management by employing the best equipment and available ingredients. You should choose a food that can be prepared in the time available. You must understand yourself enough to recognize what recipes you are capable of preparing successfully. You must also control emotions so that you don't get stirred up, but can think clearly and calmly and solve any problems that may arise.

If you had a bank that credited your account each morning with $86,400, that carried over no balance from day to day, allowed you to keep no cash amount, and every evening canceled whatever part of the amount you had failed to use during the day, what would you do? Draw out every cent every day, of course, and use it to your advantage.

Well, you have such a bank and its name is "time." Every morning it credits you with 86,400 seconds. Every night it rules off as lost whatever of this you have failed to invest to good purpose. It carries over no balances. It allows no overdrafts. Each day it opens a new account for you. Each night it burns the records of the day. If you fail to use the day's deposits, the loss is yours. There is no going back. There is no drawing against "tomorrow." It is up to each of us to invest this precious fund of hours, minutes, and seconds in order to get from it the utmost in health, happiness, and success.

Non-Human Resources

Time

Can time be managed? Yes, it can. You choose to use or not to use time. Use of time is influenced by:
- your goals, values, and standards,
- your responsibilities in life,
- your ability to plan, organize, and perform a task.

You can use a plan to help you organize your time. We tend to expect ourselves to remember everything, but we can save ourselves upsets by using a plan or by making a schedule for certain activities. What type of plan is best to help you remember what you want to do?

Roxanne enjoys learning to play the piano, but she is always neglecting to find time to practice for her next lesson. She has the tendency to postpone her practice until just before bedtime and then often is too tired. Suggest a half-hour block of time that she might use for piano practice.

Try to balance your time. This will allow you to have enough time to spend on your interests. Organizing for balance includes scheduling school, friends, leisure, health, sleep, grooming, homework, fun. Inflexible activities such as going to school or meeting an airplane or serving meals are the basis of a time plan. Flexible activities, such as hobbies or sports, are scheduled around the inflexible activities.

Money

What does money mean to you? Write down the first things that come to your mind when you hear the word money. Would you say "Money is happiness," "Money isn't everything," "Coins are round, let them roll," "Money is the root of all evil," or "Money is meant to be spent"?

Divide into pairs or groups of three. Choose one of the following phrases and write a case study to illustrate it, keeping in mind how you use this resource in making a decision. Prepare one or two questions to ask the class after you present your case study.

"Money" means . . .
- ☑ impulse buying
- ☑ label watching
- ☑ comparison shopping
- ☑ planned spending
- ☑ a bargain is not always a bargain
- ☑ consumer rights
- ☑ consumer responsibilities
- ☑ buying power
- ☑ planned obsolescence (as in fashions)
- ☑ interest charges
- ☑ savings plan
- ☑ shopping ethics
- ☑ dollar sense
- ☑ informed shopper

Career Decisions

One of the major decisions a person is faced with is choosing a career. Do you feel you have lots of time yet to think about it? Do you think if you know more about what work you want to do in the future you could start preparing yourself? Could you at least figure out what courses to take in high school?

Young people don't always know what careers are available to them. You may be familiar only with the jobs of those around you. Did you know there are about 23,000 kinds of jobs? Have you thought of some careers you may want to pursue?

Let's look at some case studies. Can these situations help you?

The guidance office has just handed out application forms for each student to choose next year's subjects. In three days' time, the application has to be handed back with choices filled in. Dave was forced to make more concrete plans about his future education. He likes people and wants to be able to help them. A career would have to be interesting, and he especially enjoys contact with children. The three jobs that are of interest to him now are pediatrician, social worker, or teacher. He knows he wants to go to college, and he investigates which subjects he needs to allow him to enter each of the three fields. Dave has made some decisions based on his interests and abilities and realizes he has to narrow his choices in the next few years.

Kimberly enjoys the outdoors. She dislikes the idea of pursuing an occupation that will mean working inside most of the time. She feels a career in forestry will be ideal, although she is rather vague about what a forester actually does. Kimberly wants to go to a college which is well known as having a good forestry school. She suddenly realizes when she is handed her application form that she must immediately increase her knowledge of the field of forestry and find out which courses she should be taking.

1. Identify the steps in the decision-making process used by *either* Kimberly *or* Dave.
2. Identify missing steps in the decision making of *either* Kimberly *or* Dave.

Carolyn and Bruce have no interest in going to college. Bruce was bored with high school, and left during his junior year. He subsequently had a series of jobs which included stock boy in a supermarket, farm laborer, and letter carrier. Bruce is now married, has a family, and is still trying to find the "right job." He has wished many times that he had trained to become an accountant or a drafter. Where can he obtain training for these jobs? Will he have to quit his present job? What are the employment possibilities? What salary could he make in these occupations?

Carolyn is very talented in art. She is an excellent poster designer and a skillful dressmaker. She would like to become a fashion designer. It is not possible for her to take further training after high school. In what occupations might she find satisfaction for her aptitudes and interests? What information could you give Carolyn regarding these occupations?

Dan realizes he is going to have to clarify his goals and make a firmer decision about his future. Dan is fifteen years old. He is a pleasant, popular boy with a rather happy-go-lucky attitude towards school and life, but he is failing ninth grade. His verbal and math ability scores are below average, which means that he will probably not be able to do well in an academic program. His school record is poor. His homework is not too bad since his friends help him, but on tests he nearly always scores near the bottom of the class. He does well in industrial arts, and it has been suggested he take a vocational course.

Dan is an athlete and plays on school and community teams in basketball and baseball. He has two younger sisters at home. An older sister dropped out of high school after tenth grade to get married and now lives in another state. Dan has one older brother who is twenty-one. He completed high school and has just completed community college with a diploma in building technology. He has been offered a good job in Arizona.

Dan's Abilities	Dan's School Record		
math – below average		Grade 8	Grade 9
verbal – below average	English	52	51
	Geography	54	52
	History	51	43
	Math	50	38
	Science	56	51
	Shop	74	80

Dan's father was angry over Dan's last report card. He said Dan was wasting his time in school, and if he didn't improve next year, he would have to leave school and go to work.

Dan is not anxious to leave school. He does not mind going to classes and enjoys sports and being with his friends. He has never thought much about what kind of career he would like.

His girlfriend is a good student. She keeps urging Dan to stay in school and try to graduate.

1. What reasons would you give Dan for staying in school?
2. What reasons would you give Dan for leaving school?
3. What course should Dan select to be most successful?

Careers Quiz (Use a separate sheet of paper.)

1. Job characteristics that are most important to me (rate yourself 1 to 15, 1 being highest):
   _____ interesting work
   _____ leader of other people
   _____ good chance for promotion
   _____ provides security
   _____ opportunity to travel
   _____ gives me plenty of leisure time
   _____ opportunity to help people
   _____ opportunity for individual success
   _____ gives me prestige
   _____ has my approval
   _____ provides a good income
   _____ opportunity to be creative
   _____ freedom to make my own decisions
   _____ work alone
   _____ variety of experiences

2. Copy this list.
   Draw a line through the careers that do *NOT* appeal to you.

accountant	lawyer
actor	letter carrier
anthropologist	manager
armed forces	marine biologist
banker	mechanic
carpenter	mortician
chef	musician
child-care aide	nurse
chiropractor	nurses' aide
construction engineer	ornithologist
cosmetician	pharmacist
dental hygienist	photographer
dentist	physiotherapist
designer	police officer
dietitian	real estate agent
doctor	recreation specialist
electrician	salesclerk
engineer	social worker
farmer	stenographer
flight attendant	tailor
forester	teacher
interior decorator	veterinarian
jet pilot	waiter or waitress
journalist	
lab technician	

3. Three careers that have some appeal to me are:
   _____, _____, _____.

Now that you have decided which careers appeal to you, arrange to have interviews with persons in these fields. Here are some questions that you might ask during the interview. These questions are very general. Adapt them and add others that apply specifically to the career that interests you.
- Why did you choose this career?
- What aspect of your work provides you with the most satisfaction?
- What special education is required for your job?
- What skills and abilities do you recommend for someone who is considering this career?
- Do you have to bring work home? If so, how often?
- Are you tired when you get home?
- Do you feel any pressures related to your job?
- What would be reasons for a person not succeeding in this job?
- What are some reasons for firing people in this job?
- What new skills have you learned since you started this job?
- Has this job caused you to move often?
- Could new inventions eliminate or drastically change your field?

Conclusion

Do you agree that your life is a series of decisions? There are many times when life seems very depressing or when problems are overwhelming. Because you are so emotionally involved with a situation, you don't think very clearly. By following the decision-making process, step-by-step, it becomes apparent that the problem can be worked out. You may become aware of a resource you hadn't counted on or you may think of some better alternatives. By being aware of the resources that are available to help you and by developing your own personal resources, you will find decision making easier and life more enjoyable.

Word Power

attitudes
eight steps in decision making
forced decisions
non-human resources
skills
voluntary decisions

Take Action

1. The student council is trying to get the student body to become more organized around the school. Its main concerns are: (a) the mess in the cafeteria and (b) few volunteers to plan school activities. The council launches a campaign using management and organizational slogans to get students to be more positive about the school and other resources. Suggest some management slogans, for example: "Management is using what you have to get what you want," or "This is not my school. It is our cooperative."

2. Discuss how the following situations can cause you to be a poor manager:
   (a) being extremely tired
   (b) being emotionally upset
   (c) feeling sick
   (d) being an impulsive person
3. Identify one habit that can help you save money, time, energy, and keep you from confusion. List the class ideas on the board.
4. Each student is to bring a picture or cartoon that shows people making a decision. Write original captions under each picture.
5. Discuss the obligations of using non-human resources.
6. Think of a skill that you have learned. Write a description or draw pictures to illustrate each step in your development of that skill.

Appendix

X: A Fabulous Child's Story

By Lois Gould

Once upon a time, a baby named X was born. This baby was named X so that nobody could tell whether it was a boy or a girl. Its parents could tell, of course, but they couldn't tell anybody else. They couldn't even tell Baby X, at first.

You see, it was all part of a very important Secret Scientific Xperiment, known officially as Project Baby X. The smartest scientists had set up this Xperiment at a cost of Xactly 23 billion dollars and 72 cents, which might seem like a lot for just one baby, even a very important Xperimental baby. But when you remember the prices of things like strained carrots and stuffed bunnies, and popcorn for the movies and booster shots for camp, let alone 28 shiny quarters from the tooth fairy, you begin to see how it adds up.

Also, long before Baby X was born, all those scientists had to be paid to work out the details of the Xperiment, and to write the *Official Instruction Manual* for Baby X's parents and, most important of all, to find the right set of parents to bring up Baby X. These parents had to be selected very carefully. Thousands of volunteers had to take thousands of tests and answer thousands of tricky questions. Almost everybody failed because, it turned out, almost everybody really wanted either a baby boy or a baby girl, and not Baby X at all. Also, most everybody was afraid that a Baby X would be a lot more trouble than a boy or a girl. (They were probably right, the scientists admitted, but Baby X needed parents who wouldn't *mind* the Xtra trouble.)

There were families with grandparents named Milton and Agatha, who didn't see why the baby couldn't be named Milton or Agatha instead of X, even if it *was* an X. There were families with aunts who insisted on knitting tiny dresses and uncles who insisted on sending tiny baseball mitts. Worst of all, there were families that already had other children who couldn't be trusted to keep the secret. Certainly not if they knew the secret was worth 23 billion dollars and 72 cents – and all you had to do was take one little peek at Baby X in the bathtub to know if it was a boy or a girl.

But, finally, the scientists found the Joneses, who really wanted to raise an X more than any other kind of baby – no matter how much trouble it would be. Ms. and Mr. Jones had to promise they would take equal turns caring for X, and feeding it, and singing it lullabies. And they had to promise never to hire any baby-sitters. The government scientists knew perfectly well that a baby-sitter would probably peek at X in the bathtub, too.

The day the Joneses brought their baby home, lots of friends and relatives came over to see it. None of them knew about the secret Xperiment, though. So the first thing they asked was what kind of a baby X was. When the Joneses smiled and said, "It's an X!" nobody knew what to say. They couldn't say, "Look at her cute little dimples!" And they couldn't say, "Look at his husky little biceps!" And they couldn't even say just plain "kitchy-coo." In fact, they all thought the Joneses were playing some kind of rude joke.

But, of course, the Joneses were not joking. "It's an X" was absolutely all they would say. And that made the friends and relatives very angry. The relatives all felt embarrassed about having an X in the family. "People will think there's something wrong with it!" some of them whispered. "There *is* something wrong with it!" others whispered back.

"Nonsense!" the Joneses told them all cheerfully. "What could possibly be wrong with this perfectly adorable X?"

Nobody could answer that, except Baby X, who had just finished its bottle. Baby X's answer was a loud, satisfied burp.

Clearly, nothing at all was wrong. Nevertheless, none of the relatives felt comfortable about buying a present for a Baby X. The cousins who sent the baby a tiny football helmet would not come and visit any more. And the neighbors who sent a pink-flowered romper suit pulled their shades down when the Joneses passed their house.

The *Official Instruction Manual* had warned the new parents that this would happen, so they didn't fret about it. Besides, they were too busy with Baby X and the hundreds of different Xercises for treating it properly.

Ms. and Mr. Jones had to be Xtra careful about how they played with little X. They knew that if they kept bouncing it up in the air and saying how *strong* and *active* it was, they'd be treating it more like a boy than an X. But if all they did was cuddle it and kiss it and tell it how *sweet* and *dainty* it was, they'd be treating it more like a girl than an X.

On page 1,654 of the *Official Instruction Manual,* the scientists prescribed: "plenty of bouncing and plenty of cuddling, *both.* X ought to be strong and sweet and active. Forget about *dainty* altogether."

Meanwhile, the Joneses were worrying about other problems. Toys, for instance. And clothes. On his first shopping trip, Mr. Jones told the store clerk, "I need some clothes and toys for my new baby." The clerk smiled and said, "Well, now, is it a boy or a girl?" "It's an X," Mr. Jones said, smiling back. But the clerk got all red in the face and said huffily, "In *that* case, I'm afraid I can't help you, sir." So Mr. Jones wandered helplessly up and down the aisles trying to find out what X needed. But everything in the store was piled up in sections marked "Boys" or "Girls." There were "Boys' Pajamas" and "Girls' Underwear" and "Boys' Fire Engines" and "Girls' Housekeeping Sets." Mr. Jones went home without buying anything for X. That night he and Ms. Jones consulted page 2,326 of the *Official Instruction Manual.* "Buy plenty of everything!" it said firmly.

So they bought plenty of sturdy blue pajamas in the Boys' Department and cheerful flowered underwear in the Girls' Department. And they bought all kinds of toys. A boy doll that made pee-pee and cried, "Pa-pa." And a girl doll that talked in three languages and said, "I am the Pres-i-dent of Gen-er-al Mo-tors." They also bought a storybook about a brave princess who rescued a handsome prince from his ivory tower, and another one about a sister and brother who grew up to be a baseball star and a ballet star, and you had to guess which was which.

The head scientists of Project Baby X checked all their purchases and told them to keep up the good work. They also reminded the Joneses to see page 4,629 of the *Manual,* where it said, "Never make Baby X feel *embarrassed* or *ashamed* about what it wants to play with. And if X gets dirty climbing rocks, never say 'Nice little Xes don't get dirty climbing rocks.'"

Likewise, it said, "If X falls down and cries, never say 'Brave little Xes don't cry.' Because, of course, nice little Xes *do* get dirty, and brave little Xes *do* cry. No matter how dirty X gets, or how hard it cries, don't worry. It's all part of the Xperiment."

Whenever the Joneses pushed Baby X's stroller in the park, smiling strangers would come over and coo: "Is that a boy or a girl?" The Joneses would smile back and say, "It's an X." The strangers would stop smiling then, and often snarl something nasty — as if the Joneses had snarled at *them.*

By the time X grew big enough to play with other children, the Joneses' troubles had grown bigger, too. Once a little girl grabbed X's shovel in the sandbox, and zonked X on the head with it. "Now, now, Tracy," the little girl's mother began to scold, "little girls mustn't hit little — " and she turned to ask X, "Are you a little boy or a little girl, dear?"

Mr. Jones, who was sitting near the sandbox, held his breath and crossed his fingers.

X smiled politely at the lady, even though X's head had never been zonked so hard in its life. "I'm a little X," X replied.

"You're a *what?*" the lady exclaimed angrily. "You're a little b-r-a-t, you mean!"

"But little girls mustn't hit little Xes, either!" said X, retrieving the shovel with another polite smile. "What good does hitting do, anyway?"

X's father, who was still holding his breath, finally let it out, uncrossed his fingers, and grinned back at X.

And at their next secret Project Baby X meeting, the scientists grinned, too. Baby X was doing fine.

But then it was time for X to start school. The Joneses were really worried about this, because school was even more full of rules for boys and girls, and there were no rules for Xes. The teacher would tell boys to form one line, and girls to form another line. There would be boys' games and girls' games, and boys' secrets and girls' secrets. The school library would have a list of recommended books for girls, and a different list of recommended books for boys. There would even be a bathroom marked BOYS and another one marked GIRLS. Pretty soon boys and girls would hardly talk to each other. What would happen to poor little X?

The Joneses spent weeks consulting their *Instruction Manual* (there were 249½ pages of advice under "First Day of School"), and attending urgent special conferences with the smart scientists of Project Baby X.

The scientists had to make sure that X's mother had taught X how to throw and catch a ball properly, and that X's father had been sure to teach X what to serve at a doll's tea party. X had to know how to shoot marbles and how to jump rope and, most of all, what to say when the Other Children asked whether X was a Boy or a Girl.

Finally, X was ready. The Joneses helped X button on a nice new pair of red-and-white checked overalls, and sharpened six pencils for X's nice new pencilbox, and marked X's name clearly on all the books in its nice new bookbag. X brushed its teeth and combed its hair, which just about covered its ears, and remembered to put a napkin in its lunchbox.

The Joneses had asked X's teacher if the class could line up alphabetically, instead of forming separate lines for boys and girls. And they had asked if X could use the principal's bathroom, because it wasn't marked anything except BATHROOM. X's teacher promised to take care of all those problems. But nobody could help X with the biggest problem of all – Other Children.

Nobody in X's class had ever known an X before. What would they think? How would X make friends?

You couldn't tell what X was by studying its clothes – overalls don't even button right-to-left, like girls' clothes, or left-to-right, like boys' clothes. And you couldn't guess whether X had a girl's short haircut or a boy's long haircut. And it was very hard to tell by the games X liked to play. Either X played ball very well for a girl, or else X played house very well for a boy.

Some of the children tried to find out by asking X tricky questions, like "Who's your favorite sports star?" That was easy. X had two favorite sports stars: a girl jockey named Robyn Smith and a boy archery champion named Robin Hood. Then they asked, "What's your favorite TV program?" And that was even easier. X's favorite TV program was "Lassie," which stars a girl dog played by a boy dog.

When X said that its favorite toy was a doll, everyone decided that X must be a girl. But then X said that the doll was really a robot, and that X had computerized it, and that it was programmed to bake fudge brownies and then clean up the kitchen. After X told them that, the other children gave up guessing what X was. All they knew was they'd sure like to see X's doll.

After school, X wanted to play with the other children. "How about shooting some baskets in the gym?" X asked the girls. But all they did was make faces and giggle behind X's back.

"How about weaving some baskets in the arts and crafts room?" X asked the boys. But they all made faces and giggled behind X's back, too.

That night, Ms. and Mr. Jones asked X how things had gone at school. X told them sadly that the lessons were okay, but otherwise school was a terrible place for an X. It seemed as if Other Children would never want an X for a friend.

Once more, the Joneses reached for their *Instruction Manual*. Under "Other Children," they found the following message: "What did you Xpect? *Other Children* have to obey all the silly boy-girl rules, because their parents taught them to. Lucky X – you don't have to stick to the rules at all! All you have to do is be yourself. P.S. We're not saying it'll be easy."

X liked being itself. But X cried a lot that night, partly because it felt afraid. So X's father held X tight, and cuddled it, and couldn't help crying a little, too. And X's mother cheered them both up by reading an Xciting story about an enchanted prince called Sleeping Handsome, who woke up when Princess Charming kissed him.

The next morning, they all felt much better, and little X went back to school with a brave smile and a clean pair of red-and-white checked overalls.

There was a seven-letter-word spelling bee in class that day. And a seven-lap boys' relay race in the gym. And a seven-layer-cake baking contest in the girls' kitchen corner. X won the spelling bee. X also won the relay race. And X almost won the baking contest, except it forgot to light the oven. Which only proves that nobody's perfect.

One of the Other Children noticed something else, too. He said: "Winning or losing doesn't seem to count to X. X seems to have fun being good at boys' skills *and* girls' skills."

"Come to think of it," said another one of the Other Children, "maybe X is having twice as much fun as we are."

So after school that day, the girl who beat X at the baking contest gave X a big slice of her prizewinning cake. And the boy X beat in the relay race asked X to race him home.

From then on, some really funny things began to happen. Susie, who sat next to X in class, suddenly refused to wear pink dresses to school any more. She insisted on wearing red-and-white checked overalls – just like X's. Overalls, she told her parents, were much better for climbing monkey bars.

Then Jim, the class football nut, started wheeling his little sister's doll carriage around the football field. He'd put on his entire football uniform, except for the helmet. Then he'd put the helmet *in* the carriage, lovingly tucked under an old set of shoulder pads. Then he'd start jogging around the field, pushing the carriage and singing "Rockabye Baby" to his football helmet. He told his family that X did the same thing, so it must be okay. After all, X was now the team's star quarterback.

Susie's parents were horrified by her behavior, and Jim's parents were worried sick about his. But the worst came when the twins, Joe and Peggy, decided to share everything with each other. Peggy used Joe's hockey skates, and his microscope, and took half his newspaper route. Joe used Peggy's needlepoint kit, and her cookbooks, and took two of her three baby-sitting jobs. Peggy started running the lawn mower, and Joe started running the vacuum cleaner.

Their parents weren't one bit pleased with Peggy's wonderful biology experiments, or with Joe's terrific needlepoint pillows. They didn't care that Peggy mowed the lawn better, and that Joe vacuumed the carpet better. In fact, they were furious. It's all that little X's fault, they agreed. Just because X doesn't know what it is, or what it's supposed to be, it wants to get everybody *else* mixed up, too!

Peggy and Joe were forbidden to play with X any more. So was Susie, and then Jim, and then *all* the Other Children. But it was too late; the Other Children stayed mixed up and happy and free, and refused to go back to the way they'd been before X.

Finally, Joe and Peggy's parents decided to call an emergency meeting of the school's Parents' Association, to discuss "The X Problem." They sent a report to the principal stating that X was a "disruptive influence." They demanded immediate action. The Joneses, they said, should be *forced* to tell whether X was a boy or a girl. And then X should be *forced* to behave like whichever it was. If the Joneses refused to tell, the Parents' Association said, then X must take an Xamination. The school psychiatrist must Xamine it physically and mentally, and issue a full report. If X's test showed it was a boy, it would have to obey all the boys' rules. If it proved to be a girl, X would have to obey all the girls' rules.

And if X turned out to be some kind of mixed-up misfit, then X should be Xpelled from the school. Immediately!

The principal was very upset. Disruptive influence? Mixed-up misfit? But X was an Xcellent student. All the teachers said it was a delight to have X in their classes. X was president of the student council. X had won first prize in the talent show, and second prize in the art show, and honorable mention in the science fair, and six athletic events on field day, including the potato race.

Nevertheless, insisted the Parents' Association, X is a Problem Child. X is the Biggest Problem Child we have ever seen!

So the principal reluctantly notified X's parents that numerous complaints about X's behavior had come to the school's attention. And that after the psychiatrist's Xamination, the school would decide what to do about X.

The Joneses reported this at once to the scientists, who referred them to page 85,759 of the *Instruction Manual*. "Sooner or later," it said, "X will have to be Xamined by a psychiatrist. This may be the only way any of us will know for sure whether X is mixed up – or whether everyone else is."

The night before X was to be Xamined, the Joneses tried not to let X see how worried they were. "What if?" Mr. Jones would say. And Ms. Jones would reply, "No use worrying." Then a few minutes later, Ms. Jones would say, "What if?" and Mr. Jones would reply, "No use worrying."

X just smiled at them both, and hugged them hard and didn't say much of anything. X was thinking, What if – ? And then X thought: No use worrying.

At Xactly 9 o'clock the next day, X reported to the school psychiatrist's office. The principal, along with a committee from the Parents' Association, X's teacher, X's classmates, and Ms. and Mr. Jones, waited in the hall outside. Nobody knew the details of the tests X was to be given, but everybody knew they'd be *very* hard, and that they'd reveal Xactly what everyone wanted to know about X, but were afraid to ask.

It was terribly quiet in the hall. Almost spooky. Once in a while, they would hear a strange noise inside the room. There were buzzes. And a beep or two. And several bells. An occasional light would flash under the door. The Joneses thought it was a white light, but the principal thought it was blue. Two or three children swore it was either yellow or green. And the Parents' Committee missed it completely.

Through it all, you could hear the psychiatrist's low voice, asking hundreds of questions, and X's higher voice, answering hundreds of answers.

The whole thing took so long that everyone knew it must be the most complete Xamination anyone had ever had to take. Poor X, the Joneses thought. Serves X right, the Parents' Committee thought. I wouldn't like to be in X's overalls right now, the children thought.

At last, the door opened. Everyone crowded around to hear the results. X didn't look any different; in fact, X was smiling. But the psychiatrist looked terrible. He looked as if he was crying!

"What happened?" everyone began shouting. Had X done something disgraceful? "I wouldn't be a bit surprised!" muttered Peggy and Joe's parents. "Did X flunk the *whole* test?" cried Susie's parents. "Or just the most important part?" yelled Jim's parents.

"Oh, dear," sighed Mr. Jones.
"Oh, dear," sighed Ms. Jones.
"Sssh," ssshed the principal. "The psychiatrist is trying to speak."

Wiping his eyes and clearing his throat, the psychiatrist began, in a hoarse whisper. "In my opinion," he whispered – you could tell he must be very upset – "in my opinion, young X here – "

"Yes? Yes?" shouted a parent impatiently.

"Sssh!" ssshed the principal.

"Young *Sssh* here, I mean young X," said the doctor, frowning, "is just about – "

"Just about *what*? Let's have it!" shouted another parent.

". . . just about the *least* mixed-up child I've ever Xamined!" said the psychiatrist.

"Yay for X!" yelled one of the children. And then the others began yelling, too. Clapping and cheering and jumping up and down.

"*SSSH!*" SSShed the principal, but nobody did.

The Parents' Committee was angry and bewildered. How *could* X have passed the whole Xamination. Didn't X have an *identity* problem? Wasn't X mixed up at *all?* Wasn't X *any* kind of a misfit? How could it *not* be, when it didn't even *know* what it was? And why was the psychiatrist crying?

Actually, he had stopped crying and was smiling politely through his tears. "Don't you see?" he said. "I'm crying because it's wonderful! X has absolutely no identity problem! X isn't one bit mixed up! As for being a misfit – ridiculous! X knows perfectly well what it is! Don't you, X?" The doctor winked. X winked back.

"But what *is* X?" shrieked Peggy and Joe's parents. *"We* still want to know what it is!"

"Ah, yes," said the doctor, winking again. "Well, don't worry. You'll all know one of these days. And you won't need me to tell you."

"What? What does he mean?" some of the parents grumbled suspiciously.

Susie and Peggy and Joe all answered at once. "He means that by the time X's sex matters, it won't be a secret any more!"

With that, the doctor began to push through the crowd toward X's parents. "How do you do," he said, somewhat stiffly. And then he reached out to hug them both. "If I ever have an X of my own," he whispered, "I sure hope you'll lend me your instruction manual."

Needless to say, the Joneses were very happy. The Project Baby X scientists were rather pleased, too. So were Susie, Jim, Peggy, Joe, and all the Other Children. The Parents' Association wasn't, but they had promised to accept the psychiatrist's report, and not make any more trouble. They even invited Ms. and Mr. Jones to become honorary members, which they did.

Later that day, X's friends put on their red-and-white checked overalls and went over to see X. They found X in the back yard, playing with a very tiny baby that none of them had ever seen before. The baby was wearing very tiny red-and-white checked overalls.

"How do you like our new baby?" X asked the Other Children proudly.

"It's got cute dimples," said Jim.

"It's got husky biceps, too," said Susie.

"What kind of baby is it?" asked Joe and Peggy.

X frowned at them. "Can't you tell?" Then X broke into a big, mischievous grin. *"It's a Y!"*

Bibliography

Albrecht, Margaret. *Parents and Teenagers: Getting through to Each Other*. New York: Parents' Magazine Press, 1972.

Ames, Louise Bates. *Child Care and Development*. New York: J.B. Lippincott Co., 1970.

Argyle, Michael. *Bodily Communication*. New York: International Universities Press, 1975.

Brisbane, Holly. *The Developing Child*. Peoria, IL: Bennett Publishing Co., 1980.

Cadwallader, Sharon. *Cooking Adventures for Kids*. Boston: Houghton Mifflin Co., 1974.

Childress, Alice. *A Hero Ain't Nothin' but a Sandwich*. New York: Avon Books, 1977.

Cohen, Dorothy H., and Stern, Virginia. *Observing and Recording the Behavior of Young Children*. New York: Teachers College Press, Columbia Univ., 1978.

Collier, James L. *The Hard Life of the Teenager*. New York: Scholastic Book Services, 1972.

Cooper, Terry T., and Ratner, Marilyn. *Many Hands Cooking: An International Cookbook for Girls and Boys*. New York: Thomas Y. Crowell Co., 1974.

Craig, Hazel Thompson. *Thresholds to Adult Living*. Peoria, IL: Bennett Publishing Co., 1981.

Dodson, Fitzhugh. *How to Parent*. New York: New American Library, 1973.

Down, Edith, and Pisesky, Sharon. *What's to Eat?*, rev. Tybe Kahn. Peoria, IL: Bennett Publishing Co., 1981.

Draper, Mary Wanda, and Draper, Henry E. *Caring for Children*. Peoria, IL: Bennett Publishing Co., 1979.

Emerson, Geraldine M., ed. *Aging*. New York: Academic Press, 1977.

Fowke, Edith. *Sally Go Round the Sun*. Garden City, NY: Doubleday & Co., 1970.

Freed, Alvyn M. *TA for Teens (and Other Important People)*. Sacramento, CA: Jalmar Press, 1976.

Gardner, Richard. *The Boys and Girls Book about Divorce*. New York: Jason Aronson, 1971.

Ginott, Haim G. *Between Parent and Child*. New York: Avon Books, 1973.

──────. *Between Parent and Teenager*. New York: Avon Books, 1973.

Goldberg, Stella, and Deutsch, Francine. *Life-Span: Individual and Family Development*. Monterey, CA: Brooks/Cole Publishing Co., 1977.

Good, Paul. *The Individual*. New York: Time-Life Books, 1974.

Goodwin, Mary T., and Pollen, Gerry. *Creative Food Experiences for Children*. Washington, DC: Center for Science in the Public Interest, 1977.

Hall, Edward T. *The Hidden Dimension*. Garden City, NY: Doubleday & Co., 1969.

Hildebrand, Verna. *Parenting and Teaching Young Children*. New York: McGraw-Hill Book Co., 1981.

Hurlock, Elizabeth. *Child Growth and Development*. New York: McGraw-Hill Book Co., 1978.

Kahn, Charles H., et al. *Going Places with Your Personality: A Guide to Successful Living*. Belmont, CA: Fearon-Pitman Publishers, 1971.

Kelly, Joan, and Landers, Eddye Eubanks. *Today's Teen*. Peoria, IL: Bennett Publishing Co., 1981.

Klemer, Richard H., and Smith, Rebecca M. *Teaching about Family Relationships*. Minneapolis, MN: Burgess Publishing Co., 1975.

Kowtaluk, Helen. *Discovering Food*. Peoria, IL: Bennett Publishing Co., 1978.

Lee, Joanna. *I Want to Keep My Baby*. New York: New American Library, 1977.

Limbacher, Walter J. *Becoming Myself*. Fairfield, NJ: Pflaum/Standard, 1970.

Lipke, Jean C. *Heredity*. Minneapolis, MN: Lerner Publications Co., 1971.

Maurus, J. *Growing Old Gracefully*. Canfield, OH: Alba Books, 1977.

Mayle, Peter. *What's Happening to Me?* Secaucus, NJ: Lyle Stuart, 1975.

Mead, Margaret. *Culture and Commitment – the New Relationships between the Generations in the 1970's*. Garden City, NY: Doubleday & Co., 1978.

Mitchell, J. J. *Adolescence: Some Critical Issues*. New York: Holt, Rinehart & Winston, 1972.

Papalia, Diane E., and Olds, Sally W. *A Child's World: Infancy through Adolescence*. New York: McGraw-Hill Book Co., 1975.

Queen, Stuart A., and Habenstein, Robert W. *The Family in Various Cultures*. New York: Harper & Row Publishers, 1974.

Riker, Audrey Palm, and Riker, Charles. *Finding My Way*. Peoria, IL: Bennett Publishing Co., 1979.

———. *Me: Understanding Myself and Others*. Peoria, IL: Bennett Publishing Co., 1977.

Robertson, Elizabeth, and Wood, Margaret. *Today's Child: A Modern Guide to Baby Care and Child Training*. New York: Charles Scribner's Sons, 1972.

Sasse, Connie R. *Person to Person*. Peoria, IL: Bennett Publishing Co., 1982.

Sathre, Freda S., et al. *Let's Talk: An Introduction to Interpersonal Communication*. Glenview, IL: Scott, Foresman & Co., 1977.

Satir, Virginia. *Self Esteem: A Declaration*. Millbrae, CA: Celestial Arts Publishing Co., 1975.

Schaefer, Charles E. *How to Influence Children: A Handbook of Practical Parenting Skills*. New York: Van Nostrand Reinhold Co., 1978.

Simon, Sidney, et al. *Values Clarification: A Handbook of Practical Strategies for Teachers and Students*. New York: Hart Associates, 1972.

Smaridge, Norah, and Hunter, Hilda. *The Teen-Ager's Guide to Hobbies for Here and Now*. New York: Dodd, Mead & Co., 1974.

Smart, Mollie S., and Smart, Russell C. *Adolescents: Development and Relationships*. New York: Macmillan Publishing Co., 1978.

Sterling, Nora. *You Would If You Loved Me*. New York: Avon Books, 1974.

Tanner, James. *Growth at Adolescence*. New York: J.B. Lippincott Co., 1962.

Tubbs, Stewart L., and Moss, Sylvia. *Human Communication*. New York: Random House, 1977.

White, Burton L. *The First Three Years of Life*. Englewood Cliffs, NJ: Prentice-Hall, 1975.

White, Marian E., et al. *High Interest – Easy Reading for Junior and Senior High School Students*. Urbana, IL: National Council of Teachers of English, 1979.

Index

Acceptability. *See* Social acceptability
Accidents, 21-2
Acne. *See* Skin problems
Adolescence, changes during, 3, 12; dual membership, 174-6. *See also* Puberty
Advertisements, 7, 29, 140
Alcohol, 21-2
Attitudes, 226

Baby-sitting, 154-71; and child safety, 162-3; and discipline, 161; ideas, 164-9; preparation for, 160; rules for, 157, 160; workshop, 160
Bar Mitzvah, 10
Behavior, 184; communication, 203-4; control, 32-3, 130; coping, 111-12; elementary schoolers, 159; infants to toddlers, 158; preschool, 158; responsible, 42
Beliefs. *See* Values
Beriberi, and alcohol, 22
Bias, 211-13
Birth order, 148-9
Body language, 198-200

Careers. *See* Occupations, future
Change, 106-15; body, 108; causes of, 106; coping with, 106, 111-12, 130; in expectations, 110; response to, 110; to roles, 62; social, 109; to values, 90
Child development. *See* Development, child
Chromosomes, 47
Communication, 184, 194, 204-5, 216-17; attitudes towards, 206-7; behavior, 203-4; and bias, 211-13; and body language, 198-200; components of, 201; and dating, 185, 187-90; distance, 214-15; improving, 216; and listening, 209; non-verbal, 195-200, 206-7; obstacles to, 208-13; patterns of, 203-4; problems, 194-5; signals, 204-5; and space relations, 214-16; symbolic, 196-8; verbal, 195, 201-3, 206-7
Community, influences, 131-3; resources, 132, 222
Conflict, of demands, 184; parental, 174-6, 185; peer, 174-6, 188-9; sibling, 144-7
Coping, 111-12, 130; activities, 113-15; behavior, 111; facts, 112
Creativity, 25; and heredity, 50
Culture, 10, 50; peer, 177; and values, 87, 90

Dating, 185-6; and parental conflict, 185; problems, 187-9; and sexuality, 190; and social acceptability, 182-4; tips, 190
Decisions, 218, 232; career, 228-31; how to make (process), 219-23; reminders about making, 224; and resources, 224-7
Development, child, 158-9; emotional, 98-102; of muscles, 184; personality, 23, 184-185; values, 82
Developmental tasks, 38; of adolescence, 44; of early adolescence, 40-3
Diets, 15-18; fad, 15-16, 26
Discipline, and young children, 32, 161; self-, 32
Discrimination, 187
Drugs, 21-22, 26, 29

Emotions, 5, 94-105; and body language, 200; definition, 95; development of, 98-102; expression of, 96, 184; independence of, 41, 130; management of, 102-4; negative, 95, 98; positive, 95, 98; problems with, 102-4
Environment, 48-9, 51-3, 184; compared with heredity, 50-1; defined, 48; family climate, 148; home, 130; influence of, 30-5, 46; quiz, 49; responses to, 130
Equality, sexual, 186-7
Erikson, Erik, 184

Family, 118-27; alternatives, 119-20, 125-6; climate, 148; conflicts with peers, 174-6; customs, 120; definition of, 118; functions of, 121; influences, 128-31, 142, 174-6; life cycle, 122-3; relationships, 128-30; responsibilities of, 120-1, 124; work patterns, 136
Family tree, 118
Feelings. *See* Emotions
Femininity, 186-7
Ferals, 33-4
Finger plays, 166-8
Friends, friendships, 178-81; characteristics of, 179; rating, 180. *See also* Peers

Goals, 41-4; and making decisions, 221
Gonorrhea. *See* Venereal diseases
Group, characteristics, 177

Hall, Edward T., 214
Heredity, 46-47, 51-3, 184, 226; compared with environment, 50-1; mental inheritance, 48

243

Identity, 179; and peer groups, 177; search for, 184; sexual, 186
Independence, economic, 41; emotional, 41, 130
Influences, 128-43; community, 131-3; family, 128-31; leisure-time, 133-4; mass media, 140; peer, 142; school, 138-9; work, 134-7
Intellectual development, 23; of adolescents, 25; of infants, 30; of preschool children, 24-5; and problem-solving ability, 26-8
Intelligence, 48; and heredity, 50
Interests, 226; elementary schoolers, 159; infants to toddlers, 158; preschool, 159
Isolates, 33-4

Jobs, 136-7

Knowledge, 225

Leisure, use of, 133-4
Life cycle, 63, 122-5
Lifeline, 38-9, 44
Life patterns, 122-4
Listening, 209

Masculinity, 186-7
Mass, body, reducing, 15-17
Mass media, influence of, 140; standards for, 140
Mead, Margaret, 121, 126
Money, 227
Motor coordination, 22; development of, 158-9; eye-hand, 158; muscle, 158-9, 184

Nutrition, 15-18, 22

Occupations, future, 134, 136; preparing for, 41, 44, 228-9; quiz, 230-1

Parents. *See* Family
Peers, 40; conflicts with family, 174-6; culture, 177; as friends, 178-80; group characteristics, 177; influence of, 142, 174-6; as reference group, 174
Pellagra, and alcohol, 22

Personality, 2, 4; defined, 183; development, 23, 184-5; inherited, 48; quiz, 190; and social acceptability, 182-4; and socialization, 32. *See also* Dating
Play, 133-4
Prejudice. *See* Bias
Puberty, 5, 11; changes during, 6-9; rites, 10
Pubescence. *See* Puberty

Quizzes (tests and questionnaires), bias, 212; birth order, 149; careers, 230-1; community, 132; dilemma test, 176; environment, 49; feelings, 102; friends, 180; group, 176; heredity and environment, 50; influence, 143; personality, 190; response to change, 110; roles, 58-9; self-concept, 68, 74; values, 78

Reference group, 73, 75, 174
Relationships, child, 158-9; family, 128-30; sibling, 150-2
Reproduction, 47
Resources, 224-33; community, 132; and making decisions, 222; non-human, 227; personal, 222, 224-6
Roles, 54-64; of adolescents, 59; changes to, 62; of daughter or son, 56; definition, 60; future, 41-42, 44; of older brothers and sisters, 56; of parents, 56, 58-9; and personality development, 184; playing, 60, 179; stereotyped, 60-1, 64, 186-7; swapping of, 63

Safety, child, 162-3
School, influences, 138-9
Self, ideal, 73; personal, 73; social, 73
Self-concept, 66-75; definition, 73; and others, 70-1; positive, 68, 72
Semaphore, 197
Sexual, identity, 186; stereotyping, 186-7; values, 84

Sexuality, 190
Siblings, 144-53; and birth order, 148-9; relationships among, 150-2; rivalry of, 144-7
Significant others, 176
Skills, 226
Skin, care, 20; problems, 19-20
Sleeping habits, 18-19
Smoking, 21
Social acceptability, 182-4
Socialization, 30-5; and values, 86
Social learning, 31
Space relations, 214-16
Syphilis. *See* Venereal diseases

Television, 140
Time, 227
Toilet training, 32
Twins, 47

Values, 50, 76-93; aesthetic, 80; changing, 90; clarifying, 76; cultural, 87, 90; and decisions, 221; definition, 79-80, 91; development of, 82; effects of, 88, 91; identifying, 76; moral, 84; parental, 174; peer, 174; religious, 86; sexual, 84; social, 86; system, 43-44; universal, 80
Venereal diseases, 21
Vocation. *See* Occupations, future

Work, experience, 136-7; influences of, 134-7